LITERARY RECREATIONS

LITERARY
RECREATIONS

BY

Sir EDWARD COOK

Essay Index Reprint Series

BOOKS FOR LIBRARIES PRESS
FREEPORT, NEW YORK

First Published 1918
Reprinted 1968

LIBRARY OF CONGRESS CATALOG CARD NUMBER:
68-54340

PRINTED IN THE UNITED STATES OF AMERICA

PREFACE

THE President of the Board of Education said the other day that in these dark times we were entitled to draw consolation whence we might, and that there was a legitimate source of consolation in the spread of the reading habit. Mr. Fisher has seen evidences of it in every omnibus, tram-car, and railway-carriage. Even in the trenches, he added, much reading goes on. There are probably few men who, like General Smuts, have studied the *Critique of Pure Reason* during a raid; but Mr. Fisher has known instances of officers enjoying the solace of Keats and Milton under the hottest fire, and an anecdote is recorded below (p. 46) of a man in the Lancashire Fusiliers who went into battle with a book by Ruskin. Perhaps, therefore, it may not be taken as any sign of undue detachment from the stress of great events that the author of this little book has found occasional respite from official work in putting together a few slight chapters of literary recreation.

So much had been written by way of apology when a stern sentence in one of the literary journals confronted me. A book about books can only be justified, said the reviewer, if it is itself a work of accomplished art or if the writer communicates to his readers a sincere pleasure taken by himself. I can have no hope of receiving absolution on the first score, but may put in a plea in mitigation. The commonwealth of art and letters needs for its sustenance those who study as well as those who make. The chapters here collected are conscious at least that literature is an art, and that profit may be had from considering its laws, methods, adjuncts, and vehicles. As for the second of the possible justifications for a book about books, it is certain that no pleasure can be given where none has been felt, but it does not follow, because an author has amused himself by writing, that his pleasure will be contagious. Every writer must take his chance, and I can only hope that these jottings in a library may here and there, in the hands of a sympathetic reader, serve to pass an idle hour.

The first of the papers here collected was printed in the *National Review*, April 1914, and the paper here called *Fifty Years of a Literary Magazine* was written for the Jubilee number of the *Cornhill* (January 1910). The others are now printed for the first time. One of the papers and parts of another were read before the New College Essay Society on occasions during recent years when I have been honoured by an invitation to revisit its meetings. The papers and discussions at that Society, and at similar bodies elsewhere, are among the pleasantest of many an Oxford man's recollections, and are perhaps not the least valuable part of a University education. The author of a clever novel has touched the point. " I am tempted to wonder," he says, " whether it much matters what a man be taught, so long as he meet enough men who have been taught something else." Dr. Horton, who was one of the greater lights of the New College Essay Society in my undergraduate days, has devoted a page or two of his Autobiography to memories of its free and varied debates, and in a reference to me has found not unkindly fault with my controversial tone in those far-off days. He bids us hope that the Society's sittings will be resumed in a Future World. In echoing my preceptor's pious hope, I will apply, in due humility, a story told of M. Van de Weyer. A friend went to see him during his last illness and expressed a hope that they might meet again in the Hereafter. " Ah ! let us hope so," he replied, " and that you will find me in an *editio nova et emendatior*."

E. T. C.

May 12th, 1918.

CONTENTS

I

THE ART OF BIOGRAPHY .　.　.　.　.　.　PAGE
1

II

SOME REMARKS ON RUSKIN'S STYLE .　.　.　.　34

III

THE ART OF INDEXING　.　.　.　.　.　.　55

IV

FIFTY YEARS OF A LITERARY MAGAZINE .　.　.　77

V

LITERATURE AND MODERN JOURNALISM　.　.　.　113

VI

WORDS AND THE WAR　.　.　.　.　.　.　142

VII

PAGE

A STUDY IN SUPERLATIVES 176

VIII

THE POETRY OF A PAINTER 211

IX

THE SECOND THOUGHTS OF POETS 246

INDEX 319

THE ART OF BIOGRAPHY

THE title of my Paper [1] is a challenge, not, I hope, to the better opinion, but certainly to accepted practice. From time to time, indeed, voices are raised to describe the difficulties which confront a biographer and to enumerate the qualifications required in a successful practitioner of the art. Such lists are so formidable that if they were believed, the wonder would be that any biographies should ever be written. But they are not believed. There is a larger output in biography than in any other classes of books, except those of Theology and Fiction, under which latter head it has sometimes been suggested that Biography—and History also—should be included. You remember what " Mr. Sludge the Medium " said :

> Such a scribe
> You pay and praise for putting life in stones,
> Fire into fog, making the past your world.
> There's plenty of " How did you contrive to grasp

---

[1] Read to the New College Essay Society at Oxford, March 7, 1914.

The thread which led you through this labyrinth ?
How build such solid fabric out of air ?
How on so slight foundation found this tale,
Biography, narrative ? "   Or, in other words,
" How many lies did it require to make
The portly truth you here present us with ? "

The fault in some modern biography is not, however, that it is fanciful, but that it is artless. It is the fashion in these days to write a man's life immediately after he is dead, when authentic documents are numerous and personal recollections still fresh. The difficult thing is to make the documents tell a coherent story and to fuse the varied recollections into a living impression. The difficulty is sometimes not recognised, and in other cases is deliberately avoided. It is thought that personal acquaintance with the subject is a sufficient qualification. Or, on the other hand, the task is put, as it were, into commission ; different friends are invited to contribute their recollections, and no attempt is made to weld them into a whole. A picture to which one brush contributed the eye, another the mouth, and so on, would only by a miracle present an intelligible likeness. There is indeed a certain interest in the composite biographies which give impressions of the subject from a succession of different angles. It is the same kind of interest that belongs to *The Ring and the Book* ; but Edward FitzGerald thought that even Browning

had failed to work the book into a ring, and that
the poem remained " a shapeless thing." Lord
Tennyson's Life of his father, admirable in some
respects, is from this point of view rather material
for a biography than itself a finished work of art.

A very high authority is responsible for opinions
which might lead to the conclusion that biography
is not a conscious art at all, but that anybody or
everybody is competent, with luck, to write a
good Life of somebody else. The book which
by common consent is the greatest biography in
the English language was written, said Lord
Macaulay, by " one of the smallest men," " of
the meanest and feeblest intellect," that ever
lived. Many of the greatest men that ever lived
have written biography, he added, but a dunce
and a fool has beaten them all. Macaulay's
critical authority once reigned paramount, and
his judgment on the Boswell of Johnson's Life
dies hard. The Professor of English Literature
in this University has, I am aware, pronounced
Boswell to be a man of genius ; adding that " the
idle paradox which presents him in the likeness
of a lucky dunce was never tenable by serious
criticism, and has long since been rejected by all
who bring thought to bear on the problems of
literature." This, I hope you will agree, is the
better opinion ; but I am not sure that it prevails
quite so fully among serious critics as Professor
Raleigh's words suggest. Another Professor of

English Literature—also a member of this University—has recently published some observations on the same subject; and, while he does more justice than Macaulay to Boswell's skill, he yet seems to me not quite to hit the real point. Boswell's chief virtues as a biographer are, says Sir Sidney Lee, those of "the faithful hound" and "the parasitical temper"; his book is great because he "did much which self-respecting persons would scorn to do"; and "the salt of his biography is his literal reports of Johnson's conversations, reports in the spirit of the interviewer." I cannot agree here with Professor Lee. For one thing, as an old journalist, I must demur to the suggestion that the spirit of the interviewer is literalness. I am afraid that there are politicians and ambassadors, more perhaps in other countries than in this, who know to their cost that it is nothing of the kind; and where the medium of the interview is rightly and truthfully used, its method is never simple literalness. The ablest interviewers I have known were Mr. Stead and Edmund Garrett. The general accuracy of their interviews was seldom, if ever, impugned; but they never took a note, and did not attempt to reproduce with slavish literalness every word that was said by their subjects. I have always regarded as a masterpiece in this sort of journalism an interview, so called, between Garrett and Cecil Rhodes. I know of no state-

ment within so short a compass—I do not think
that there is any statement of whatever compass—
which embodies so vividly so much of the manner,
character, and ideas of Mr. Rhodes as this presentation by Garrett of the substance of several
conversations.   It does so not because Garrett
was a faithful hound or a parasite—he was neither ;
but because he had quick perception and was a
literary artist.   And so with Boswell.   Call him
by what contemptuous names you will, for the
opportunities which he sought and used ; but
do not suppose that any faithful hound with
like opportunities could have written Boswell's
Johnson.   The book is no doubt unique in a
fortunate conjunction — of Johnson, a great
man and a good, willing to talk, with Boswell
at hand to draw him out, to remember, and
to collect.   But the unique conjunction would
have failed of its actual result if Boswell had
not been possessed of biographical genius.   He
had an instinct for what was interesting and
characteristic ; he knew how to arrange, select,
plan, and present.

The point can be enforced by comparing
another famous biography, in which also there
was a peculiarly fortunate conjunction.   Every
one, I imagine, would include Lockhart's *Life of
Scott* among the six best biographies in the English
language, and some good judges have placed it
second to Boswell's *Johnson*.   Scott was almost

as good a biographical subject as Johnson, and
Lockhart had intimate knowledge of his father-
in-law.   Nevertheless Lockhart's book is not so
good a biography as Boswell's.   On the one hand,
Lockhart's *Scott* is often spun out with letters and
diaries of other people which add very little to
our knowledge of Scott himself.   On the other
hand, those who have delved deep sometimes
complain that Lockhart misses many things which
he must have known or could easily have found
out, and which lovers of Scott would dearly like
to know.   Ruskin, one of whose many abandoned
literary projects was a Life of Sir Walter, goes
so far as to say that " Lockhart is always incon-
ceivably silent about the little things one most
wants to know."   But what is all this except to
say that Lockhart was not so fine an artist in
biography as Macaulay's dunce ?

Biography, then, is an art.   What are its
conditions and laws ?   The rule which is most
commonly and most strongly laid down by those
who discourse on the subject is Brevity ; and
doubtless many biographies, perhaps most, are
too long.   But there are some awkward facts
which the preachers of biographical brevity have
to face.   One is that two of the best biographies
in the English language are also two of the
longest.   Sir Sidney Lee, as is natural in an
editor, has laid great stress on brevity ; but I
have noticed that many—I am not sure that I

might not say all—of the very longest articles in
the *Dictionary of National Biography* are from the
pen of the professor of brevity.   And nobody,
I am sure, who has read those articles has ever
wished that they had been shorter.   Professor
Lee's biographies are models of condensation.
If they are longer than others, it is because their
subject-matter was of more importance.   In a
recent review of a somewhat long biography, the
author was asked with some asperity why he had
not modelled his work on Tacitus and Plutarch.
To require of an ordinary practitioner genius such
as theirs seems to be rating the art of biography
a little high ; nor is the collocation of the two
names particularly happy, for the method and
scope of Tacitus and Plutarch severally are as
different as is their style ; but the reviewer's
remark suggests some observations.   Tacitus, the
supreme master of biting brevity, was short in
his biographies because he was writing not
biography but history.   Plutarch's *Lives*, though
by one standard of comparison short, are by
another long.   He wrote not so much individual
biography, as collective ; and if his scale be
compared with a collection such as the *National
Dictionary*, it will be found that Plutarch's *Lives*
are long.

Length or shortness in biography must
obviously be relative, not only to the importance
of the subject and the quantity of appropriate

material, but also to the design of the book as
a work of art.   In the kindred art of graphic
representation there may be sketches and finished
portraits, and among the latter whole-lengths, half-
lengths, and heads.   An intelligent critic does not
say that the sketch of a head in half-a-dozen lines
by Phil May is bad because it is not wrought
with the minuteness of a portrait - piece by
Holbein ; nor is a play in five acts by Shakespeare
declared too long because Browning gave a life's
drama in the fifty-six lines of " My Last Duchess."
Southey's *Life of Nelson*—that " immortal monument raised by genius to valour "—was not too
short because Lockhart's *Life of Scott* was long.
The question whether a sketch or a full-length
is in any particular case the more appropriate
biographical method depends upon another factor.
Has the person's life-story been told before, are
most of the relevant facts already known, or is
there material available which is both new and
important ?   In the former case, the better
method is that which the French call a " study,"
and in which, for grace and lucidity, they are
unsurpassed.   Brevity is therein the wise counsel.
Yet the pursuit of brevity by those who might
have told us more about great and interesting
people has involved us in much loss.   " Many
other things I could now say of him," wrote
Anthony à Wood in closing his too short account
of a famous Oxonian, " relating either to his most

generous mind in prosperity, or dejected estate
in his worst state of poverty, but for brevity's
sake I shall now pass them by." Much that we
would gladly know about Richard Lovelace is
therefore lost to us. Let us be thankful that no
evil genius was at Boswell's elbow to persuade
him for brevity's sake to cut down his anecdotes
of Dr. Johnson.

The proper criterion to apply to products of
the art of biography is concerned not with size
but with Relevance. The pages in a biography
may be rightly many and rightly few. The book
is condemned unless they are relevant ; just as in
the case of a picture detail can only be right if
it is pertinent. But relevant to what ? In considering this question we shall come nearest, I
think, to the essential conditions of the art ; and
the words with which the Father of Biography
prefaces one of his most famous *Lives* will carry
us far on the way to the heart of the matter.
" We shall now proceed," says Plutarch, " to give
the lives of Alexander the Great and of Cæsar
who overthrew Pompey ; and, as the quantity
of material is so great, we shall only premise that
we hope for indulgence though we do not give
the actions in full detail and with a scrupulous
exactness, but rather in a short summary ; since
we are writing not Histories, but Lives. Nor is
it always in the most distinguished achievements
that men's virtues or vices may be best discerned ;

but very often an action of small note, a short saying, or a jest shall distinguish a person's real character more than the greatest sieges or the most important battles." How many biographies would have been better done had these words been taken to heart ! Yet Plutarch's instructions may be pushed too far. " He is the greatest of biographers," says Mr. Frederic Harrison in a pleasant chapter of *Among My Books*, " because he thoroughly grasped and practised the true principle of biographic work—to make a living portrait of a man's inner nature, not to write the annals of his external acts. The conventional biography records what the person *did* ; the true biography reveals what the person *was*." That is a true saying, and every biographer should bind it about his neck when setting himself to his task. Yet it is not quite the whole truth. In the case of a man of action, a Life which left out what he did would be absurd. Who would be satisfied with a Life of Gladstone which said nothing of his Budgets, his Midlothian campaign, his fight for Home Rule ? You cannot show what such a man *was* except in relation to what he *did* ; but the essential thing is at the same time to bring out the relation between what he did and what he was. Few, I suppose, will dispute Mr. Harrison's judgment that Plutarch's *Life of Alexander* is " the most masterly portrait ever painted with the pen—far more true, more real, and more

graven on the memory of ages, than are all the
laborious studies of all the annalists ancient and
modern " ; though Professor Freeman, I think,
preferred Arrian to Plutarch.   Yet Plutarch tells
us a great deal about what Alexander did.   His
Life is a masterpiece of biography, not because
Plutarch left out actions and events, but because
he made them the index of a mind and a character.
There is a remark to this effect in a British
classic which in the opinion of at least one competent judge [1] may be set up as a rival to Boswell's
Johnson.   " If," says Roger North in his Life of
the Lord Keeper, " the history of a life hangs
altogether upon great importances such as concern
the church and state, and drops the peculiar
economy and private conduct of the person that
gives title to the work, it may be a history and a
very good one ; but of any thing rather than of
that person's life."   To keep the man in the
foreground, to make him stand out as a person
from the background of event, action, and circumstance : that is the essential duty of a biographical
artist.   It is also his greatest difficulty ; and that,
perhaps, is a reason (though others might be
suggested) why, as has often been remarked, the

[1] Robert Louis Stevenson, who used to take the *Lives of the Norths* with
him on his travels.   It was not only that as a Scot he had to be critical of
Johnson.   It might be argued that as a work of art Roger North's should
be counted the better, because, unlike Boswell's, it owes nothing of its
excellence to the subject.   Unlike Johnson the Norths were dull.   I owe
this note to my friend the late Mr. B. R. Wise.

best biographies are more often of men of letters than of men of action.

The biographer, then, must be relevant to individual character. He is to remember Plutarch's words; he is to write not Histories, but Lives. Often he may from the nature of his material make fresh contribution to history; and it is worth noticing in this connection that Plutarch, in another place, explains that his reason for passing lightly over much in the *Life of Nicias* is that he has nothing to add to the inimitable narrative of Thucydides. If, on the other hand, a biographer find new material at hand, he must become a historian; yet even so, if he desires to make his book a work of art, the history must be subordinated to the biography. A book which proclaims itself the *Life and Times of Somebody* is a hybrid little likely to possess artistic merit as biography. The true biographer will similarly beware of *Somebody and his Circle*. His work is to be relevant to an individual. Of course a man's family and friends, and his dealings with them, are always some part, and often a large part, of his own life. Such dealings come within Plutarch's category of " things which serve to decipher the man and his nature." Who could gain a true idea of Dr. Johnson apart from his friends ? But one of Boswell's many artistic merits is that the Doctor is always at the centre of the circle. A like reason is not available in the case of men who lived aloof ; and thus, if Lord Rosebery's book on Chatham were to be regarded as a biography—a description, however, which it expressly disclaims—there are sketches in it which cannot be considered wholly relevant ; though, to be sure, their omission would remove some of the most brilliant pieces of that admirable torso. If there be a fault in Sir George Trevelyan's *Early Life of Charles James Fox*, it is a tendency to discursiveness ; though, here again, it were ungrateful to wish anything away from what is one of the most delightful biographical studies in our language.

It is, however, in relation to the family of the subject of a biography that the rules of relevance are most often and most flagrantly disregarded. For my part I generally find the conventional first chapter on Ancestry as tiresome as—dare I say it ?—the introduction to a Waverley novel. I am aware that there is a school which claims that biography should adjust itself to the newest scientific lights or theories, and trace the hero's descent in such a way as to serve the need of students of heredity and genetics. Sir Sidney Lee has, however, dealt with this claim so admirably in his *Leslie Stephen Lecture on Biography*, that I shall pass it over lightly. Except in special cases such researches into hereditary influences, even in the first degree, are often a snare to the biographer. Plutarch set the fashion, and after telling us, in the introduction to the *Life of Alexander*, aforesaid, that he is concerned only with what throws light upon a person's real character, proceeds forthwith to relate Alexander's descent from Hercules and to give us particulars of his father and mother on the eve of their marriage. I leave them aside in the decent obscurity of a foreign tongue. The greatest expert in genetics would derive no light from them. The dreams and omens of ancient biographers reappear in the pages of the moderns as ancestral incidents or circumstances invested with far-fetched significance. Mr. Chesterton makes some excellent remarks in this connection at the beginning of his *Life of Browning*. There is a theory that the poet was descended from feudal barons ; another, that he was of Jewish blood ; a third, that there was in him a strain of the negro. We are shown how easily each of these hypothetical descents can be made from the poet's writings to appear significant ; " but," asks Mr. Chesterton, " is there in the world a biographer who could lay his hand upon his heart and say that he would not have seen as much significance in any three other nationalities ? " And he proceeds in a passage of excellent chaff to show how significant it might have been if Browning's ancestors had been Frenchmen, his grandfather a Swede, or his great-aunt a Red Indian. Mr. Chesterton here hits on the head

what is a very common " sin and snare of biographers." They " tend to see significance in
everything ; characteristic carelessness if their
hero drops his pipe, and characteristic carefulness
if he picks it up again." When such characteristics are traced back to ancestors in the third and
fourth degree, the thing becomes as tiresome as
ridiculous. Until at least the laws of heredity
are better determined, I suggest that biographers
would be well advised to draw the line before
they reach great-grandfathers. For the biographical relevance of grandfathers there does
seem to be a case ; the classic instance is that of
Governor Pitt, whose fiery blood descended, in
Lord Rosebery's phrase, " like burning lava " to
his grandson, the Earl of Chatham. As for a
man's brothers, sisters, aunts, uncles and cousins,
many biographies are full of them most
superfluously.

Another danger of biographical irrelevance
lurks in a *Life and Letters*. " It is too much the
habit of modern biographers," says Ruskin, " to
confuse epistolary talk with vital facts." The
letters which a man writes, as also those which
he receives, may indeed be relevant and vital
biographical fact. They may or they may not.
In the case of the letters written by him, it depends
much upon his powers of expression and habits
of self-revelation. In the case of letters received
by him, it depends entirely upon whether they do

or do not throw light on his own actions and character.[1]   These rules of the art of biography are more obvious than observed.   Many biographies are packed with letters which have no closer relation to the subject of the book than that he was the recipient of them.   Here is an extract from a modern biography : " The following interesting letter from Chichester Fortescue deserves to be included in these pages, if only for the remarkable prophecy of a Home Rule party in the House of Commons which it contains."   *Qui s'excuse, s'accuse*.   In a Life of Chichester Fortescue his prophecy in 1866 might be relevant, but the biographer was writing the Life of an altogether different person, in relation to whom the letter has no relevance whatever. Of course a biographer's temptation in this matter is great.   He finds interesting things in the papers before him, and rather than pass them over, he flings relevance aside and brings them in.   It is a temptation which requires some strength of artistic conscience to resist ; but the resistance may find its reward.   The man who writes a biography full of irrelevant good things will have them picked out by others who will fit them into their proper places.   He does but

---

[1] In a review of Lord Morley's *Recollections* it was complained that the author allowed himself to have all the best of it in his correspondence with the Government of India because he gave all his own letters and none of Lord Minto's.   Lord Morley might reasonably have replied that he was writing not a Life of Lord Minto, but his own.

open a quarry. He who writes with strict respect for the conditions of his art may carve a statue.

Sometimes there are accidents in the making of biographies whereby letters which would have been more relevant in one place are given where they are less relevant in another. There is a curious instance in the case of two important biographies which recently appeared almost simultaneously of men who for part of their lives were in close official relations—Lord Clarendon and Lord Lyons. One of the most memorable events in the diplomatic career of Lord Clarendon was his proposal for general disarmament in 1870—a proposal which anticipated certain suggestions of our own day, and which at the time was promptly followed by the outbreak of the Franco-German War. *Absit omen!* [1] In Sir Herbert Maxwell's *Life of Lord Clarendon* the affair receives bare mention in a few lines. In Lord Newton's *Life of Lord Lyons* it is the subject of a most interesting chapter, and many documents relating to it are published. Yet the initiative was Lord Clarendon's. He was, indeed, prompted in the first instance by the French Government; but he made the proposal his own, and pushed it *con amore*. Lord Lyons, on the other hand, was in this matter nothing but a rather unwilling and wholly sceptical intermediary. It cannot be said

---

[1] This was written in March 1914.

that the letters are irrelevant to the *Life of Lord Lyons*, but they would have been far more relevant in the *Life of Lord Clarendon*.   One is tempted to wish that some biographical clearing-house or exchange could be established whereby the proper material might find its way to the proper place.

Next to Relevance, in the canons of the biographer's art, come Selection and Arrangement. Anything that is irrelevant should be excluded, but not everything that is relevant can be included. Selection must depend primarily of course upon the determined scale ; but even in a full-length, two - volume biography, wholesale rejection is necessary.   It is, however, quite as easy to err by leaving out as by putting in.   The portrait may be rendered incomplete, and even false, by undue reticence, as well as by inconsiderate babbling.   Biographical " indiscretion " is a term commonly applied only to the latter error, but the former sometimes merits it no less.   There was a striking instance in the biographical treatment of a modern man of letters.   The authorised account of his life took the form of a selection of his private letters.   Singularly frank in some directions, the selection was so severely reticent in others that the editor took a subsequent occasion to correct the entirely misleading impression—obscuring some of the hero's " most characteristic traits "—which the original volumes had necessarily created.   I think that the editor's

second thoughts were well-advised ; but who can
be sure that the correction will catch up the
misleading picture ? Every one is familiar with
such phrases in a biography as " Of his domestic
relations this is not the place to speak," or " There
are some aspects of his life and character too
sacred to be here put down." Such remarks show
a misconception of what biography is, and are a
confession of failure. To tell " sacred " things
aright requires the nicest tact, but to leave them
altogether untold is to strip the biography of the
things best worth telling. It is to turn the key
on the heart of the subject.

Arrangement is a difficulty no less great than
selection. By the laws of human life, a biographer has, it is true, a beginning and an end
prescribed to him ; but between the birth and
the death of his subject, how great is the call upon
his art for proportion, order, convenience, lucidity
and all the other branches of arrangement ! The
infinite variety among the lives of different men,
their differences in number and kind of interests,
occupations and actions, require a corresponding
variety in the method best adapted to each
particular case. Any practitioner of the art must
be accounted peculiarly fortunate and successful if he is not told, whatever method he has
adopted, that he would have done better to follow
another. In the case of a full and varied life,
the severely chronological method, consistently

applied throughout, is almost certainly the worst. It becomes worse than ever, in a biography which is mainly composed of letters, if these too are given in mere chronological order. The object of the biographer is to produce an ordered impression, not the effect of a kaleidoscope. To give within the compass of a few hundred pages a coherent account of the innumerable facts, thoughts, reasons, circumstances, which make up a human life calls far more insistently than is always recognised for architectonic art.

One condition of the biographer's art remains to be noticed, but it is so obvious that very few words about it will suffice. The biographer must be honest. He must have general sympathy with his subject, for without it he cannot hope to gain the insight which will enable him to understand and to interpret. Lewes's *Life of Goethe*, which Leslie Stephen, than whom there could be no higher authority, accounted one of the greatest of English biographies, fails, if at all, only because Lewes's " general prepossession against German style and dislike of the mystical and allegorical may disqualify him for adequate appreciation of some aspects of Goethe's genius." But a biographer's sympathy should be neither blind nor undiscriminating. I will quote words from two modern masters of the art. " No partiality, no grudge," says Lord Morley, after Cicero. " I had no choice," says Sir George

Trevelyan in the second edition of his famous *Life of Macaulay*, " but to ask myself, with regard to each feature of the portrait, not whether it was attractive, but whether it was characteristic." There is danger in each extreme. The great biographies may reveal the hero's faults, but they do so frankly, and the predominant note is sympathy. A touch of ambiguity or a scratch of over-candid friendship may spoil the effect. Mr. Purcell's *Life of Manning* is to my thinking one of the best of modern biographies, but it just missed the very highest rank by leaving an uncomfortable sense of ambiguity in the writer's standpoint. What has set some readers against Froude as the biographer of Carlyle—though for my part I rank the *Life of Carlyle* among the masterpieces—is a suspicion that he bore some grudge. Charles Eliot Norton, who, however, is hardly an impartial witness, found the book " artfully malignant." The sugar-candied mood is as dangerous as the too candid. What spoils Dowden's *Life of Shelley* is a partiality passing the bounds of common sense. Of the excessive partiality of many a biography written by adoring relatives, it is needless to speak.

In discussions about art the dispute is perpetual over the relation, in sphere and importance, between subject and treatment. In painting let us agree that you may make a fine work of art out of a pumpkin or a hide ; but in the art of biography there is no purse to be made out of a sow's ear. Half the battle is won when the artist has got hold of a good subject. A bad biography can, indeed, be written on a good subject ; but it is almost as difficult to make a complete failure with a good subject as to make even a passable success with a bad subject. It is not always recognised, however, wherein the goodness of a subject from the point of view of biography consists. Moral goodness is of course not in itself a sufficient recommendation. There are excellent biographies, and autobiographies, of rascals, and there are very dull books about saints. Neither is it sufficient alone that the subjects should be persons of importance in their day. The first qualifications of a good subject are that the life of the man or woman should be really memorable, that there should be a marked personality behind the actions, that the character should be distinctive and interesting. The practice of biography differs widely in its choice of subjects from these requirements of the art. It is held that Cabinet rank, or membership of the Royal Academy, or the episcopal bench and so forth, qualifies a man *ipso facto* to become the subject of a biography in two volumes. Everybody, I expect, could name a political biography —and if a dozen people were asked to do it, a dozen different books would very probably be named—from which the resulting impression was

only a wonder how and why the hero attained
his high place.   Such a result, it may be said, is
true to life, for the wonder is sometimes expressed
of living Cabinet Ministers or of other persons
officially stamped as great, wise, and eminent.
But this is an inadequate result of a work of art,
and is never what the author intended.   The
failure arises sometimes from the simple fact that
the politician, though eminent in place, was in
truth a very commonplace person ; and in other
cases because the hero's life was too entirely
political.   Politics in themselves are among the
most intractable forms of biographical material.
The temptation to write history and not lives is
then peculiarly strong ; the difficulty of sub-
ordinating the background to the figure is great ;
and, moreover, the outward actions are often not
an index of the man, the political medium is a
distorting mirror.   " Bismarck, reading a book
of superior calibre, once came upon a portrait of
an eminent personage whom he had known well.
Such a man as is described here, he cried, never
existed ; and he went on in graphic strokes to
paint the sitter as he had actually found him.
' It is not in diplomatic materials, but in their life
of every day that you come to know men.' " [1]
One comes to know more of Bismarck from
Busch's Diary than from any collection of the
Chancellor's public acts.   The official lives of

[1] Lord Morley's *Notes on Politics and History*, p. 52.

contemporary politicians, though rarely forming first-rate biographical material, may nevertheless afford valuable material, or footnotes, to history, and by that standard they may perhaps fairly claim to be judged.

A second element in the goodness of biographical subject is the existence of material of self-expression clothed in attractive and intelligible language. Such material may exist in the shape of diaries, memoranda, letters, or recorded conversations. It is sometimes laid down as a general rule that a biographer should not interpose between the reader and the subject but should leave the subject to reveal himself. There is a large element of truth in this rule, but it may be stated far too absolutely. The practice of some of the best biographers conforms least to it, and only in the rarest cases will strict adherence to it produce a full, true, and sufficient picture. Persons vary infinitely both in their gifts of self-expression and in their candour. Some are morbidly self-abasing ; others are careful always to give themselves *le beau rôle* ; others leave no key under their own hand with which to unlock their hearts. There are, as somebody has said, three forms of truth about every man : there is what he seemed to himself, to his friends, and to his enemies. The biographical artist has to seek a final impression of " the true truth " by considering and condensing all the factors. But the existence of such material as was indicated just now is an enormous help. The greatest of mankind are sometimes, however, the most lacking in the gift or habit of self-expression, and this is one reason why biographies of great men are often the least satisfying. There is an awful aloofness about such men, and the best art of biography cannot bridge the gulf :

> Thin, thin, the pleasant human noises grow,
>   And faint the city gleams ;
> Rare the lone pastoral huts—marvel not thou !
> The solemn peaks but to the stars are known,
> But to the stars, and the cold lunar beams ;
> Alone the sun arises, and alone
>   Spring the great streams.

Dr. Johnson was a great man, but he was clubbable and communicative, and so Boswell had a perfect subject. The elder Pitt screened himself from his fellows. His letters on public affairs are pompous and involved ; his family letters are for the most part stilted. It is difficult to come into close touch with a man who writes to his favourite son that " all the Nine will sue for your Love " and that the College is " not yet evacuated," he supposes, " of its learned garrison." Lord Rosebery wrote some interesting pages on this topic in the preface to his fragment on Chatham, concluding, in consequence of the lack of suitable biographical material, that " the complete life of Chatham is not merely difficult to write, but impossible.   It is safe, indeed, to assert that it never has been written and never can be written."   He did not know that the word impossible is unknown to the learned garrison of this College.   Mr. Basil Williams in his recent *Life of William Pitt, Earl of Chatham*, has filled what had been a conspicuous and even a discreditable lacuna in English literature.   He has given us a biography of one of the glories of our race and State, which is well-proportioned, admirable in style, and sane in judgment.   It would be interesting to know whether Lord Rosebery finds reason for withdrawing his *obiter dictum*. If he does not, it will not be from any fault on the part of the author of the new *Life of Chatham* ; it will be from defect, which even he was unable to supply, in the material.   The account of the statesman's speeches, triumphs, difficulties, schemes and efforts, could hardly be bettered ; of the inner springs of his action, of the life of the man in undress, there is still something to seek.   The great Commoner had no taste for self-revelation, and would have brooked no Boswell.

The puissant English Minister of a later age was, from one point of view, an ·ideal subject for a biographer's art.   Mr. Gladstone was not only a great man concerned in great actions, but his character was of many - sided interest and of fascinating complexity.   " Robert Browning,

writer of plays," might in him have found " a
subject to your hand." But from another point
of view, the subject was less ideal. Mr. Gladstone was voluminously communicative in letters
and in speeches—the speeches reported verbatim,
not conjecturally pieced together like Chatham's.
He was the greatest speaker of the age, but the
speeches were oratory, not literature, and much
of their fascination disappears with the flashing
eye, the resonant voice, the eloquent gesture, the
eager personality of the man. And then as a
writer of letters, diaries, and memoranda Mr.
Gladstone did not shine by any habitual concision
or pungency of phrase. The biographer of
Disraeli will here be at the advantage ; and not
less the biographer of Lord Salisbury, if I may
judge by such few private letters and notes as I
have seen. Lord Morley's private material for
the *Life of Gladstone* was, I imagine, rather
voluminous than easily tractable. And this is
the reason of a judgment which I once heard
passed upon the book by a friend. " Whenever
Morley fills the page by direct recital or otherwise, the book is uniformly interesting ; when
he brings Mr. Gladstone on *in propria persona,*
it sometimes tends to drag." I was too good a
Gladstonian and too much absorbed in the
contents to have noticed this difference when I
first read the book, but I perceive what my friend
meant. Mr. Gladstone as a writer was not light

of hand, and this was one of many difficulties
the consideration of which must enhance any
craftsman's admiration for Lord Morley's great
achievement.

One of Mr. Gladstone's contemporaries has
more recently been the subject of a biography
which also is markedly successful. John Bright
was a great orator, but you cannot make a good
biography merely out of speeches, even though,
as in this case, they possess literary form. He
was a great man, but his scope was somewhat
limited. His mind was not very flexible ; his
interests did not cover a very wide range. Nor,
except in his best speeches, was his manner of
self - expression particularly attractive. I took
up Mr. Trevelyan's Life of him with somewhat
anxious curiosity. In Garibaldi's romantic adventures he had the advantage of a splendid
subject, which he treated with contagious gusto
and with perfect art. But what would he be
able to make of a subject so different, and by
comparison so humdrum, as John Bright ? I
think that most readers have found that the book
holds them from the first page to the last. Mr.
Trevelyan has overcome the difficulties of the
subject by due subordination of external circumstances to personality, and by impressing the
force of a noble and simple character upon every
chapter of the Life.

Mr. Trevelyan's books suggest another re-

flection on the materials in the art of biography.
Unchastened hero-worship is, as we have seen,
out of place in biography ; but generous sympathy is essential, and in biography, as in the
novel or the drama, contrasts and foils are often
useful.   The hero demands a villain ; and the
subject for a sympathetic biography may be
accounted additionally fortunate if the material
aptly provides a villain of the piece.   When Mr.
Gladstone is the hero, the villain is ready-made
to the biographer's hand in Mr. Disraeli.   As
soon as Disraeli's biographer reaches the point
at which those two dominant personalities fill the
stage with their conflict, the parts will of course
be reversed.   Did not Mr. Gladstone himself say,
in a speech here in Oxford, which I well remember
hearing as an undergraduate, that his mission in
life had become " to dog the footsteps of Lord
Beaconsfield " ?   In   Mr.   Trevelyan's   *Life of
John Bright*, where the hero is the opponent of
the Crimean War and the popular tribune on
behalf of Reform, the villain is Lord Palmerston,
who carried through the war, and in domestic
affairs pursued from the Liberal side a Con-
servative policy.   But in the books about Garibaldi the same statesman plays, among the sub-
sidiary characters, the part of hero to Austrian
and other villains.   Thus in the biographer's
pages " one man in his time plays many parts."
I hasten to add that Mr. Trevelyan is obviously

alive to the humour of the situation ; and in the Life of Bright pleads the necessity of biographical art for dealing so harshly with the stalwart English gentleman who " snapped his fingers in the face of the priests and despots."

One of the ironies of the art of biography is that the lives which, from some points of view, are best worth writing are those which nobody will read and which, therefore, are seldom written. The Lives for which a loud demand creates a constant supply are of the people who have made open mark in the world ; but they are not always those which are inherently most memorable. " Lives in which the public are interested," says Ruskin, roundly, " are scarcely ever worth writing. For the most part compulsorily artificial, often affectedly so—on the whole, fortunate beyond ordinary rule—and, so far as the men are really greater than others, unintelligible to the common reader, the lives of statesmen, soldiers, authors, artists, or any one habitually set in the sight of many, tell us at last little more than what sort of people they dealt with, and of pens they wrote with ; the personal life is inscrutably broken up —often contemptibly, and the external aspect of it merely a husk, at the best. The lives we need to have written for us are of the people whom the world has not thought of—far less heard of— who are yet doing the most of its work, and of whom we may learn how it can best be done."

There is some exaggeration in this, though
Ruskin saves himself, it will have been noted,
by saying of the lives in which the public are
interested that they are, not never, but scarcely
ever, worth writing. But that there is truth in
his statement will be admitted, I think, by any
one who is fond of biography and who recalls
how many of his favourite " Lives " are of little-
known persons. Ruskin's words come from his
preface to *The Story of Ida*, a very charming and
touching biography of a Tuscan peasant-girl by an
American writer, Miss Francesca Alexander. In
an able critical article I saw that some one named
as the best biography in the English language
the *Life of Dr. John Brown* by Dr. Cairns. I read
the book in consequence, and though I think
that judgment of it capricious, it is certainly a
very interesting and well-written biography. Yet
the book is, I imagine, little read, and the subject
of it is perhaps little remembered except as the
father of another Dr. John Brown, the author of
Rab and *Marjorie*. There have been good critics
—Dr. Garnett among them—who accounted
Carlyle's *Life of Sterling* not merely a biographical
masterpiece, but the author's most completely
satisfactory performance. Carlyle may perhaps
be given the curious distinction of having written
both one of the best short biographies in the
language and one of the worst, by which latter
description I have heard a competent authority

call his *Life of Schiller*. For the writing of the
Life of John Sterling, two men of genius and one
of high literary ability contended—Mill, Carlyle,
and Archdeacon Hare. Yet Sterling achieved
little, and made small mark in the world. Mr.
Chesterton, from a different aspect, touches a
point somewhat similar to Ruskin's, and, again,
with a note of paradoxical exaggeration. The
real gospel of Dickens, he says, is " the in-
exhaustible opportunity offered by the liberty and
the variety of man. Compared with this life,
all public life, all fame, all wisdom, is by its nature
cramped and cold and small. For on that defined
and lighted public stage men are of necessity
forced to profess one set of accomplishments,
to rise to one rigid standard. It is the utterly
unknown people who can grow in all directions
like an exuberant tree. Many of us live publicly
with featureless public puppets, images of the
small public abstractions. It is when we pass
our own private gate, and open our own secret
door, that we step into the land of the giants."
What Mr. Chesterton says of the sphere of fiction
and caricature may be paralleled, I think, in that
of biography. I know of readers who make the
Dictionary of National Biography their supper book
or bed-side book. They would tell us, I expect,
that its fascination resides not so much in the apt
and lucid biographies of the more famous men,
but rather in those of many of the lesser known,

men whose lives have never formed the subject
of biography elsewhere, but who disclose un-
expected points of vivid oddity or otherwise of
marked character ; or of men, again, whose
capacities found no favouring tide of circumstance.
What is really memorable, even for influence and
effect, is not always what has been marked by the
world's coarse thumb. " The growing good of
the world," said George Eliot, in closing the story
of a life of partial failure, " is partly dependent
on unhistoric acts ; and that things are not so
ill with you and me as they might have been, is
half owing to the number who lived faithfully a
hidden life and rest in unvisited tombs."

II

SOME REMARKS ON RUSKIN'S STYLE

Mr. Asquith, in a scathing depreciation of the literature of art-criticism, makes exception of Ruskin for his "intellectual independence," "spiritual insight," and "golden-tongued eloquence." And indeed the concurrent judgment of the best authorities places Ruskin very high among the great masters of English prose. Lord Morley, by no means sympathetic to Ruskin's point of view, has named him as one of the " three giants of prose style " who strode across the literature of the nineteenth century. Matthew Arnold, who disliked Ruskin personally, has cited a passage from *Modern Painters* as marking the highest point to which the art of prose can ever hope to reach. Tennyson, on being asked to name the six authors in whom the stateliest English prose was to be found, gave : Hooker, Bacon, Milton, Jeremy Taylor, De Quincey, and Ruskin. And Lord Acton mentioned Ruskin among those who " doubled the opulence and significance of language and made prose more penetrating than anything but the highest poetry."

What are the secrets of Ruskin's mastery ? Elsewhere I have written at length on his models, his studies, and his methods ; but I think that at bottom it nearly all comes to this : that he had something to say, that he said it in the way that was natural to him, and that nature had endowed him with exquisite sensibility.   You may analyse a style into its component parts as systematically as you like ; you may trace, label, and collate as diligently as you can ; and you will be little nearer in the end than in the beginning to the secret of a great writer's charm and power. The essential features are those which are underived and incommunicable.   The style is the man.

In the case of Ruskin's writing the child was father of the man.   The essays on " The Poetry of Architecture," which under the *nom de plume* of Kata Phusin he contributed to the *Architectural Magazine*, were written while he was an undergraduate át Christ Church.   They indicate already his point of view, and contain in germ much of his maturer work.   And, as he said of them in later years, these boyish pieces " contain sentences nearly as well put together as any I have done since," and show " the skill of language which the public at once felt for a pleasant gift in me." The gift was of nature.   The glow, the colour,

the music, the exuberance of language, are found
in his notes and diaries, as Mr. Frederic Harrison
has truly said, no less than in his finished books.
Mr. Harrison had seen diaries of 1849.   In the
Library Edition of Ruskin's Works many are
given of earlier date, and the same thing is true
of them.   He was to see more, to feel more, and
to learn more ; but throughout his working life
he saw with his own eyes, he felt with his own
heart, and what he learnt was knowledge at first
hand.   He read widely and discursively, avoiding
commentaries and seldom entering into critical
or historical inquiries.   The original texts were
all he cared to consult in literature ; and in
scientific inquiries, if he consulted other researches, he soon came to the conclusion that he
had better begin over again from the beginning
for himself.   He confesses it in a playful letter,
which I think is one of the happiest of all his
exercises in that gentle art.   He is apologising
to Mrs. Carlyle for delaying to call, and, after
giving other excuses, goes on thus :

Not that I have not been busy—and very busy, too.
I have written since May, good 600 pages [of *Modern
Painters*], and am going to press with the first of them on
Gunpowder Plot Day, with a great hope of disturbing
the Public Peace in various directions.   In the course of
the 600 pages I have had to make various remarks on
German Metaphysics, on Poetry, Political Economy,
Cookery, Music, Geology, Dress, Agriculture, Horti-

culture, and Navigation; all which subjects I have had to read up accordingly, and this takes time. During my studies of Horticulture I became dissatisfied with the Linnæan and Everybodyelseian arrangement of plants. I have accordingly arranged a system of my own. My studies of political economy have induced me to think, also, that nobody knows anything about *that*, and I am at present engaged in an investigation, on independent principles, of the Natures of Money, Rent, and Taxes, in an abstract form, which sometimes keeps me awake all night. My studies of German Metaphysics have also induced me to think that the Germans don't know anything about *them*; and to engage in a serious inquiry into the Finite realisation of Infinity; which has given me some trouble. . . . But I am coming to see you.

Ruskin's habit of studying only original texts, or actual phenomena, regardless of what other people had written around the texts or discovered about the phenomena, is obviously a source both of weakness and of strength. It accounts for some of his waywardness and ingenious perversity, but it encouraged the suggestiveness of his thought and preserved that " intellectual independence " of which Mr. Asquith speaks and which was noted by John Stuart Mill also as characteristic of Ruskin's writing.[1]

---

[1] In John Stuart Mill's Diary of 1854 there is this passage : " It is long since there has been an age of which it could be said, as truly as of this, that nearly all the writers, even the good ones, were but commentators : expounders and appliers of ideas borrowed from others. Among those of the present time I can think only of two (now that Carlyle has written himself out, and become a mere commentator on himself) who seem to draw what

Ruskin, then, had something of his own to say, and he said it in his own way, but this does not mean that he took no pains in saying it. He tells us in his autobiography that his literary work was done " as quietly and methodically as a piece of tapestry," but he took infinite trouble in getting the stitches right. His command of language was due, he says elsewhere, to " the constant habit of never allowing a sentence to pass proof in which I have not considered whether, for the vital word in it, a better could be found in the dictionary." The study of his manuscripts that was made by Mr. Wedderburn and myself for the Library Edition shows that Ruskin's search for the right word, for the fitting sentence, was often long, and paragraphs and chapters were written over and over again before they satisfied him.[1] And this revision was applied not only to his more elaborate passages, but no less to his most simple writing. Cardinal Newman—a great master of simple and lucid English, greater in these particular respects, if we take the whole

they say from a source within themselves : and to the practical doctrines and tendencies of both these, there are the gravest objections. Comte, on the Continent ; in England (ourselves excepted) I can only think of Ruskin."

[1] Ruskin carried on his revisions to the stage of proofs, revises, and re-revises. Dr. Furnivall was told by Ruskin's father that the publisher came to him one day exhibiting a thickly scored final revise and explaining that continuance in such practices would absorb all the author's profits. " Don't let my son know," said the old gentleman ; " John must have his things as he likes them ; pay him whatever would become due, apart from corrections, and send in a separate bill for them to me." Few authors, it may be feared, are blessed with so indulgent a parent.

body of their writings, than Ruskin—submitted to the same discipline. " I have been obliged," he said, " to take great pains with everything I have written, and I often write chapters over and over again, besides innumerable corrections and interlined additions."

In the *Note-Books of Samuel Butler*, the " Enfant Terrible of Literature " (as his editor calls him) has this passage :

I never knew a writer yet who took the smallest pains with his style and was at the same time readable. Plato's having had seventy shies at one sentence is quite enough to explain to me why I dislike him. . . . Men like Newman and R. L. Stevenson seem to have taken pains to acquire what they called a style as a preliminary measure—as something that they had to form before their writings could be of any value. I should like to put it on record that I never took the smallest pains with my style, have never thought about it, and do not know or want to know whether it is a style or whether it is not, as I believe and hope, just common, simple straightforwardness. I cannot conceive how any man can take thought for his style without loss to himself and his readers.

It was wicked of the author of *Erewhon* to lay hands on his father, the author of the *Republic*, and his remark on Newman is unintelligible to me, for the ease and limpidity of Newman, with however great pains attained, are always felt rather than seen. Yet there is an element of truth in what Butler says, and it is necessary to distinguish. He who takes overmuch thought for his style is in danger of losing the way to excellence ; but the mischief comes, not from taking pains about his manner of saying a thing, but only when the manner begins to be of more moment than the matter. " In the highest as in the lowliest literature," says Mr. Pater, " the one indispensable beauty is, after all, truth—truth to bare fact in the latter, as to some personal sense of fact, diverted somewhat from men's ordinary sense of it, in the former ; truth there as accuracy, truth here as expression, that finest and most intimate form of truth, the *vraie vérité*."

All the masters of good style say the same thing. Renan, for instance (of whom Mommsen characteristically admitted that he was " a true *savant* in spite of his beautiful style "), said of St. Sulpice that its contempt for literature made it " perforce a capital school for style, the fundamental rule of which is to have solely in view the thought which it is wished to express." " The absolute condition of Good Writing," said Edward FitzGerald, " is the saying in the most perspicuous and succinct way what one thoroughly understands. This, of course, includes Good English, or it would *not* be perspicuous to others, however clear to oneself. Really, the Perfection is to have all this so *naturally* that no Effort is apparent ; and so the very best *Style* where there are no marks of it."

Butler wrote with admirable lucidity, and if he did it with artless facility he was by so much the more fortunate than most other writers. John Stuart Mill, whose writing is eminently smooth and lucid, has recorded in his *Autobiography* the assiduous course of reading by which he sought to clarify his style; and even so, " after revision and re-revision of a piece he felt so little satisfied of its exact conformity to its purpose that he could only bring himself. to send it to the printer by recalling how he had felt the same of other writing that people thought useful." [1] Butler succeeded for the most part in conveying to understanding readers the exact sense, or nonsense, which he desired. But how difficult this is—to secure the absolute accordance of expression to idea—to find the exactly right words for conveying from one mind to another the facts, perceptions, fancies, impressions, associations which a writer intends ! It is so difficult that in the straining after the effect there is always a danger of the manner overcoming the matter.

Ruskin, in his earlier writings especially, did not escape this danger; and, as he often bemoaned, he had to pay the penalty. " All my life," he said in conversation with Mr. Spielmann, " I have been talking to the people, and they have listened not to. what I say but to how I say it; they have cared not for the matter, but only

[1] Lord Morley's *Recollections*, vol. i. p. 59.

for the manner of my words." He became increasingly conscious of this disadvantage, and his middle and later writing is, with some exceptions, better than his earlier. In one of his Oxford lectures he pointed this out to us.[1] It was a lecture upon Style illustrated by a wide range of literary and artistic references to Turner and Carpaccio, to Virgil and Pope, and Sir Walter Scott and the Book of Job, and I remember not to whom else, and incidentally by citations from his own books. He began with the old maxims that *ars est celare artem* and that the foundation of right expression in speech or writing is sincerity. The two principles are closely related. " Whenever art is visible there is a trace," he said, " of insincerity, a certain degree of coldness. When there is perfect sincerity, the art, however magnificent, is never visible—the passion and the truth hide it. The drawing of the Greta and Tees, for instance, of Turner—it is the best I have [2]— it looks as if anybody could have done it. And in the best writing it will seem to you as if, whether it speak of little things or great, it couldn't have been said in any other way."

The fault of Ruskin's earlier writing is that it calls attention to its manner by palpable display ; the improvement in his later style is that

[1] The lecture was for the most part extempore. I gave a few recollections of it in my *Studies in Ruskin* (1890). Ruskin's own notes for it are printed in vol. xxii. of the Library Edition.

[2] Now in the Collection of the Ruskin Drawing School at Oxford.

the manner is seen less distinctly and the matter thereby gains weight. In the lecture to which I have referred Ruskin himself illustrated these points by reading, first, a passage, much admired when it appeared in the first volume of *Modern Painters*, and, then, the peroration, much derided at first, of *Unto this Last*. The earlier passage is this :

He who has once stood beside the grave, to look upon the companionship which has been for ever closed, feeling how impotent *there* are the wild love and the keen sorrow, to give one instant's pleasure to the pulseless heart, or atone in the lowest measure to the departed spirit for the hour of unkindness, will scarcely for the future incur that debt to the heart, which can only be discharged to the dust.

" With my present knowledge of literature," said Ruskin, " I could tell in an instant that the person who wrote these words never had so stood beside the dead. Being capable of deep passion, if he had ever stood beside his dead before it was buried out of his sight, he would never, in speaking of the time, have studied how to put three *d*'s one after another in *d*ebt, *d*ischarged, and *d*ust." And then he turned to what he called the central book of his life and read this :

And if, on due and honest thought over these things, it seems that the kind of existence to which men are now summoned by every plea of pity and claim of right may,

for some time at least, not be a luxurious one;—consider
whether, even supposing it guiltless, luxury would be
desired by any of us, if we saw clearly at our sides the
suffering which accompanies it in the world.   Luxury is
indeed possible in the future—innocent and exquisite;
luxury for all, and by the help of all; but luxury at present
can only be enjoyed by the ignorant; the cruellest man
living could not sit at his feast, unless he sat blindfold.
Raise the veil boldly; face the light; and if, as yet, the
light of the eye can only be through tears, and the light
of the body through sackcloth, go thou forth weeping,
bearing precious seed, until the time come, and the kingdom, when Christ's gift of bread and bequest of peace
shall be Unto this last as unto thee; and when, for earth's
severed multitudes of the wicked and the weary, there
shall be holier reconciliation than that of the narrow
home, and calm economy, where the Wicked cease—not
from trouble, but from troubling—and the Weary are
at rest.

Now that passage is better, said Ruskin, than
the other, " because there is no art of an im-
pudently visible kind in it, and not a word which,
as far as I know, you could put another for,
without loss to the sense.   It is true that *plea*
and *pity* both begin with *p*, but *plea* is the right
word, and there is no other which is in full and
clear opposition to *claim*."   As we are on points
of style, I will add that Ruskin went on to mend
the passage somewhat.   " Were I writing it
now," he said, " I should throw it looser, and
explain here and there, getting intelligibility
at the cost of concentration.   Thus when I say :

Luxury is possible in the future — innocent and exquisite ; luxury for all, and by the help of all—

that is a remain of my old bad trick of putting my words in braces, like game, neck to neck, and leaving the reader to untie them. Hear how I should put the same sentence now :

Luxury is indeed possible in the future—innocent, because granted to the need of all ; and exquisite, because perfected by the aid of all.

You see," he said, " it has gained a little in melody in being put right, and gained a great deal in clearness."

Such are among the points in which Ruskin's style shows a progressive improvement, and which, as I often noted in editing his works, he kept constantly in mind when he revised his sentences. It may have surprised some readers —especially such as know Ruskin only from selections of his purple patches—to hear him speaking of conciseness as characteristic of him. But so it is. He was a master not more of rhetorical pomp and of the long rolling sentence than of concentration closely packed with thought. Here is a passage—not irrelevant to some discussions of the day—which is among those which he was happiest, he said, in having written. It comes from a lecture delivered at Bradford and called " Traffic " :

The only absolutely and unapproachably heroic

element in the soldier's work seems to be—that he is paid
little for it and regularly: while you traffickers, and
exchangers, and others occupied in presumably benevolent
business, like to be paid much for it, and by chance. I
never can make out how it is that a *knight*-errant does
not expect to be paid for his trouble, but a *pedlar*-errant
always does ;—that people are willing to take hard knocks
for nothing, but never to sell ribands cheap; that they
are ready to go on fervent crusades, to recover the tomb
of a buried God, but never on any travels to fulfil the
orders of a living one ;—that they will go anywhere bare-
foot to preach their faith, but must be well bribed to
practise it, and are perfectly ready to give the Gospel
gratis, but never the loaves and fishes.[1]

If this passage has a literary fault, it is over-
concentration. And here is another piece of
concentrated thought—a passage which Mr.
Frederic Harrison has " always taken as a masterpiece of wit, wisdom, and eloquence " :

In a community regulated only by laws of demand
and supply, but protected from open violence, the persons
who become rich are, generally speaking, industrious,
resolute, proud, covetous, prompt, methodical, sensible,
unimaginative, insensitive, and ignorant. The persons

---

[1] The passage comes from *The Crown of Wild Olive*, about which
book this anecdote is told. "Ruskin would have appreciated the gratitude
of a man of the Lancashire Fusiliers, of whom a sergeant of the Lancers
wrote : 'He had two ghastly wounds in his breast, and I thought he was
booked through. He was quietly reading a little edition of Ruskin's *Crown
of Wild Olive*, and seemed to be enjoying it immensely. As I chatted with
him for a few minutes he told me that this little book had been his companion all through and that when he died he wanted it to be buried with
him. His end came next day, and we buried the book with him'" (*Westminster Gazette*, March 23, 1915).

who remain poor are the entirely foolish, the entirely wise, the idle, the reckless, the humble, the thoughtful, the dull, the imaginative, the sensitive, the well-informed, the improvident, the irregularly and impulsively wicked, the clumsy knave, the open thief, and the entirely merciful, just, and godly person.

These passages both belong to Ruskin's middle period. Of his altered manner of writing in descriptive passages, a good instance may be obtained by comparing the pieces which he wrote at different periods about his favourite among the sepulchral monuments of Italy, the Ilaria of Quercia in the cathedral of Lucca. His affection for his beautiful work is shared by the peasantry. "We have often," says the Arundel Society's note on its engraving, "seen the Lucchesi, on leaving the Duomo by the door beside which the monument is placed, stoop and press their lips for a moment to the sweet up-turned face." [1] There are four descriptions of the monument in the Library Edition of Ruskin's works. The earliest is given in a letter written to his father after first sight of it. This is chiefly interesting as showing how first impressions were worked up, as in this case in the following passage in the second volume of *Modern Painters* :

In the Cathedral of·Lucca, near the entrance-door of the north transept, there is a monument by Jacopo della

---

[1] The monument, then placed against the wall of the north transept, was in 1891 removed to the centre and protected by an iron railing.

Quercia to Ilaria di Caretto, the wife of Paolo Guinigi. I name it not as more beautiful or perfect than other examples of the same period, but as furnishing an instance of the exact and right mean between the rigidity and rudeness of the earlier monumental effigies, and the morbid imitation of life, sleep, or death, of which fashion has taken place in modern times. She is lying on a simple couch with a hound at her feet; not on the side, but with the head laid straight and simply on the hard pillow, in which, let it be observed, there is no effort at deceptive imitation of pressure. It is understood as a pillow, but not mistaken for one. The hair is bound in a flat braid over the fair brow, the sweet and arched eyes are closed, the tenderness of the loving lips is set and quiet; there is that about them which forbids breath; something which is not death nor sleep, but the pure image of both. The hands are not lifted in prayer, neither folded, but the arms are laid at length upon the body, and the forms of the limbs concealed, but not their tenderness.

If any of us, after staying for a time beside this tomb, could see, through his tears, one of the vain and unkind encumbrances of the grave, which, in these hollow and heartless days feigned sorrow builds to foolish pride, he would, I believe, receive such a lesson of love as no coldness could refuse, no fatuity forget, and no insolence disobey.

It is a fine passage: Mrs. Laurence Binyon includes it, I see, in her interesting selection of *Nineteenth Century Prose*, but Ruskin's later descriptions of the same monument (1874, 1878) are, I think, better. They are too long to quote, but I will give one extract :

Her hands are laid on her breast—not praying—she has no need to pray now.   She wears her dress of every day, clasped at her throat, girdled at her waist, the hem of it drooping over her feet.   No disturbance of its folds by pain of sickness, no binding, no shrouding of her sweet form, in death more than in life.   As a soft, low wave of summer sea, her breast rises; no more: the rippled gathering of its close mantle droops to the belt, then sweeps to her feet, straight as drifting snow   And at her feet her dog lies watching her; the mystery of his mortal life joined, by love, to her immortal one.

If any reader cares to refer to the descriptions in full, he will see that all the points noticed in *Modern Painters* are included, but that greater simplicity is attained, while the art of the writing is less obtrusive, the intensity of the feeling is enhanced, and in some details there is closer fidelity to fact.   One point was noticed by Ruskin himself. " In *Modern Painters*," he said, " I foolishly used the generic word *hound* to make my sentence prettier.   He is a flat-nosed bulldog."

All this illustrates a fact than which none impressed me more in the course of my long work in editing Ruskin.   He revised and elaborated in order to clarify, to chasten, to deepen, and to impress.   Elsewhere I have illustrated this statement by setting out from his manuscripts and proofs the stages through which some of his most eloquent pages passed on the way to their ultimate form.[1]

---

[1] See my *Life of Ruskin,* vol. i. ch. xviii.   Many other instances may be found by reference to the Index to the Library Edition.

" It is the chief provocation of my life," he
wrote to a friend, "to be called a word-
painter." He *was* a word-painter, but he painted
always "with his eye on the object" and with
his mind on the thought. This is especially
true of his work as a descriptive writer. Sir
Charles Walston has a chapter on " Ruskin
as the founder of Phænomenology of Nature."
The claim had already been made by Ruskin
himself. Of his studies, in *Modern Painters*,
of the nature and form of clouds he says that
they are "usually thought of by the public
merely as word-painting," but that they " are in
reality accurately abstracted, and finally concentrated, expressions of the general laws of
natural phenomena." He instanced a passage
in the chapter of the fourth volume called " The
Firmament." " The sentence, ' Murmuring only
when the winds raise them or rocks divide,'
does not describe, or word-paint, the sound of
waters, but (with only the admitted art of a
carefully reiterated *r*) sums the general causes of
it ; while, again, the immediately following
sentence, defining the limitations of sea and
river, ' restrained by established shores and
guided through unchanging channels,' attempts
no word-painting, either of coast or burn-side,
but states, with only such ornament of its simplicity as could be got of the doubled *t* and
doubled *ch*, the fact of existing rock structure

which I was, at that time, alone among geologists in asserting." Of his writing in such sort he was " not ashamed to express my conviction that it was unlikely to be surpassed by any other author." In editing his Works, which included a study of things drawn as well as of things written, I saw reason for thinking that Ruskin's conviction was not too thrasonical. There was in him a combination of gifts and studies which must always be very rare. It was not only that he was possessed of acute sensibility and of a most original mind, together with a great mastery of language. To his work as a descriptive writer he brought the further qualifications of an amateur in some branches of natural science and of an accomplished and most industrious draughtsman. He was something of a botanist and more of a geologist and mineralogist. Of his drawings the catalogue which I compiled for the Library Edition, though it is mainly limited to engraved or exhibited drawings, contains 2145 pieces. " People sometimes praise me as industrious," he says in his autobiography, " when they count the number of printed volumes which Mr. Allen can now advertise. But the biography of the waste pencilling and passionately forsaken colouring, heaped in the dusty corners of Brantwood, if I could write it, would be far more pathetically exemplary or admonitory." He used to say that he kept skies " bottled like his father's sherries,"

and I doubt if he ever sat down to describe anything with the pen which he had not spent hours
in drawing with the pencil. He *was* a word-
painter, but he was much else.

The matter may be brought to a test. Take
any of his good passages of description and see.
I will name five examples, not as being the best,
but as having some interesting association :

The chapter on " The Region of the Rain-
Cloud " in the first volume of *Modern Painters*.
This chapter ends with a comparison of the
rendering of the phenomena by Turner and
Claude respectively and is referred to in this
scene of Morris's Oxford life : " He would often
read Ruskin aloud. He had a mighty singing
voice, and chanted rather than read those weltering
oceans of eloquence as they have never been
given before or since, it is most certain. The
description of the Slave Ship or of Turner's skies,
with the burden, ' Has Claude given this ? '
were declaimed by him in a manner that made
them seem as if they had been written for no end
but that he should hurl them in thunder on the
head of the base criminal who had never seen
what Turner saw in the sky."

The description of the narcissus fields on the
mountain-side above Vevay in the third volume
of the same book. This is the passage which
Matthew Arnold selected. " There," he said,
" is what the genius, the feeling, the tempera-

ment in Mr. Ruskin, the original and incommunicable part has to do with, and how exquisite it is ! "

The description of the old tower of Calais Church in the fourth volume. A " glorious thing," said Rossetti of it. In the Library Edition I have printed the first draft of the passage, and by comparing this with the final form a reader may note how the author omitted superfluous words, pared down alliterations, and knit the sound into closer harmony with the sense.

The description of an old boat at the beginning of *The Harbours of England.* " No book in our language," says Mr. Frederic Harrison, " shows more varied resources over prose-writing, or an English more pure, more vigorous, more enchanting," and of this hymn to the sea-boat he adds that it is " as fine and as true as anything ever said about the sea, even by our sea-poets, Byron or Shelley."

And, last, the description of the Rhone at Geneva in *Præterita.* This is of peculiar interest as being the latest piece of the kind which Ruskin wrote with any elaboration. I had heard Sir Charles Walston in a lecture at the Royal Institution select this passage, as a masterpiece of observation, analysis, selection and rhythm, for a test which he suggested, and I was curious to know when it was written. Chancing to meet

Ruskin not long afterwards, I asked the question.
He told me (and indications in his diary confirm
his recollection) that it was written in May 1886
—a date some months after one of his serious
illnesses and a few weeks before another.

Now take the subject of any of these passages,
or sit down to write out a description of anything
else touched by Ruskin—a cathedral front, a
blade of grass, or a picture by Tintoret—or
where a corresponding passage from some other
author can be found, bring that into account
and then compare the result with Ruskin's work.
Wherein would the difference be found to consist ? Not merely, I think, in difference of
eloquence and rhythm ; but we should most of
us find that we had stated, or that most of the
other authors had stated, fewer facts and conveyed
the impression of fewer or less significant thoughts.
To Ruskin's writing at its best may be applied
what he lays down about the art of painting.
" Finish," he says, " simply means telling more
truth "—truth, in the words already quoted from
Mr. Pater, " either to fact or to some personal
sense of fact, diverted somewhat from men's
ordinary sense of it."

III

THE ART OF INDEXING

A servant with this clause
  Makes drudgery divine :
Who sweeps a room as for thy laws
  Makes that and th' action fine.

THERE is no book (in the category of general
literature) so good that it is not made better by
an index, and no book so bad that it may not
by this adjunct escape the worst condemnation.
Carlyle, the foe of Dryasdust, reserved his
heaviest fire for those members of the species
who had not even the decency to index themselves.   He gives a list of books at the beginning
of his *Cromwell*: " Enormous folios, these and
many others have been printed, and some of them
again printed, but never yet edited—edited as
you edit wagonloads of broken bricks and dry
mortar, simply by tumbling up the wagon.   Not
one of those monstrous old volumes has so much
as an available Index !"   And again at the
beginning of his *Friedrich* :

Books born mostly of Chaos, which want all things,
even an index, are a painful object. . . . The Prussian

Dryasdust, otherwise an honest fellow and not afraid of labour, excels all other Dryasdusts yet known.   . . He writes big books wanting in almost every quality; and does not even give an Index to them.   Enough : he could do no other : I have striven to forgive him.

The strife was hard and not, I imagine, successful, for Carlyle is credited with the saying that a publisher who issues a book without an index should be hanged.   The Roxburghe Club, thinking that trial should precede execution, proposed that the omission of an Index, " when essential," should be an indictable offence, and Lord Campbell, in a more practical spirit, proposed that in such a case an author should be deprived of copyright.   In spite of such fulminations, authors and publishers continually offend, and even when an index is given it is too often done in a perfunctory and slovenly manner.   " A dreary book crowned by a barren index," says Lord Rosebery of Forsyth's *Captivity of Napoleon at St. Helena*, writing as one who had barely survived " the hideous task " of reading his way through those " indigestible " and massive three volumes.   The fact is that the importance of the art of indexing is little understood.   Many people do not even know that it is an art at all.

Two classes of books in particular should always have a good index—the best books and the most unreadable books.   The best books, because there is so much in them that a reader

will want to find again ; the worst books, because
lacking an index they are without any reason for
existing at all.   Take, for instance, the Parliamentary Debates.   No man of sense reads them
for pleasure.   They are valuable only for reference, and a book of reference without a complete
index is almost a contradiction in terms.   For
many years *Hansard* was indexed as badly as
could be.   It is now much better done, because
the entries are fuller and more numerous.

Should even a novel have an index ?   There
is high authority for answering, as the parlia-
mentarians say, in the affirmative.   Dr. Johnson,
in writing to Mr. Richardson about *Clarissa
Harlowe*, said :

I wish you would add an index rerum, that when the
reader recollects any incident, he may easily find it, which
at present he cannot do, unless he knows in which volume
it is told ; for Clarissa is not a performance to be read
with eagerness, and laid aside for ever ; but will be
occasionally consulted by the busy, the aged, and the
studious ; and therefore I beg that this edition, by which
I suppose posterity is to abide, may want nothing that
can facilitate its use.

The egregious Mr. Croker has it that Johnson's
proposition was so absurd that it can only be
ascribed to a desire on his part to minister to
Richardson's vanity.   But not every one is, like
Lord Macaulay, a walking index to *Clarissa*,
who, it should be remembered, is in seven or

even eight volumes, and there is a great deal to be said for Johnson's suggestion. A biography cannot be considered complete without an index. Why not also a novel ? The great characters of fiction are much more worthy of memory, and do in fact live much longer, than the subjects of most biographies. " For the life after death," says Samuel Butler of Hamlet, Don Quixote, Mr. Pickwick and some others, " it is not necessary that a man or a woman should have lived." [1] It must, however, be admitted that for a novelist still alive to furnish his books with an index would be a dangerous presumption. Richardson might have carried it off, for his Pamela and Clarissa went forth conquering and to conquer, but hardly another could so venture. When time has set its seal on a novelist's work comes the day for an index. The *Dickens Dictionary* and the *Key to the Waverley Novels* have deserved well of two or three generations of readers already.

If it be a sin to put out any good book without adding an index, still more is he to be condemned who edits the Collected Works of a good author without doing so. The more voluminous and the more miscellaneous the author, the greater is the need of a full and analytical index. Carlyle

---

[1] Disraeli had said something like this in his speech at the Royal Literary Fund dinner in 1868 : " Without books those imaginary characters as they are called, but which are really much more vital and substantial than half our acquaintances, would no longer exist. There would be no Hamlets, no Don Quixotes, no Falstaffs."

had this service done to his Works during his
life; Ruskin has had it done to his after his
death, for though he sometimes nibbled at undertaking the task himself he lacked time to fulfil
it. He knew the need acutely. " I have left
the system of my teaching widely scattered and
broken," he lamented. " Alphabetical indices,"
he says elsewhere, " will be of little use unless
another and a very different kind of index be
arranged in the mind of the reader," and he
proceeded to analyse the contents of one of his
books in logical sequence. This is what the
elaborate Index at the end of the Library Edition
aimed at doing for the whole body of his writings.
" The work of Ruskin," says a French expositor,
" is a forest where paths and branches cross each
other without end." " One must feel," says
another critic, " that true justice would only be
done to the works of Ruskin if with infinite labour
some sympathetic and congenial spirit possessed
of much sobriety and system were to arrange the
whole of the works and to distribute passages
taken from them all under new heads, with a
simple, intelligible, and orderly classification."
Of these requirements, the infinite labour was
forthcoming; and with the Index just mentioned
in hand, any reader of Ruskin has the means of
doing the thing for himself. There are other
modern writers in whose case the need is not so
sore, but yet is felt. Take Matthew Arnold, for

instance. He was discursive ; he touched many
subjects lightly, he leapt (as Mr. Birrell has it)
from bough to bough, and he often returned to
the same bough in different books. If you
want to know all that he had to say in defining
the essence of poetry or in description of the grand
style, you have to collate passages scattered in
many different essays, and there is no index to
help you in the search. The late Lord Coleridge,
in a Prefatory Note to the second series of *Essays
in Criticism*, says that Arnold intended to write
something more about Shelley. Lord Coleridge
added, what is very true, that " in order to gather
the mind of Mr. Arnold on the whole of any
subject it is necessary to read more than one paper,
because in each paper he frequently deals with
one aspect of a subject only, which requires for
sound and complete judgment to be supplemented
or completed by another. It is especially necessary to bear this in mind in reading what has
become his last utterance on Shelley." Yet the
editor of his complete works gives us no index
at all. Another book which badly wants indexing
is Froude's ever-delightful *Short Studies on Great
Subjects* in four volumes. I have often thought
that the money spent in producing Editions de
Luxe is all very well, but necessaries should come
before luxury, and an index is a necessary. I
have even wondered whether some of those who
have edited modern authors would not have

done better service by indexing than by " introducing " them. A friend of Francis Douce,
the antiquary, had a curse of his own for those
who sent out a book without an index where one
was obviously wanted. He damned them " ten
miles beyond Hell." For my part I think that
simple damnation is enough in the case of a
single book, and that the extra ten miles of Douce's
friend might be reserved for those who collect
an author's works without indexing them.

A specious defence against indexes has sometimes been made out of the argument that every
one ought to read, mark, learn, and inwardly
digest a book as he goes along, that therein he
makes an index for himself, and that if he
finds it ready-made he is spared this wholesome
discipline. Public men, when they address
Institutes or Students' Unions, make much of
various mechanical aids to serious reading. We
are told how Sir William Hamilton used to make
an abstract of a book as he went along, distinguish-
ing different groups of subjects by different-
coloured inks ; or how Gibbon, reversing the
process, made an abstract before he read a book
of what he expected to find therein, subsequently
noting any new points ; or how Horne Tooke
made notes of books on visiting-cards, slipt them
through a slit into his desk—" put it into the
post-office " was his phrase—and afterwards
sorted them out for reference. And so forth and

so forth. It is quite true that no printed index is
likely to fill the same place as these private aids
to memory. But that is no reason why the
printed index should not first be supplied. It is
intolerable presumption on the part of an author
to suggest that his words are too precious, too
worthy of being learnt by heart, for an index to
be given. Thomas Fuller long ago disposed
of such pretence in a passage of sound sense and
quaint humour :

An Index is a necessary implement, and no impediment
of a book, except in the same sense wherein the carriages
of an army are termed *impedimenta*. Without this, a
large author is but a labyrinth without a clue to direct the
reader therein.   I confess there is a lazy kind of learning
which is only *indical*; when scholars (like adders which
only bite the horse's heels) nibble but at the tables, which
are *calces librorum*, neglecting the body of the book.   But
though the idle deserve no crutches (let not a staff be used
by them, but on them), pity it is the weary should be
denied the benefit thereof, and industrious scholars pro-
hibited the accommodation of an index, most used by
those who most pretend to contemn it.

Let it be granted, then, that every book which
is worth anything should have a good index.
But what is a good index ? There is much
ignorance on this point, and many indexes are
skimble-skamble performances. Take such a
simple thing as an index to a poet's poems. The
other day I wanted to refer to Tennyson's two

translations from the *Iliad*, and turned for quick help, as I supposed, to the " Index to the Poems " ; but the help was not forthcoming, for only one of the pieces was indexed under " Iliad," the other appearing under "Achilles." The maker of that index worked without brains. But we shall better be able to discuss errors in indexing if we start from first principles. An index is meant to be a pointer and to serve as a time-saving machine. It should enable a reader, first, to find readily the place where the author has said a particular thing, and, secondly, it should enable him to find all that the book has said on a particular subject.

In applying these principles, I lay down as the first rule, One book One index. It was once a custom to have several indexes to one book, in order, I suppose, not to mix up titles incongruously. There would, for instance, be an index of persons and places, a second of subjects, a third of words, and so forth. The practice was common in editions of the classics, and the Latin phrases were often used in English books —*index locorum, rerum, verborum*, and so forth. Such multiplication of indexes is an unmitigated nuisance. It makes reference less easy. One index alphabetically arranged is the only right plan.

But what should be included in the index ? How many and what kind of titles should there be ?   Macaulay has a saying on this subject from which I must take liberty to dissent strongly :

"I am very unwilling," he wrote to his publisher, "to seem captious about such a work as an index.   By all means let Mr. —— go on.   But offer him with all delicacy and courtesy from me this suggestion.   I would advise him to have very few heads except proper names. A few there must be, such as Convocation, Nonjurors, Bank of England, National Debt.   These are heads to which readers who wish for information on such those subjects will naturally turn.   But I think that Mr. —— will on consideration perceive that such heads as Priest-craft, Priesthood, Party Spirit, Insurrection, War, Bible, Crown, Controversies, Dissent, are quite useless.   Nobody will ever look at them ;   and if every passage in which party-spirit, dissent, the art of war and the power of the Crown are mentioned is to be noticed in the Index, the size of the volumes will be doubled.   The best rule is to keep close to proper names, and never to deviate from that rule without some special occasion."

This may be a good rule in the case of a history, and proper names are what should always be included in an index whatever else be omitted.   In the case of Macaulay's own History his rule is the more appropriate because the work is stronger in its personal sketches and in appeal to the imagination than in discussion of general problems.   But Macaulay had interesting things to say on many subjects, and Mr. ——, to the great advantage of Macaulay's readers, did not confine himself to the few general heads for which he had the author's express permission. " Nobody will ever look for them," said Macaulay of this and that suggested title ; but how could he tell ? Lord Rosebery in a speech a few years ago, foresaw a day when the world itself could not contain the books that should be written : libraries would cover all the ground, and the only help was, he suggested, a periodical bonfire. He forgot, by the way, that this is the age of tubes. Space may be extended downwards, and the underground store-rooms of the Bodleian Library at Oxford have provided accommodation for ages to come. It is a chastening thought for all literary men that, bonfire or no bonfire, most of what is written to-day will be as dead a hundred years hence as though it had never been. But who can say to-day what will be wholly valueless then ? Nobody can. The scientific world has been all agog with Mendelism. The new " ism " is revolutionising biology, and if the biologists have their way it may revolutionise politics and social reform. But what was the origin of Mendelism ? where was the sacred script found ? It was a stray article which lay ignored for thirty-five years in an obscure periodical, just the sort of thing that a hustling librarian might have turned out as fodder for Lord Rosebery's bonfire. An index-maker, then, should have no prejudices or partialities, and every subject on which he finds any

F

substantial discussion in the book should be included in the index. He is working for an unknown future and for readers whose tastes and interests he cannot know. Of course, in making an index exhaustive, he must use some discrimination. Opie's answer to the man who asked how he mixed his colours—" With brains "—is applicable to all arts and crafts, however humble.

A good index, then, will have a great many titles. Double entries are sometimes advisable if an index is to be adapted to ready reference. I agree with the writer who said that " time is of more value than type and the wear and tear of temper than an extra page of index." Take, for instance, the case of *Hansard* already mentioned. A speech should be indexed under the speaker's name, but also under its main subject. Every indexer must have certain rules before him, but he will do well not to follow them slavishly. In the construction of an index there are cases when it is necessary to do, as some architects have to be told, and make a sacrifice of symmetry to convenience. The one thought which an indexer should never forget is how best to save the time of those for whom he is working.

Next, how are the entries under any given head to be arranged ? Wrong answers to this question cover most of the vices which an index can exhibit. The most frequent and the most heinous is the practice of following a subject-heading by long strings of page numbers without any indication of what you will find on the several pages. This is to fob you off with an index which is no index. Of course, if the references to a particular person or subject are few or unimportant, a simple reference to the pages may be excused ; but when they are many and varied, an index of that kind sets you, if you are in search of a particular passage, to look for a needle in a bundle of hay. Some indexers know that this will not do, but they weary in doing better, and, after sorting out a certain number of the references, fall back into simple numbers under the sub-heading " Otherwise mentioned." Here, again, there is sometimes reasonable excuse for the practice : it is a sound plan to preserve proportion and to distinguish between substantial references and mere passing allusions : the latter may rightly be lumped together under " Otherwise mentioned." On the other hand, it is very tiresome to find, after long search, that an important reference is concealed under that head. Lord Morley's *Life of Gladstone* is furnished with an admirable index, as was meet and right in a work which, besides its other merits, is a most valuable book of political reference. I remembered that somewhere there was record of Mr. Gladstone's attitude towards Mr. Chamberlain at the opening of the Irish controversy in 1885.   The references to Mr. Chamberlain are for the most part clearly distinguished in the index, but the particular passage which I had in mind only disclosed itself after search among the " other mentions " (iii. 191).

Where, then, a book contains many mentions of a person or a subject, the indexer must analyse them and tell you not only on what page each mention will be found, but also what is the subject of the mention on each page.   This is the most difficult and least mechanical part of an indexer's work.   If the reader thinks that anybody can do it, let him try his hand and he will learn better. It needs much time, thought, and judgment to seize the true sense of a passage, to decide what description will best facilitate reference, and then to make the entry with the concision required in an index.   Nearly as bad as an index which omits a proper reference is one which gives you a blind reference.   The classical instance in this sort is alleged to occur in a law book :

Best, Mr. Justice, his great mind, p. 101.

On turning to the page one is supposed to have found the statement that " Mr. Justice Best said he had a great mind to commit the man for trial."   I believe that the entry has never been traced to any authentic source, but it serves as an example of how not to do it.   If the entry does really exist, it may have been the jest of a bored or spiteful indexer, and this possibility suggests a further point. The maker of an index to another man's work must be impartial. His business is to be a sign-post, not a critic. Mr. Wheatley in his exhaustive monograph has given instances of the way in which in the eighteenth century the index was sometimes used as an instrument of party propaganda. Thus William Bromley had published a platitudinous book of Travels, and his Whig opponents put out as an election squib an index in which all his most platitudinous passages were collected; as, for instance :

BOULOGNE, the first city on the French shore, lies on the coast, p. 2.
FEBRUARY, an ill season to see a garden in, p. 53.

The squib missed fire, for Bromley was returned and was elected Speaker. It must be attributed to the intellectual arrogance of the Whigs that an addiction to platitude was thought likely to count against a parliamentarian. Still, Macaulay who knew all these things may well have said (as reported) to his publisher, " Let no damned Tory index my History."

We may now suppose our indexer to have read through the book. He has the stock of slips on which the purport of each passage which he intends to index is indicated. He has sorted them out under proper names or subjects. How is he to arrange the entries under each heading? It is at this stage, as it seems to me, that most indexers go wrong. The plan generally adopted is to arrange the entries in the order in which the passages indicated by them occur in the book. Now if the author is a very methodical and orderly writer, if you know the order in which he treats his subjects, if you remember roughly whereabout in a book or a volume a passage occurs, such an index may serve you. But it is seldom that these conditions exist, and if they do not, the index compiled on the assumption that they do will serve you very badly. An instance will make the point clear.

The indexes and summaries which are supplied to Carlyle's complete works were, it is believed, the work in main of his neighbour and volunteer assistant, Mr. Henry Larkin, who " helped me," says Carlyle, " in a way not to be surpassed for completeness, ingenuity, patience, exactitude, and total and continual absence of fuss." " You wanted work," said Carlyle to him, " and you are likely to get it." This can well be believed, for Mr. Larkin had first volunteered his services when *Friedrich* was in progress. The indexes to that book and to Carlyle's works generally are well done, but in one respect they are deficient. The index to *Friedrich* contains under his name twenty-one half columns of close print. The entries give well enough the subject of each reference, but they are not sorted out under any sub-heads, being arranged, irrespective of subject, in the order in which they occur in the seven volumes. The index is hopeless and helpless if you want to find readily where Carlyle reports a particular saying or to trace the author's scattered references to the gifts or character of his hero. Of course, where the essence of the matter is chronological and the book itself is so arranged, the arrangement of index entries in a corresponding order may serve, but even so a certain amount of subdivision is desirable.

With this proviso I should lay down two rules : in every long heading in an index there should be sub-headings, and the order of arrangement under each should be alphabetical. The observance of these rules greatly adds to the labour of the indexer, but it also greatly helps facility of reference. It is impossible to carry general rules much further. The number and kind of sub-heads must depend on the nature and volume of the matter in hand. But a few hints, suggested by common mistakes in indexes, may be offered. In the case of entries dealing with persons it is clearly desirable to separate general references from those which deal with particular books, speeches, letters, or whatever else they may be. In the case of a voluminous writer, it may often be helpful to divide his references to general subjects into (1) leading ideas and principal passages, and (2) general references. In the case of (2), entries should be alphabetical, but in the case of (1), the order may well be explanatory and logical.

Who should make the index? In old days an author generally did the work himself, and Bayle cites with approval the whimsical remark attributed to a Spanish bibliographer that the index of a book should be made by the author even if the book itself were written by some one else. Certainly there is a flavour about an index made by an author himself, especially if he is a humorist, which is lacking from others. One shares the chuckle which Lowell must have enjoyed when he put into the " Index to the *Biglow Papers* " : " Babel, probably the first congress, 164 ; a gabble-mill, *ib.* " ; or Ruskin, when in an index which he began for his hotch-potch called *Fors Clavigera* he wrote down : " Parliamentary talk, a watchman's rattle sprung by constituencies of rascals at sight of an honest man, 37." [1] The author of *Erewhon*, too, was fond of indexing or beginning to index his books, and must have enjoyed this entry for a new edition of *Alps and Sanctuaries* : " Crossing, efficacy of,

---

[1] The humour of the following reference to *Fors Clavigera*, in an index by another hand, was perhaps unconscious. Ruskin had written : "If you have to obey the whip as a bad hound, because you have no nose, like the members of the present House of Commons, it is a very humble form of menial service indeed." What an indexer made of the passage was this :

" House of Commons, its members have no noses, 28."

1 52," remembering how the *Tablet* had read his remarks on that subject in a devotional rather than a biological sense. The same author obviously enjoyed himself in making the elaborate index which he added to the second edition of his *Evolution Old and New*, as in this entry referring to one of his pet aversions :

GENIUS, Mr. Allen says I am a, 388.

There is a serious reason why an author should make his own index, or, if he does not, should let the indexer work at his elbow. There is nothing like making an index for discovering inconsistencies and needless repetitions.

Few authors, however, have the patience to make their own indexes, but those who have not should recognise the importance of this adjunct to their work and make due acknowledgment of the collaboration. To do this would tend to establish indexing as one of the minor literary arts. There was a time when indexers had a certain status. Macaulay gives them a place, albeit the last, in the press which occurred to get near the chair where Dryden sat at Will's coffee-house. " There were Earls in stars and garters, clergymen in cassocks and bands, sheepish lads from the universities, translators and index-makers in ragged coats of frieze." It is better to have your ragged coat noticed than not to be noticed at all. How seldom it is in modern

books that the name of the index-maker is given!
I should like to believe that whenever nothing
is stated to the contrary the author has made the
index himself. But a bitter cry which I read a
few years ago in *The Book Monthly* makes this
belief difficult. " Why is it," asked the writer,
" that the erector of sign-posts through copious
volumes gets so little public recognition ? Those
useful pages have involved much reading, skill,
judgment in the marshalling of scattered references into orderly companies. ' Index by So-
and-so ' in the forefront of a book would be at
least as reasonable as ' Wigs by Thingummy '
on the programme of Hamlet."

What, it may be asked, is the proper scale
of an index ? No general answer can be given.
The scale must be governed by considerations
which differ with the nature of each individual
book or author. I have had the curiosity to
measure some of the ample indexes mentioned
in this paper. Carlyle's index-scale is, roughly,
as 1 to 36. Ruskin's Works (Library Edition)
are in thirty-eight volumes : the index makes a
thirty-ninth volume, but its print is very small.
The index to Morley's *Life of Gladstone* is on the
scale of 1 to 30. The scale of Butler's index to
Evolution Old and New is as 1 to 17. The record
for length of index in proportion to the length of
the book was held until the other day by Freeman's *Norman Conquest* : the scale is as 1 to 14,

but in this case the print of the index is large.
Lord Morley's *Recollections* has now easily beaten
this record.   The book itself occupies 760 pages ;
the index, in small print and double column,
76—precisely as 1 to 10.   Another feature of
this index, besides its length, is worth notice.
Here and there Lord Morley's index discloses
a name or a reference not given in the text : this
is often a good plan, as saving a footnote and
rewarding the user of an index by a piece of
information withheld from a less careful or curious
reader.

A perusal of the pages of an index, and even
the process of making it, are not dull, dead things.
I confess that when I look into a new book,
especially if it be one which I have not yet bought,
I turn first to the index.   If the index be at all
full there is no better way of sampling a book.
From reviews you never can tell.   The reviewer's
taste, if he blames, may not be yours.   And if
he praises and gives you specimens you may find
that he has picked out all the plums and that
the rest is leather and prunella.   An index gives
you a taste of the quality at once, which perhaps
may be why some authors and publishers are so
shy of it.   As for index-making, it is very labour-
some, especially in the case of editing a book or
collected works by some one else, but the work
has its alleviations.   " I find index - making,"
wrote Ruskin, " more difficult and tedious than

I expected.   It is easy enough to make an index, as it is to make a broom of odds and ends, as rough as oat straw ; but to make an index tied up tight, and that will sweep well into corners, isn't so easy."   It is not easy, but if you persevere you may find the same sort of satisfaction that a good housewife is said to find in a spring-cleaning or a scholar in rearranging his books. Then again an index, if it be adequately full and analytical, brings the compiler and the user into a close relation with the mind, work, and method of the author which is hardly possible in any other way.   The satisfaction of finding order evolve itself out of seeming chaos, the pleasure of noting intellectual connections have relieved, I doubt not, many a long day, month, and year of an indexer's otherwise dull labour.   Still, when all is said in this sort, the art of indexing is long and tiresome.   A master of worldly wisdom gave this among other injunctions to his pupils : " Never drudge."   The scholar, when trial is made of his patience, acts on a different precept : " Never grudge."

FIFTY YEARS OF A
LITERARY MAGAZINE

1001. *Cornhill Magazine,* from its commencement to the present time, *illustrated with several hundred engravings, clean, in the original wrappers,* in all 599 parts, forming 100 volumes. *A Bargain,* being a remarkably cheap series of this important and interesting periodical, from the library of a gentleman in the country, containing most valuable information not to be found elsewhere, contributed by writers of eminence, on subjects biographical, historical, literary, etc., and stories by the most celebrated writers of fiction. Invaluable to the general reader.

I NEVER come upon an entry of this sort in a catalogue without a certain pleasure, which the bookseller's zeal cannot utterly destroy, nor yet without a certain pang, which his wiles cannot wholly assuage. *Habent sua fata libelli!* So, then, popular magazines which in these days one sees casually bought, roughly opened, lightly discarded—the moment's plaything of a listless reader in the railway—were once carefully stored, each number set scrupulously in its appointed place, preserved " in the original wrappers," too, and " clean " ; yes, and by readers not a few are so kept even unto No. 599—not the least valued possession, it may be, in some " King's treasury " of the rectory, the manse, or the house in the wold.   In looking up an old volume of the *Cornhill* the other day, I came upon " A Scribbler's Apology."   It is unsigned, but was written, if I mistake not, by a valued contributor whose articles on popular science were for many years one of the attractions of the Magazine. He seems to have had a premonition that before long he would lay aside his pen for ever.   He makes his retrospect and concludes, in the scribbler's favour, that he has been " earning his livelihood, not indeed like the shoemaker with a clear consciousness of social worth, but in a relatively harmless and unblameworthy fashion." It is a too modest claim.   The thoughts, the information, the reflections contributed by him and hundreds of " scribblers " besides, on other subjects, have fired many a spark, aroused many an interest, thrown light on many a dark place, we cannot doubt, among thousands of readers. The *Cornhill*, or other favourite magazine, has been the monthly visitor, eagerly expected, gladly welcomed, and sometimes, as we have seen, never allowed to leave.   And in this continuity

of life even the occasional article by some unknown
pen—the happy thought which perhaps once
only moved an else silent mind to effective expression, or the one successful essay, it may be,
of an often-rejected contributor—shares equal
place, by right of inclusion between the yellow
covers, with the papers of some great master of
style, or the stories " by the most celebrated
writers of fiction." Such are the pleasant
thoughts which my bookseller's catalogue suggests.

But then comes the pang. " A complete set
of the *Cornhill*." It is to be found in many
libraries, public and private. But of the many
copies printed of each number, how few, in the
case of any magazine, can ever hope to survive !
And then, even when each copy has been preserved, there comes the time of dispersal or
dissolution. What will be the fate of my bookseller's set ? Honoured place and worthy binding, let us hope (with a good impression of the
cover duly pasted in), in some other library.
But sets are often broken up, and the disjointed
members enjoy but a precarious spell of life.
A large mass of the literature contributed to
magazines is doomed by inevitable laws to
oblivion. One reads a striking article, and
says, " I must keep this " or " make a note of
that." But few of us do it. The *Cornhill*,
however, by resolute adherence to one good
practice, encourages us. It is lightly stitched

with honest thread, and the favourite article can
be readily taken out for preservation, if we will.
The inventor of wire-stapling, which prevents
ready opening of the pages, which rusts and
which requires a carpenter's operation for its
removal, will have to endure, I warn him, long
years of penance in the bookman's purgatory.
Thackeray's latest books, the last pages of Charlotte Brontë, the first appearances of many a
poem by Tennyson, Robert Browning, Mrs.
Browning, Meredith, and Swinburne, and of
many a collected volume by Matthew Arnold,
by John Addington Symonds, by Leslie Stephen,
by Robert Louis Stevenson, and a host of other
"writers of eminence," are all to be found in the
back numbers of the *Cornhill.* If a book-lover
has not the requisite space to keep the whole set
of the *Cornhill,* what a collection of "first editions"
he might make by cutting its threads ! But
this is a counsel of perfection which few follow.
"A back number" ! It has become a proverbial phrase for what is dead and done with.
Many of the contributions made by the great
men survive, indeed, in collected books ; but
they are often prodigals, and discard much of
their original writings. A considerable amount
of their work, and a great mass of admirable
work by lesser known authors, survive only in
the back numbers, and it is a shadowy survival.
Well, the handiwork of the happy shoemaker

of the " Scribbler's Apology " does not last for
ever ; it is something, in literature also, even to
serve the passing hour.   To those whose occasional writings are buried in a magazine I would
commend a vision of the bookman's paradise
as seen by William Blake ; and in such comfort
as it may bring, let me include the sorrows of
rejected contributors.   " Ah, well, my dear,"
said he to his wife when publishers proved
unkind, " they are printed Elsewhere—and
beautifully bound."

.   .   .   .   .   .

I have referred to the novels in the *Cornhill*.
It was out of the serial publication of fiction that
the idea of the *Cornhill* and of other popular
magazines at low prices arose ; and this chapter
in the history of the British publishing trade is
curious in that the offspring, as it were, absorbed
its parent.   Fifty years ago it was a common
practice to issue novels in monthly instalments.
A happy thought occurred thereon to Mr.
George Smith, the only begetter of the *Cornhill*.
There had been the monthly reviews for a century
and more, and there was the serial publication
of novels.   Smith's idea was to combine the two,
giving to the public, at the price of the then
cheapest magazine, both the contents of a general
review and the monthly instalment of fiction.
In the popular price he was not absolutely first
in the field, for *Macmillan's Magazine*, also at

a shilling, had started two months ahead of him, but it made at that time no great speciality of fiction. The best fiction by the best writers was Smith's plan. On this side of it, the history of the *Cornhill* with its successive contributions from Thackeray, Anthony Trollope, Charles Lever, George Eliot, Mrs. Gaskell, Wilkie Collins, Charles Reade, William Black, James Payn, Henry Seton Merriman—to speak only of those who have passed away—is the history of British fiction. The magazines with their serials have continued from that day to this ; the serial publication of novels, apart from them, has ceased to be.

.   .   .   .   .   .

The mainstay of the new Magazine, as conceived by Mr. George Smith, was to be a monthly instalment of a novel by Thackeray, and as soon as he had made terms to that effect he went ahead with his scheme. It was a happy afterthought which led him to persuade Thackeray to become editor as well as chief contributor. Anthony Trollope has left it on record that in his opinion Thackeray was an indifferent editor. Trollope was a large contributor and a warm friend, and he ought to have known ; but the reasons he gives do not carry conviction. Thackeray had too thin a skin, it seems ; had not the necessary hardness of heart ; found it painful to reject contributions from widows and orphans with nothing but the *res angusta domi* to recommend them.   Thackeray hated doing it, we know ; he has told us so in his *Thorns in the Cushion* ; but the question is, " Did he do it all the same ? " If he did, the pang of the kind heart interfered nothing with the efficiency of the editor.   I have looked for the articles of which Trollope may have been thinking as palpably below the *Cornhill* standard, and protest that I cannot find them. FitzGerald, it is true, speedily scented a taint of decline, but he was an epicure.   " Thackeray's First Number," he wrote, " was famous, I thought : his own little Roundabout Paper so pleasant : but the Second Number, I say ; lets the Cockney in already : about Hogarth : Lewes is vulgar : and I don't think one can care much for Thackeray's novel."   What a standard does FitzGerald set in ruling out G. A. Sala's illustrated paper on Hogarth, and George Henry Lewes's *Studies in Animal Life*, and *Lovel the Widower* as not good enough for the *Cornhill* !   A second count in Trollope's indictment is that Thackeray was unmethodical ; never took to his desk, I suppose, at the same hour each day, to turn out a regulation number of words by the clock ; did not, it is more specifically alleged, answer letters promptly and decide the fate of contributions *instanter* ; dilly-dallied with troublesome affairs ; even lost a manuscript now and then.   All this one can well believe.   A letter

has been printed from Thackeray to Sir Henry
Thompson which bears upon the point.
" Hurrah," he wrote, " have found your leg ! "
—a sentence cryptic enough until it is explained
that the great surgeon had at Thackeray's request written a paper for the first number of
the Magazine describing an operation " Under
Chloroform," that the editor mislaid the manuscript, but that " the leg " turned up in time for
a later number.   No harm was done.   It was
a capital article, equally good at any time.

Again, Thackeray was not afraid of what,
if it appeared in the newspaper Press of to-day,
might be called sensational journalism.   In one
of his earlier numbers he published under the
title " Stranger than Fiction " a sufficiently
startling account of some spiritualistic séances,
which excited much attention and controversy
at the time.   The editor's note was as follows :
" As Editor of the Magazine I can vouch for
the good faith and honourable character of our
correspondent, a friend of twenty-five years'
standing ; but as the writer of the above astound-
ing narrative owns that he would refuse to believe
such things on the evidence of other people's
eyes, his readers are therefore free to give or
withhold their belief."   An ingenious exercise
in the art, not unknown to some other editors,
of making the best of both worlds !   Thackeray
had, too, what the journalists call " a keen eye

for copy." There is a letter from him to Anthony Trollope which well expresses a craving common to all "enterprising editors":

> I hope you will help us in many ways besides tale-telling. Whatever a man knows about life and its doings, that let us hear about. You must have tossed a good deal about the world, and have countless sketches in your memory and your portfolio. Please to think if you can furbish up any of these besides a novel. When events occur, and you have a good lively tale, bear us in mind.

"A good lively tale"! The "new" journalist calls it, I believe, "a good news story."

.   .   .   .   .   .

What were the worst thorns in the editorial cushion? The necessity, I imagine, for one thing, of hurting the susceptibilities of contributors by considering those of Mrs. Grundy.

The lady's decrees vary from generation to generation, and the fortunes of a magazine are from this point of view a chapter in the history of conventions and taste. In these days stronger meat is often presented in public than was permissible in mid-Victorian times. "Thackeray has turned me out of the *Cornhill*," wrote Mrs. Browning in May 1861, "but did it so prettily and kindly that I, who am forgiving, sent him another poem. He says that plain words permitted on Sundays must not be spoken on Mondays in England, and also that his 'Magazine is for babes and sucklings.'" "Lord

Walter's Wife," though it contained " pure
doctrine, and real modesty, and pure ethics,"
was thus ruled out on account of Mrs. Grundy.
Thackeray's letter was printed by Lady Ritchie
in the *Cornhill* for July 1896, and appears also in
the *Letters of Mrs. Browning*. Every one who
remembers the letter, or cares to turn it up, will
know how greatly Thackeray hated doing the
thing, and with what admirable and gracious
taste he did it. He had his reward. He lost
a good poem, it is true, but he got another, and
he kept a deeply valued friendship. The biography of a later editor of the *Cornhill* admits
us behind the scenes of another tragi-comedy
of a like kind. It was one of the *Cornhill's* privi-
leges to print Mr. Thomas Hardy's *Far from
the Madding Crowd*. Leslie Stephen admired
the tale greatly ; but there was a point at which,
he averred, " three respectable ladies had protested," and they were representatives, he doubted
not, of other Mrs. Grundys. " I am a slave,"
he wrote, in pleading for " gingerly treatment,"
and afterwards in declining *The Return of the
Native*. " Such were noses," comments Stephen's
biographer characteristically, " in the mid-
Victorian age." Happily Stephen's sacrifice to
Mrs. Grundy left no more sting behind it than
Thackeray's.

The nose of orthodox convention was equally
acute in spheres other than the relations of the

sexes. To the early numbers of the *Cornhill*
Ruskin contributed some papers on political
economy (*et de quibusdam aliis*), entitled *Unto
this Last*. At the present day, when economic
thought and political practice have come largely
into line with Ruskin's ideas, it requires some
effort of the historical imagination to realise the
storm of indignant protest which the essays
raised. It was as fast and furious as any theological heresy-hunt. Ruskin's papers were denounced in the Press as "eruptions of windy
hysterics," "utter imbecility," "intolerable
twaddle"; he himself was held up to scorn as
a "whiner and sniveller," screaming like "a
mad governess," "a perfect paragon of blubber-
ing." Even a cool and detached observer like
Philip Gilbert Hamerton was shocked at "those
lamentable sermons appearing in the *Cornhill
Magazine*. When a great writer is once resolutely
determined to destroy his own reputation," he
wrote in "A Painter's Camp," "it is no doubt
well to do it as speedily, as publicly, and as
effectively as possible ; but Mr. Ruskin's real
friends cannot help regretting that he should
have given his crudest thoughts to a million
readers through the medium of the most popular
Magazine of the day." By other critics the
attack was pressed against the editor and the
proprietor of the Magazine. "For some in-
scrutable reason," wrote one, "which must be

inscrutably satisfactory to his publishers, Mr.
Thackeray has allowed, etc. etc." Such blows
went home, and after four of the essays had
been published, the conductors of the Magazine
bowed before the storm. Thackeray had to convey to his friend a sentence of excommunication.
Ruskin did not quarrel either with Thackeray
or with Mr. Smith, but he was deeply hurt.
He believed that *Unto this Last* was his best book
—most pregnant in ideas, and most successful
in style. His repute at the time was as an art-
critic, but great men seldom accept the popular
judgment of their several achievements. Heine
dismissed his lyrics as " not worth a shot," but
accounted himself great as a tragedian. Goethe
took no pride in his poems, but much in his
scientific researches. Mr. Gladstone was prouder,
I suspect, of his studies in Olympian theology
than of any political exploit ; and Paganini,
when complimented after a concert on his violin-
playing, asked impatiently, " But how were you
pleased with my bows ? " The more Ruskin
was acclaimed as an art-critic and a word-painter,
the more he resented not being appreciated as
an economic thinker. He has had his will, for
at the present day it is a fashion to discard his
art theories and accept his economics. *Unto
this Last* has become the most widely dispersed,
and perhaps the most influential, of all his writings. But this is not to cast any reflections upon

Thackeray's judgment at the time.   An economic heretic, like the poet of Wordsworth's Prefaces, " has to create the taste by which he is to be admired."   The conductor of any popular magazine or other " organ of public opinion " may well be a little ahead of his public, but he cannot afford to be too much ahead.   Ruskin fared no better under Froude in *Fraser's Magazine* than under Thackeray in the *Cornhill*.   The economic essays were resumed in *Fraser's* shortly afterwards, and met there with a like suspensory order.

" Thou shalt not shock a young lady " : this Leslie Stephen used to say was the first editorial commandment ; nor shock accepted creeds either. Yet it is difficult to draw the line, and Stephen printed W. E. Henley's *Hospital Outlines* and several chapters of Matthew Arnold's *Literature and Dogma*.   The difficulty of steering a course between the " three respectable ladies " on the one side and the critical judgment, unfettered by conventions, on the other, must always be among an editor's most annoying worries.   Thackeray was neither a pachyderm nor a man of business habits ; and after two years and a half of " thorns in the cushion " he resigned the editorial chair.   His editorship (Anthony Trollope notwithstanding) was a brilliant success.   The success of the Magazine had indeed been ensured from the day when Thackeray's editorship was known.

The *Cornhill*, as Dickens said, was " before-hand accepted by the public through the strength of his great name." He made notable contributions himself, and was able to ensure them from others. Not that he was alone in the field, but his friendships and his literary standing enabled him to come off never second best. One would like to have been an unseen spectator at Farringford when Mr. Alexander Macmillan and Thackeray successively journeyed thither to cozen contributions out of Tennyson. *Macmillan's* had " Sea Dreams "; the *Cornhill*, " Tithonus." I do not know which of the friendly rivals had first choice, or that any choice was given to either ; but who will dispute that " Tithonus " is the better poem ? Tennyson himself did not. Thackeray's first six numbers included contributions, besides his own and Tennyson's, from Matthew Arnold, Charlotte Brontë, Emily Brontë, Mrs. Browning, Mrs. Gaskell, Tom Hood, Washington Irving, Charles Lever, G. H. Lewes, Lytton, George Macdonald, Monckton Milnes, Laurence Oliphant, Adelaide Procter, Father Prout, Ruskin, Fitzjames Stephen, Anthony Trollope, and (among artists) Leighton and Millais. Did ever a first volume make a braver show ? Thackeray, however, did not rely merely on names, and indeed, in 1860, not all of these names had yet the full authority which they afterwards acquired. The signed stories,

poems, illustrations were all of their authors'
best, and there were added unto them many
articles in which the subject-matter was certain
to attract popular attention. The success of
the Magazine was instantaneous and well sustained. The circulation reached what was then
the unprecedented figure of 100,000. An
American friend of Thackeray has recorded a
pleasant scene showing the editor's delight.
Thackeray had gone for a holiday jaunt to Paris,
where he met J. T. Fields. They walked about
together, and whenever they passed a group of
excited talkers on the boulevards, Thackeray
would stop and say, " There, there, you see !
The news has reached Paris. The circulation
has gone up since my last accounts from London."
The proprietor was equally pleased, and in his
generous way doubled Thackeray's already not
inconsiderable salary, as editor, forthwith. Thackeray's resignation had little effect, I think, on the
success of the Magazine. For two good reasons.
He continued to contribute, and the Thackeray
tradition long survived. Also, he had founded
something of a school in magazine literature :
there was always somewhat of the Thackeray
touch in the *Cornhill*.

  .   .   .   .   .   .

 " Have newspapers souls ? " The question,
which I have seen debated in ingenious articles,
has a morbid interest for some of us. " The

soul, doubtless, is immortal—where a soul can be discerned." It is not easily to be discerned even in long-lived newspapers ; though as these have sometimes a policy which does not always change with every passing gust, the rudiments of a soul may now and then be traced. But can a magazine, which is professedly a miscellany, which brings together articles on all subjects, often with no link except that they are contained within the same cover—can a magazine have a soul ? In turning over the pages of the hundred volumes of the *Cornhill*, I have been on the search, and I believe that I have found it. The range of subjects is very wide, the methods of treatment are infinitely various. Politics and public affairs have for the most part been avoided, though the fringe of them is often touched. They are not always touched to the same effect. So, again, in the innumerable articles on literature and morals, of travel, of anecdote, and of criticism, the writers have different opinions, different manners, different points of view. Sometimes in turning from Leslie Stephen to J. A. Symonds, from Fitzjames Stephen to Matthew Arnold, or in passing from " The Great God Pan " to " Parrots I have Known," I have given up my search for the common soul of the *Cornhill*. Yet on a general retrospect I seem to have a clear impression of a certain unity. The " note " of the *Cornhill* is the literary note, in the widest sense of the term ; its soul is the spirit of that humane culture, as Matthew Arnold describes it in the pages, reprinted from the *Cornhill*, of *Culture and Anarchy*. Any collector of the *Cornhill* who treasured his or her 599 numbers in the original parts was well qualified, I dare aver, to graduate *in literis humanioribus*.

The form in which this spirit has most particularly expressed itself in the pages of the *Cornhill* is the essay—not necessarily the essay on literary subjects, but the essay which, whatever its subject, treats it in the temper of humane letters. Thackeray set the model in his *Roundabout Papers*—masterpieces of style, and " models," as Leslie Stephen has said, " of the essay which without aiming at profundity gives the charm of the playful and tender conversation of a great writer." This was what I meant by " the Thackeray touch " which had never forsaken the *Cornhill*. It reappears, with equal grace if with somewhat slighter texture, in the essays which during many years past have appeared in its pages from the pen of his daughter, and perhaps most notably in those " Blackstick Papers," even the first of which, in December 1900, many of its present readers remember. Leslie Stephen was a prince of essayists, and the number of his contributions in that sort to the Magazine is very large. Many were reprinted in *Hours in a Library* ; the identity of several others, not reprinted, was disclosed in Professor Maitland's *Memoir*, but these are only a tithe of the whole number. Stephen sometimes sought to put readers off the scent by appending to his essays initials other than his own. I know not why; perhaps because he modestly but unnecessarily feared that readers might have " too much Stephen." Stephen's *Cornhill* essays were in many respects unlike Thackeray's; they were more strenuous, connected, and direct; perhaps the sap was a little drier, for Stephen was no sentimentalist; but they have a very pleasant flavour of their own, and a refreshing common sense which is not so common as it might be in the modern essay. " The only sting in it," said George Meredith of Stephen's " *Cornhill* style," " was an inoffensive humorous irony that now and then stole out for a roll over, like a furry cub, or the occasional ripple on a lake in grey weather." After many years of " L. S.," readers of the *Cornhill* found a new series of essays signed " R. L. S."—" not the Real Leslie Stephen," as was explained to Mr. Gosse, " but a young Scot whom Colvin has discovered." Nine of the essays which Stevenson collected in *Virginibus Puerisque*, and several of those in *Familiar Studies of Men and Books*, made their first appearance in the *Cornhill*. The first so to appear, on " Victor Hugo's Romances " (August 1874), was also

the first piece, Stevenson used to say, in which
he had found himself able to say things in the way
in which he felt they should be said.   " L. S."
did a good turn to " R. L. S." in taking so much
of his early work, and not less a good turn to
readers of the *Cornhill*, who for some years had
the pleasant chance of finding an essay by Stevenson in its pages.   And here let the great army
of the rejected take comfort.   Even the most
discerning of editors sometimes make mistakes,
and even " R. L. S." did not always find the
door open.   The essay on Raeburn, included
in *Virginibus Puerisque,* was rejected by Leslie
Stephen and by at least two other editors.   The
series of " *Cornhill* essays " has been continued
in later days in the *Pages from a Private Diary*
and the *Provincial Letters* of Dean Beeching,
and in many a page signed " E. V. L.," or
" A. C. B."   But it were invidious to particularise
further.   I have said enough to establish my
point that the *Cornhill* has been an Alma Mater
of the essay.

   .   .   .   .   .   .

   Magazines, like newspapers, often have a
tradition which survives many changes of editors.
I do not think that all the changes in the editorship of the *Cornhill* could be detected by in-
ternal evidence, but there are certain landmarks.
Thackeray resigned in March 1862, and then the
editorial labours were for a time in commission,

so to speak, shared by Dutton Cook, Frederick Greenwood, and George Smith himself. In 1871 Leslie Stephen was appointed to the chair. I can detect little difference in the character or quality of the Magazine during the first twelve years (1860–71). There is a reason for this, I suspect, other than the one already indicated. In the land of *Cornhill* there was a succession of Prime Ministers, but the Sovereign remained the same, and his influence, though exercised with unostentatious tact, was, I suspect, great and constant. Mr. George Smith was strong where Thackeray was weak. If the editor was unmethodical, the proprietor was the soul of punctuality and orderliness, sparing no trouble, entering into every detail. The method and the handwriting sometimes proclaim the man. I have been permitted to unlock and peep at the most sacred *arcana* of the *Cornhill Magazine*. They consist of a series of leather cases, each containing half a dozen little ledgers. In these Mr. Smith entered, month by month, in his own minute and pleasant hand, the subjects of all the articles and illustrations, the prices paid to every author and artist, the number of copies sold of each number and of each volume. For many years there is no trace of any assistance from clerk or deputy. It is easy to see that the *Cornhill* was among the dearest to him of his many and multifarious enterprises. Thackeray called him " the Carnot of our Recent Great Victories." Thackeray's immediate successors would not, I imagine, have said otherwise.

.   .   .   .   .   .

With the accession of Leslie Stephen in 1871, Mr. Smith may have somewhat relaxed his direct control upon the Magazine. The Master of Peterhouse is quoted by Stephen's biographer as saying, " It may safely be asserted that from Thackeray's day to our own no English Magazine has been so liberally interfused with literary criticism of a high class, and at the same time remained such pleasant reading, as the *Cornhill* under Stephen's management." I believe that Dr. Ward's verdict will be endorsed by all who remember or refer. The fiction was as strong as ever, and the general contents were varied and readable. Stephen's editorship was the time not only of very many pieces from his own pen, but of Stevenson's essays, as aforesaid, of Symonds's *Greek Poets* and *Sketches and Studies in Italy*, of many articles on art or literature by Mr. Gosse and Sir Sidney Colvin, of Tennysonian and other studies by Churton Collins, of Johnsonian studies by Dr. Birkbeck Hill. Comparing the *Cornhill* of Stephen's reign (1871–82) with that of his predecessors, I find that the purely literary element had become more emphasised, and we know from Stephen's biography that this increase in pure literature was accompanied by no corre-

H

sponding accession of popular vogue.   Did Leslie
Stephen provide a Magazine of which the times
were unworthy ?   I do not think so, but we will
consider somewhat of this question on a later
page.

.   .   .   .   .   .

In 1882 Stephen resigned, and a new era in
the history of the *Cornhill* was inaugurated.   He
had recommended his friend, James Payn, as his
successor, and Payn's editorship lasted for fourteen years.   The price of the Magazine was
reduced from a shilling to sixpence, and the
illustrations were gradually dropped.   The *Cornhill* note remained in many a pleasant essay,
Payn's own *Literary Recollections* among the
number, and the articles on popular science—
always a feature of the *Cornhill* from the earlier
times of R. A. Proctor to the later of W. A.
Shenstone—were regularly contributed by Grant
Allen.   Never did philosopher insinuate his
doctrine so persistently as Allen when he used
to describe the evolution of the colour of flowers,
or trace back the genius of Michael Angelo to
the savage's scrawls upon a cocoanut, or assure
us blandly that we can draw no true line between
a baby's admiration for a bunch of red rags and
the critic's admiration of a Sistine Madonna.
But the predominant feature during Payn's
editorship was an abundance of short stories.
They were excellent, for Payn had a shrewd

judgment in such things, and no popular magazine is complete without some of them. But there were many other caterers in this service, and some Cornhillers were not ill-pleased when the price was restored under his successor to the familiar shilling, and there was room again for a larger supply of the miscellaneous articles in the old style.

. . . . . .

Payn's health broke down in 1896, and from the middle of that year, for several months onward, I seem to detect a new hand at the helm. We become more military, more consciously patriotic. We have an Englishman's Calendar provided for us each month, to remind us of great deeds. We seem invited to a new way of life. But here, again, the true *Cornhill* note was well maintained, and at this period we make first acquaintance in the Magazine with the " Private Diarist " and " E. V. L." Of the editorial conduct of the Magazine in these and in later years it would be unseemly to speak at large. Nevertheless, it would be ungrateful for the *Cornhill* and its readers to forget the debt they owe to the short reign in the editorial chair of Mr. St. Loe Strachey. One of the pleasantest features of the early history of the *Cornhill* was, we have been told on authority, the monthly dinner which Smith gave to Thackeray and his contributors, and it is likely enough that in a different form the same friendly relations among those chiefly concerned in the Magazine have from time to time been revived. But the Thackeray touch counsels silence. Was it not in connection with such a gathering that he wrote his scathing piece " On Screens in Dining-Rooms " ? If there have been friendly tables, oval or round, for consultation or conviviality, of such gatherings, as of other august councils in the realm, no records are taken. One remark alone I will permit myself. " That such letters as passed between George Smith and Leslie Stephen are often passing, we may hope — if we are optimists." So Professor Maitland, in his characteristic way. That optimism is here no vain creed will be admitted by every one who had the good fortune to be brought into touch with another editor of the *Cornhill*, the late Reginald Smith, whom to have known was itself a liberal education in human kindliness, in thoughtful courtesy, and in love of letters.

.   .   .   .   .   .

As I open the little *Cornhill* ledgers once more, turning, as any particular entry chances to attract me, to the volumes of the Magazine itself, I am struck by the vast quantity of " good copy " which lies buried in its pages—" copy " good now for the sake of its authorship, now for its intrinsic merit, now for its anecdotic interest, and often for all three. What a mine

for the bibliographer—and for such studies in
" The Second Thoughts of Poets " as I have
made in another chapter—are these volumes
and these little ledgers ! Here, to take an instance or two, in No. 7 of the *Cornhill* was the
first version of a piece familiar to readers of
Matthew Arnold's poems under the title " The
Lord's Messengers." " Men of Genius " he
called it in the *Cornhill*, where also there is this
additional stanza at the beginning of the poem :

> Silent, the Lord of the world
> Eyes from the heavenly height,
> Girt by his far-shining train,
> Us, who with banners unfurl'd
> Fight life's many-chanc'd fight
> Madly below, in the plain.

I suppose it was the " Us " that caused the poet
to withdraw the stanza. The rest of the poem
was much revised, sometimes for the better.
Again, every one knows the first line of Tennyson's " Tithonus " :

> The woods decay, the woods decay and fall,

and some of us have listened to lectures in which
the repetition has been dwelt upon as a peculiar
beauty. And so no doubt it is ; but it was
adopted by the poet only as a way out of a weak
beginning, for in the original *Cornhill* version
(February 1860) the first line is this :

> Ay me ! ay me ! the woods decay and fall.

In another of the poet's contributions to the *Cornhill* (No. 48), the "Attempts at Classic Metre in Quantity," the student of Tennyson will find many revisions and some added notes, with here and there an alternative rendering. The "barbarous experiment, barbarous hexameters"—suggested, I suppose, by Matthew Arnold's then recent lectures on Homer—show no alteration in the final text, but the "Specimen of a Translation of the *Iliad* in Blank Verse" is very different.

A bibliographer, unless he have access to the little ledgers, will find it less easy to trace the articles unsigned and never collected which were contributed by men or women who were famous already, but for one reason or another withheld their identity, or whose names were not then given because they were as yet unknown. Sir Joshua Reynolds once said to Dr. Johnson, what Boswell had "often thought, that he wondered to find so much good writing employed in the Reviews when the authors were to remain unknown and so could not have the motive of fame." "Nay, sir," replied Johnson, "those who write in them write well in order to be paid well." Mr. George Smith has told us himself that he did not stint his prices. A single number of the Magazine, he said, once cost him £1183, and I find that during four years he paid no less than £32,280 to literary contributors, in addition

to £4376 to artists for illustrations. But those
were the days of Thackeray and George Eliot,
when twelve guineas a page were paid for the
Roundabout Papers and a single month's instalment of *Romola* cost £583.

"I have had two applications for the lecture
["Heine"] from magazines," wrote Matthew
Arnold to his mother, "but I shall print it, if
I can, in the *Cornhill*, because it both pays best
and has much the largest circle of readers."
Johnson's answer to Reynolds gave only half
the truth; Arnold's remark gives the other half.
Good writers wrote well for the *Cornhill*, whether
they signed their articles or not, both "in order
to be well paid" and to be well read.

.   .   .   .   .   .

The biographer no more than the bibliographer
can afford to neglect searching the files of the
Cornhill. The invaluable Poole will help him,
but that index to the periodicals does not include
incidental references. Take Leigh Hunt, for
instance. Lord Houghton said that the best
thing in Thackeray's first number was an essay
on Hunt, entitled "A Man of Letters of the
Last Century." It was written by Hunt's son,
and is a very good account. But a personal
reminiscence by George Smith, thrown in casually
many years later, is better. Smith had given
Hunt a cheque. "And what am I to do," asked
Skimpole-Hunt, "with this little bit of paper?"

Smith exchanged it for bank-notes. When Hunt reached home they were accidentally burnt. Next day he returned to Smith in great agitation. This, however, had not prevented him from purchasing on the road a little statuette of Psyche, which he carried, without any paper round it, in his hand. Smith volunteered to go with Hunt to the Bank, and they were shown into a room where three elderly gentlemen were transacting business :

They kept us waiting some time, and Leigh Hunt, who had meantime been staring all round the room, at last got up, walked up to one of the staid officials, and addressing him said in wondering tones, " And this is the Bank of England ! And do you sit here all day and never see the green woods and the trees and the flowers and the charming country ? " Then in tone of remonstrance he demanded, " Are you contented with such a life ? " All the time he was holding the little naked Psyche in one hand, and with his long hair and flashing eyes made a surprising figure.

A surprising figure indeed, and a delicious picture ! It is worth many pages of less vivid, though more formal, portraiture. Many such biographical glimpses will reward a diligent searcher in the *Cornhill* files—of Cardinal Wiseman, for instance, and Cardinal Newman, of Jowett, of Landseer, of Leighton, and above all of Thackeray. It is pleasant to light upon an appreciation of him, in which Charles Dickens recalls times " when he unexpectedly presented himself in my room, announcing how that some passage in a certain book had made him cry yesterday, and how that he had come to dinner because he couldn't help it and must talk such a passage over."

.   .   .   .   .   .

Another feature which strikes me as I turn over the files is the large number of what may be called footnotes to history. The earlier numbers of the *Cornhill* were rich, for instance, in fragments of the Garibaldian epic recorded by actors in the scenes or by friends who had the accounts at first hand. It was fitting that Mr. George Trevelyan, who made that epic live again in a more material age, should have been the medium in the *Cornhill* only a few years ago of printing some further instalments in this sort. The history of the *Risorgimento* involves the ambiguous character of the Emperor of the French. Some aid towards the solution of that problem may be found in the *Cornhill* picture of " Louis Napoleon painted by a Contemporary." " He likes to be absolute himself, but he wishes all who are not his subjects to be free." So wrote Senior in his journal : a shrewd reflection. The politicians of to-day say that this is a trait of human character which explains the attitude of a good many people towards the rival claims of Protection and Free Trade. Is there anything

new beneath the sun ?   The world of to-day
is all agog about flying.   So it was thirty-six
years ago : turn up the *Cornhill*, No. 159, and
you will see.   It was unkind of Grenville Murray,
though, to recall an old saying that the taste of
the French for aerostatics—from the days of
Froissart's apprentice of Valenciennes and Cyrano
de Bergerac's voyage to the moon onwards—
was " due to their natural and national levity " ;
but he made a good shot at the end of his article :
" Men of the present day say that the dirigible
airship is impossible ; our grandchildren or our
great-grandchildren may prove the contrary."
He was only out by a generation or two.   R. A.
Proctor was not so happy in his patriotic confidence (December 1876) that " Arctic voyages
by seamen of other nations than our own will
not succeed."   Again, turn to the *Cornhill*,
No. 13, and you will find an article of protest
written round a description in the *Times*—not
the *Telegraph*—of rain as a " pluvial visitation."
I turn a few more pages, and come upon one of
Richard Doyle's " Bird's-Eye Views of Society."
It is entitled " Small and Early," and the letterpress preaches a little sermon against " asking
more than your rooms will hold."   The mid-
Victorian crinolines have gone, but only to make
room for a yet more populous crush.   The more
the world changes, the more it remains the same.
Illustrations of the saying are one of the things

that always reward a search among old records
or old files.

.   .   .   .   .   .

And then, again, there is what I have called
the anecdotic interest, to which the bookman
may add the bibliographic interest.   The early
files of the *Cornhill* are rich in such associations.
The first number was issued in December 1859.
On the 28th of the month Macaulay died in his
library ; the *Cornhill* was on the table beside
him, open at the first page of Thackeray's *Lovel
the Widower*.   The collector of the Magazine
" in the original parts " has that interest, dear
to collectors of first editions, of handling the
number or the volume in the self-same form in
which it issued from the press.   With heightened
interest one may turn to the beautiful " Roundabout " in No. 2—" the outpouring of a tender,
generous nature," said Macaulay's brother—
in which Thackeray applied to Macaulay, Scott's
dying words to Lockhart : " My dear, be a good
man.   Nothing else will give you any comfort
when you come to lie here."   I like, too, to
handle the very page, as it first appeared, on
which Thackeray introduced the opening chapter
of Charlotte Brontë's unfinished novel—" those
few and fine words of introduction " which
Swinburne characterised as " among the truest
and noblest, the manliest and the kindliest, that
ever came from his pen."

.   .   .   .   .   .

For the amateur of English engraved illustrations the back numbers of the *Cornhill* are an equally rich mine.   Here is to be found much of the work of Leighton and Millais, of Frederick Walker and George Pinwell and Frederick Sandys, of du Maurier and Helen Allingham, of G. D. Leslie and F. Dicksee, translated for the most part by the sound school of woodcutting of the brothers Dalziel.   Leighton's illustrations to *Romola* showed, said Ruskin, his " advancing power," and Leighton's biographer truly accounts it a fortunate coincidence that George Eliot should have written a Florentine story at a time when the painter was available to illustrate it.   I gather, however, from George Eliot's letters that she must have been a little exacting.   Leighton's pictures, though " deliciously beautiful," were sometimes " not just the thing " she wanted.   Two gifted workers, each steeped in Florence, were moving on parallel lines which would not meet.   Trollope, whose novels were illustrated for the *Cornhill* by Millais, was less particular, or the artist was more complaisant ; for Trollope in his *Autobiography* is warmly enthusiastic over the skill with which Millais interpreted his characters and situations. But none of the *Cornhill* illustrations are, I think, more pleasing than those of Frederick Walker. " Who of our readers," asked Sir Sidney Colvin in a memoir of the artist in the Magazine, " has not known and taken delight in that sympathetic touch ? Have we read about Philip in church beside the children ? We may follow and see him there, the great rough head bent beside those smooth cheeks and ringlets. Have we delighted in the manly spirit of the young Huguenot of Winchelsea ? We turn the page and see how Denis Duval and Tom Parrott, for their good luck, went upstairs to look at Denis Duval's box with the pistol in it ! " These and many a score of other dainty images meet the eye as one turns over the old volumes. The reproduction, made necessarily from electrotypes, is sometimes a little rough ; to see the illustrations at their artistic best one should go to the impressions from the wood-blocks themselves in the " *Cornhill* Gallery," which was issued separately, reviving pleasant memories of Lucy Robarts and Lord Lufton, of Baker and Lovel, of Philip on his way through the world, of Cousin Phillis, of Lily Dale and Adolphus Crosbie, of Romola and Tito. The " illustrations of the 'sixties " are now in favour with collectors, who do not find any abiding satisfaction in the mechanical output of the photograph and the process-block. The *Cornhill Magazine* played a great part in sustaining during the 'sixties and the 'seventies a now expiring art.

A word or two on the *Cornhill* cover, and I have done. Why *Cornhill* ? Mr. George Smith

named the Magazine from the then seat of his
publishing house. " It has a sound of jollity
and abundance about it," wrote Thackeray.
The same kind of note was struck in the colour
and design of the cover. The design takes us
back to mid - Victorian days and the artistic
schemes which the Queen and the Prince Consort
centred " in her halls of glass " (as the original
version of Tennyson's Dedication has it). The
cover was designed at Sir Henry Cole's suggestion
by Godfrey Sykes, a student at the newly founded
schools at South Kensington, and the original
design is still to be seen at the Victoria and
Albert Museum, in the Department of Engraving.
George Smith used to say that he was chaffed
about the sower scattering with his left hand.
Well, the artist might reply, " I am not an
agricultural labourer," and a left-handed sower
is at any rate less of a solecism than a mower
swinging his scythe from left to right—a spectacle
which may be witnessed on the walls of a certain
public gallery in London. But I protest that
the artist had a deep meaning in his apparent
deviation from realism ; he intended to signify
that the editor of the *Cornhill* would distribute
good seed and overflowing measure even with
his left hand. I like, too, the absence of any
advertisement of contents from the cover. Good
wine needs no bush. A " Contents slip " is
indeed now lightly attached, but that, I take it,

is only a concession to chance customers. The regular Cornhiller was advised by the cover from the first that he would always find good cheer within. Whether it were an article by " L. S.," let us say, or " R. L. S.," whether a story by Thackeray or Trollope or George Eliot, he would duly find on turning the pages ; there was no need to anticipate his pleasurable excitement. So I read the cover.

> With Fudge, or Blarney, or the Thames on fire
>   Treat not thy buyer ;
> But proffer good material—
>   A genuine Cereal,
> Value for twelve pence, and not dear at twenty,
> Such wit replenishes thy Horn of Plenty.

So wrote " Father Prout " in introducing No. 1 of the *Cornhill Magazine*. The promise of cover and of inaugural ode has been kept through all the changes and chances of fifty years. I close the old volumes and turn to No. 599. The names are different, and the subjects ; the quality of the contents and the nature of the treatment are the same. There is still the Thackeray touch ; still the *Cornhill* note.

That the tradition may be handed on from pen to pen for another fifty years will be the pious wish of every lover of humane letters. It is sometimes feared, however, that the palmy days of the literary magazine are numbered, and in a certain sense this is true. The *Cornhill* at its start attained, as we have seen, a circulation unprecedented at that time in the history of magazines. In the present day the greatest circulations belong to periodicals of a very different kind. We hear much in this connection about a decadence in the popular taste. I do not believe it. The fallacy consists in an implied assumption that persons who fifty years ago would have read the *Cornhill* or *Macmillan's* or the *Temple Bar* now read the more frivolous of the illustrated magazines. The fact is that the latter class of readers were fifty years ago reading either nothing or periodicals far more rubbishy. That is one side of the case, and there is another. The market for good literature, whether in books or in periodicals, is larger to-day than it has ever been, but the supply is provided by many more competitors. "Beware of the English periodicals," wrote Mrs. Browning to a friend in 1864; "there's a rage for new periodicals, and because the *Cornhill* answers, other speculations crowd the market, overcrowd it; there will be failures presently." A shrewd forecast. In old days the literary demand was concentrated upon a few periodicals. At the present time any one periodical which desires to attract the larger public has to consult many tastes, and the supply of literary articles is scattered in many places. There are fewer literary magazines, but in the magazines there is as much literature.

V

LITERATURE AND MODERN
JOURNALISM

I WONDER if any public man of our time, in
making a speech about books, has ever refrained
from having a fling at the newspapers. " I am
not going," said Mr. Birrell the other day,[1] " to
say anything about the superiority of books over
newspapers." When an old parliamentary hand
or a lawyer says " Far be it from me to say,"
one knows what to expect. And though Mr.
Birrell's good sense saved him from the absurdity
of implying that everything which is bound up
as a book thereby becomes literature, he yet
allowed us to see clearly enough that he shares
the common belief that the newspapers are
dangerous rivals, if not the open foes, of good
books. Is this belief well founded ?

It finds some countenance in the fact that
journalism, which in the eighteenth century was

[1] At the reopening of the Gladstone Library at the National Liberal
Club, October 30, 1917.

closely and honourably connected with literature, fares badly at the hands of the Victorian writers. When a new editor goes to the *Daily News*, his friends think to say something kind by hoping that he will enjoy sitting in the chair of Charles Dickens.   They forget that though Dickens was the first, he was also probably the worst and certainly the shortest-lived editor that the *Daily News* ever had ;   he occupied the chair for precisely twenty-six days—a period which must be accounted short even in these days of frequent changes in Fleet Street.   He did, indeed, leave a friend to take his place, but Mr. Forster seems to have found the work equally uncongenial. After a few months he in turn departed, and Dickens warmly congratulated him.   " I certainly am very glad," he wrote, " of the result of the *Daily News* business, though my gladness is dashed with melancholy to think that you should have toiled so long.   I escaped more easily." Having turned his back on journalism, Dickens cast no regretful glances.   On the contrary, he gave   a   parting   kick.   In republishing some *Daily News* articles—the *Pictures from Italy*—he referred to the " mistake " he had made in contributing them to a newspaper, and apologised to his readers for his indiscretion, pleading that it was only a " brief " one.   I am afraid, therefore, that in any study of modern journalism Dickens must figure less as the creator of the

Daily News than as the creator of certain famous types in fiction. Every one remembers the *Watertoast Gazette*, " at whose double extra numbers Queen Victoria shakes in her royal shoes." Without naming them as shall be nameless, I think it would not be difficult to recall writers of to-day who, in more pompous terms perhaps, but with like assurance, claim earth - shaking powers. So, again, the magnanimous Pott was a very ridiculous creature— very unlike, I am sure, the great editors of to-day. But in all Dickens's grotesques there is a basis of truth to nature, and the suspicion haunts me that even in my own time and experience I have heard some echoes — far-away echoes, perhaps, but still echoes—of the fierce rivalries of the *Eatanswill Gazette* and *Eatanswill Independent* :

The Independent, Sir, is still dragging on a wretched and lingering career, abhorred and despised by even the few who are cognisant of its miserable and disgraceful existence ; stifled by the very filth it so profusely scatters ; rendered deaf and blind by the exhalations of its own slime, the obscene journal, happily unconscious of its degraded state, is rapidly sinking beneath that treacherous mud which, while it seems to give it a firm standing with the low and debased classes of society, is, nevertheless, rising above its detested head and will speedily engulf it for ever.

But journalists are not the only professional people who are deeply sensible of each other's

shortcomings.   That Dickens's caricature was
not exaggerated in point of style is shown by this
piece which I cut out of a London newspaper
not many years ago :

They are the only faction in the world which seeks
to identify themselves with the passions of helots and the
manners' of the gutter.   Contemptible in the spirit of
their hatred as they are impotent in its display, the sorry
spectacle they present is that of the ecstasy of venom with
which the viper renews the attempt to gnaw the file until
it is cured of its appetite by its diet.

But Dickens poured ridicule on everything that
deserved it.   For instance :

Mind and matter glide swift into the vortex of im-
mensity.   Howls the sublime, and softly sleeps the calm
Ideal, in the whispering chambers of Imagination.   To
hear it, sweet it is.   But then outlaughs the stern philosopher, and saith to the Grotesque, " What ho ! arrest
for me that Agency.   Go bring it here ! "   And so the
vision fadeth.

This passage was the production of one of the
Literary Ladies.   And pages not unlike it may
be found within the bound copies of books
to-day.   I do not mean to suggest, however,
that it is only as " literature " that stuff and
nonsense are palmed off.

Then there was Thackeray, who was the creator
of the *Pall Mall Gazette* of fiction.   He called
it " a journal written by gentlemen for gentlemen."   But I think that anybody who reads

Philip carefully will come to the conclusion that
the paper edited by Mr. Bickerton for Mr.
Mugford was a paper edited by a snob for a
vulgarian.   All the literary men of the period
seem to have combined to guy the journalists.
There is Matthew Arnold, for instance, with his
conversation in *Friendship's Garland* on the
character of Mr. Bottles.   Mr. Arnold had
ventured the opinion that Mr. Bottles was
hardly a man of delicacy.   The remark, we are
told, had an extraordinary effect upon the only
journalist present :

> Delicacy, said he,—delicacy—surely I have heard that
> word before.   Yes, in other days, he went on dreamingly;
> in my fresh enthusiastic youth, before I knew Sala.

Even Lord Morley, journalist as well as man
of letters, dismissed the newspaper press, in his
famous piece on " Compromise," as " that huge
engine for keeping discussion on a low level."
I really believe that the only Victorian writer who
has a good word for the better possibilities of
modern journalism is Carlyle.   He scoffed, indeed,
at the able editors and their unwearied thrashing
of straw.   That they could do it and live was,
he said, a crowning instance of human vitality.
But at any rate he recognised that journalism had
or might have a mission :

> A preaching Friar settles himself in every village, and
> builds a pulpit which he calls Newspaper.   Look well,

thou seest everywhere a new Clergy of the Mendicant Orders, some bare-footed, some almost bare-backed, fashion itself into shape, and teach and preach zealously enough for copper alms—and the love of God.

Praise, or even recognition, from Carlyle is praise indeed ; but then a journalist may perhaps be haunted by a fear that the Sage may in reality have been making a Gargantuan guffaw — a literary attitude not unusual to him.   It is on record that Carlyle replied to a young man who said that he wrote for the papers, " Journalism is just ditch-water."   As for Carlyle's disciple, Ruskin dismissed the output of modern journalism as " so many square leagues of dirtily printed falsehood."

Skits and tirades of this kind, though they have served to encourage the idea of literature and journalism as antagonistic forces, do not carry us very far.   Certainly a man of supreme literary genius such as Dickens does well to keep away from journalism.   He should not sacrifice even to the best of papers or parties powers which were meant for mankind.   If Dickens had taken his editorial duties seriously and stuck to his chair, he would no doubt have made a great name for himself as an editor ; but at what a loss !   *Hard Times* we might still have had, perhaps, for that book was almost an educational and political tract ; but in all probability we should have had no *Dombey* and no *Copperfield*.

If there be any journalist who feels that he has the power of writing a *David Copperfield*, by all means let him quit journalism; though if his present engagement be a good one, he would be well advised to be sure before throwing it up that his unwritten masterpiece be indeed a *Copperfield*.

A quieter and more subtle thrust was delivered at modern journalism by another man of letters. It is in Leslie Stephen's biographical introduction to the *Letters of J. R. Green*. Stubbs, Freeman, and Green belonged to a mutual admiration society. Thorold Rogers bade us look where

> ladling from alternate tubs
> Stubbs butters Freeman, Freeman butters Stubbs.

What was left over was bestowed on Green, but there was one thing about him which the other two could not forget or forgive. Green wrote for the newspapers. Perhaps that alone might have been condoned—even Freeman wrote in the papers—but Green wrote and was widely read. He was, in other words, a good journalist, and Stubbs and Freeman exchanged laments on this lapse from the drier paths of history. Leslie Stephen cannot deny the impeachment. So, like a loyal biographer, he seeks to blunt its edge. It is quite true, he says, that Green wrote habitually, successfully, and profitably for the journals, but he was not therefore and of necessity a journalist, for " by journalism we mean writing for pay upon matters of which you are ignorant." It is fortunate for journalism that Leslie Stephen's words appeared after the great *Oxford Dictionary* had passed the letter J, or this might have been added to other mordant definitions. There is a horrid element of verisimilitude in it. There was once a journalist, it is true, who belied the definition. " Mr. Lowe will be very happy to undertake to write for the *Times* on any subject on which he possesses sufficient information." But this modesty of limitation is, I imagine, rare; and, besides, what is sufficiency of information for journalistic purposes ? I doubt if many confirmed journalists could truthfully say that they had never written for pay upon matters of which they were largely ignorant. A moment's reflection will show that it must be so, and Stephen's is a true definition, so far as it goes, because it covers some of the distinctive features of journalistic writing, though it is not only in journalism that men and women write for pay upon subjects of which they are ignorant. One reason why a certain superficiality is inherent in daily journalism is that newspapers are written in a hurry. Take, for instance, the conditions of dramatic criticism. The critic has no brief, and no time to get up his case. He has to form his impression of the play in circumstances by no means conducive to calm judgment. As

quickly as he can he has to describe the story—
if he can find it ; to give an idea of the dialogue—
if he can remember it ; and then to add some
general critical remarks on the performance and
the performers, making due allowance for first-
night nervousness and sometimes for first-night
hitches.   And all the while the editor is sending
messages, less or more polite, to know how much
longer he will be, and the printer, impatient
devils, to fetch the final slips.   I was amused to
read an outburst about the superficiality of the
dramatic critics.   " How many of these gentlemen," asked the writer indignantly, " ever sit
down with their heads on their hands to ponder
for hours and attempt to do justice to work
which may have cost months and even years of
toil ? "   The answer must be, Not one of them.
I am afraid that a dramatic critic, working under
the conditions just described, who should rest
his head on his hands to ponder for hours, would
be liable to have that head somewhat rudely
bruised.   I believe that the difficulty is at the
present day met to some degree by inviting the
critics to dress rehearsals ; but the case may
serve as an illustration of one of the reasons for
superficiality in the work of journalism.   And
there is another.   A journal written only by the
learned would not appeal to capitalists as a
" commercial proposition."   The salary list would
be prohibitive ; and even if it were not, and a

newspaper written only by experts were produced, hardly anybody would read it. The journalist, it seems to me, stands in a middle position between the expert and the complete ignoramus. When he starts upon a subject he often knows very little about it, but he sometimes picks up much as he goes along. In this respect I do not know that journalism is very unlike a good deal of literature. At any rate I know of one charming and successful author who applied to himself a saying, first coined, I think, by Disraeli. " When I want to learn a subject," he said, " I sit down to write a book about it."

Let it be admitted, then, that there is a large element of truth in Leslie Stephen's definition. But it is not the whole truth. The case from which it started shows this. Green's *Stray Studies* were written for the papers, and were good as journalism. What appears in the papers may be well or ill informed and well or ill written, and if Stephen choose to say that only the latter is journalism, the dispute becomes one about words. The point I wish to make is that during the time when Victorian writers were pouring scorn as men of letters upon journalism, the men of letters themselves were busy at it, and that many men whose principal work was in journalism were hardly less entitled to be so called. Matthew Arnold's *Friendship's Garland* was written for the *Pall Mall Gazette*. J. A. Symonds, Pater,

Oscar Wilde, and many other well-known literary writers, were reviewers. Churton Collins wrote turn-overs for the *Globe*. Andrew Lang was a leader-writer. And will any one deny that Frederick Greenwood and his successor John Morley wrote admirably as journalists ? And what is worth adding is that these and many other writers in the press formed something of a school. It must often have been noticed by those behind the scenes that in popular belief the name of a particular writer was erroneously attached to examples by a different hand of what had become a model. The connection between literature and journalism is still close, and there is as much good writing in the press as at any earlier time (though also, for reasons presently to be noticed, there may be more worse writing) ; but it would be impertinent for me to particularise.

It may be true—I think it is—that there is a sharper differentiation of functions, a more trenchant division of labour, than was once the case in English journalism. Delane would be much surprised to hear that in most great newspapers of to-day there is not only *the* editor, but a City editor, a News editor, a Literary editor, and so forth. A " good story " does not mean in these days a literary story; and what is called live journalism is not literary journalism. Literature has, as I suppose some would say, been taught its place. But the place is still consider-

able, and in some respects it is larger than it
was in an earlier generation.   The differentiation
of functions of which I have spoken has been
made necessary by the greater width of range
in modern journalism :

> Quicquid agunt homines, votum, timor, ira, voluptas,
> Gaudia, discursus, nostri est farrago libelli.

The lines may not inaptly be taken as the " bill "
of the modern newspaper, and is not this in accord
with the spirit of literature ?   In this widening
of interest, which is characteristic of modern
journalism, literature itself has had a share.   I
can remember the time when a column of book-
notices in a daily newspaper was a daring in-
novation.   In old days the notice of a book in
the *Times* newspaper was an exceptional event.
The fact was recalled to me when I was compiling
a bibliography of Ruskin.   The appearance of
Modern Painters was at the time a great literary
event, but from the first volume to the last,
1843 to 1860, the *Times* never noticed the book ;
though, strangely enough, when some of Ruskin's
verses had appeared in a Christmas Annual—a
false literary start—they were hailed as marking
the advent of a new poet.   Who can imagine
either the ill-timed neglect or the ill-founded
notice in the *Times* of to-day ?   It seems to me
that the weekly Literary Supplement of that
paper shows a higher and a more evenly sustained

level of literary merit than I can remember in
any newspaper of my time. And I might point,
too, to the leading theatrical notices in the same
paper. I have heard actors and dramatists and
actor-managers complain of them sometimes. I
always beg them in reply to remember the claims
of literature—and Aristotle. The increased allot-
ment of space to literary affairs somewhat puzzled
and irritated printers who had served their
apprenticeship under the old régime. On one
occasion an editor sent up to the composing-
room a rather long account of Matthew Arnold.
" Who is this M. Arnold ? " one of the printers
was heard to ask, " and how many more columns
of him is the editor going to shovel up ? " " You
wait," replied a more literary and a more tolerant
" companion," " till Ruskin goes off, and then
you'll see something ! " And they did, but
that was in another paper, and there was not a
murmur of surprise. Even in papers with large
circulations, the publication of a great book or
the death of a great man of letters has come to
be recognised as an event no less, or not so very
much less, than a Test Match or the affairs of a
cinema artist. The newspapers even sell books,
and the skill of some of them in passing off old
books for new would do no discredit to an
auctioneer who was passing off new pictures for
old. Even at a critical period of the great war,
and at a moment when they were talking about

a politico-military crisis at home, the newspapers all treated the publication of a book by Lord Morley as a principal event of the day.[1]   The war itself has illustrated incidentally the literary strain in modern journalism.   For various reasons, some of which I have noticed in another place,[2] the war correspondent's work is very different in function and in opportunity from what it was in the times of Russell and Forbes.   It has been in the hands of able writers, and the effects at which they have aimed have been in large measure literary.   The importance which modern editors seem to attach to literary opinion has been shown by the fact that many of them turn to the popular novelists of the day to tell their readers how the war may be lost or won.

All this, it may be said, is perhaps true ; but when in these days the newspapers are held up as the enemies of good books, reference is made to the prevalence of a class of papers newer than that of which Matthew Arnold spoke when he coined the phrase " The New Journalism." [3]

The newer journalism is often denounced for its personalities, and it is implied that in former times the newspapers were in this respect other and better.   Nothing could be more untrue.

---

[1] *Recollections*, published on November 16, 1917, a few days after Mr. Lloyd George's speech in Paris.

[2] In my study of Delane, p. 82.

[3] In the *Nineteenth Century* for May 1887, the reference being to Mr. Stead's *Pall Mall Gazette*.

There are more personalities published because there are more newspapers, but the personalities are much less offensively personal. The fact is of course that the press in its tone and manners reflects those of the world of which it is a mirror, and only forgetfulness of the past can lead anybody to suppose that the tone and manners of to-day are not an improvement upon those of a century ago. Take the evidence of caricature. The distance that separates Tenniel or his present successors and Gould from Gillray and Rowlandson is enormous. The character of some of Gillray's pictures must be seen to be believed. One or two instances may be recalled of the way in which he represented the leaders of the Whig party on the news of the Battle of the Nile. One caricature shows the Duke of Norfolk with many empty port bottles beside him in a revolting state, while saying that Nelson and the British fleet is a sickening toast. Another represents Nelson bringing home two uncommon fierce French crocodiles from the Nile as a present to the King : they are Sheridan and Fox. In 1802 the Peace of Amiens had caused the First Consul to be treated with more show of civility. But Fox's visit to him gave the caricaturist another chance. Mrs. Fox was represented as a sphere of vast circumference in every direction, while Fox, equally rotund, is made to bow so low as to produce sartorial dissolution. The social caricatures of the time are coarser and not less ferocious. The English caricatures of to-day are refinement itself compared with them.

The idea that modern journalism is harmful to literature because its scrappiness encourages triviality and desultoriness is founded, I submit, on a misconception akin to that noticed in the preceding chapter. It is quite true that a journalism of scraps has come into existence during the last generation. I have often read the account which Sir George Newnes is said to have given of the fateful hour of its birth. He and Lady Newnes were turning over some daily newspaper and voting it dull. At last a paragraph caught their eye which seemed really interesting. " Now that, my dear, is what I call a tit-bit." " You are right," said the other, and " why should we not start a paper to consist of tit-bits all the time ? " At that moment the eggs of an enormous brood of Tit-Bits, Answers, Scraps, Scrapings, Cuts, and the foundations of fortunes and reputations afterwards enhanced in other spheres were laid. There is no authority for the surmise that the parent tit-bit was a paragraph which calculated the number of postage-stamps which, arranged in a row, would reach from the earth to the moon. It is a mistake, I may add, to suppose that the world of Tit-Bits journalism is entirely occupied with the diffusion of useless knowledge. It should also be remembered to its credit that it has always abstained from seeking to raise the blush of shame on the cheek of modesty, which is more than can be said of some forms of modern literature.   It may even be claimed that the " Home Journals " of which I am speaking have in some dim and incipient degree a literary scope. I have been told by one who was likely to know that the real secret of their popularity is to be found in the answers to correspondents or women's pages, which serve up moral platitudes.   Every one who has glanced at such pages knows the kind of thing.   " Cheer up, little woman, and remember that every cloud has a silver lining." Or, " Do not let sad thoughts grow upon you. The clouds may be dark, but yet there will be light."   What are these things but crude and prosaic echoes of the Tennysonian School with its

> O let the solid ground
>   Not fail beneath my feet
> Before my life has found
>   What some have found so sweet—

or

> Somewhere beneath the sun,
>   These quivering heart-strings prove it,
> Somewhere there must be one
>   Made for this soul, to move it ?

But I must not press this point too far.   Perhaps the best that can be said for scrappy journalism is that it affords to millions of people an innocent pastime.   But does that constitute an

K

offence against literature ?   From some of the
tirades levelled against it one might suppose
that the fascination of *Tit-Bits* and its like had
seduced serious minds from the immensities,
that if the great public were not reading daily
scraps and weekly snippets it would be sending
into ever and ever new editions all the weighty
books which now miss that felicity.   But the
fact surely is that the journalism of scraps is read
to-day by people who in an earlier generation
would have read nothing at all.   It is a delusion
to suppose, when one sees, say during the luncheon
hour in the City, boys and girls in St. Paul's
Churchyard devouring their favourite *Scraps* or
Cuts that they would otherwise be immersed in
contemplation of the Cathedral or the study of
philosophy.   The vogue of this new journalism
has been due to the coincidence of a great cheapen-
ing in the cost of paper with the opening of new
reading strata by the spread of popular education.
It is probable that the newspapers are school-
masters which bring a certain number of the
great public to read other things.   It is certain
that the extension of the popular newspaper
press has synchronised with an extension of cheap
editions of classical literature, and it is unlikely
that the publishers put these reprints upon the
market solely from a disinterested love of good
literature.   They are issued, one must suppose,
because they are bought.   Whether they are

always read is, I admit, a further question. " No furniture so charming," said Sydney Smith, " as books " ; the saying has a new meaning in these days when books are sold at drapery stores and commended, like lingerie, for their daintiness. An ingenious friend of mine once wrote, or intended to write, a paper on the connection between modern literature and bijou residences.

The gravest indictment in the name of literature against modern journalism was drawn a few years ago by the President of the Authors' Society. In acknowledging the award of the gold medal of the Royal Society of Literature, Mr. Hardy said :

An appreciation of what is real literature, and efforts to keep real literature alive, have become imperative, if the taste for it is not to be entirely lost, and with the loss of that taste its longer life in the English language. While millions have lately been learning to read, few of them have been learning to discriminate ; and the result is an appalling increase every day in slipshod writing that would not have been tolerated for one moment a hundred years ago. I don't quite like to say so, but I fear that the vast increase of hurried descriptive reporting in the newspapers is largely responsible for this in England ; writing done by men, and still more by women, who are utterly incapable of, and unconscious of, that grin of delight which William Morris assured us, comes over the real artist either in letters or in other forms of art at a close approximation to, if not an exact achievement of, his ideal. Then the increasing influx of American journals, fearfully and wonderfully worded, helps on the indifference to literary form. Their influence has been strongly apparent of late years in our English newspapers, where one often now meets with headlines in staring capitals that are phrases of no language whatever, and often incomprehensible at a casual glance. Every kind of reward, prize, or grant, therefore, which urges omnivorous readers and incipient writers towards appreciating the splendours of English undefiled, and the desire of producing such for themselves, is of immense value.[1]

As for journalese, as it is called, the thing is horrible, but a journalist may be pardoned for quarrelling somewhat with a term which seems to imply that the style in question is peculiar to newspapers. No doubt there are reporters, and leader-writers also, who make it a rule always to vary a word when the same would do, and never to use one word if two can be found.

Of the first of these sins that beset the journalist, the gentlemen who summarised the cricket results for the papers, used before the war to furnish every day a terrible example; as, for instance :

At Lord's, Leicestershire scored 334 against M.C.C. and Ground. Kent, at Leyton, hit up 426. At Brighton, Sussex made 315. Hampshire, at Southampton, compiled a score of 381. At Bristol, Gloucestershire were dismissed for 100.

Delane must have turned in his grave at such senseless variations of phrase—Delane of whom

---

[1] *Times*, June 4, 1912.

we are told that he applied even to the smallest paragraphs a constant vigilance in order that a standard of correct English should be maintained. " I remember," says Dean Wace, " his being particularly indignant with the use of the slipshod phrase that a marriage, or a funeral, or a race had taken place.   It was mere slovenliness of expression, he said, instead of saying that a marriage had been solemnised or a race run."

Of the second fault, a report of a royal wedding which I have by me may serve as an example.   No simple word is used.   The marriage was the nuptials, small was exiguous, black clothes were sable habiliments, the bishop was the sacerdotal dignitary.   And then everything was doubled— slip or hitch, uncertainty or delay, smoothly and securely, accessories and embellishments, and so forth throughout.   It were superfluous to name the paper.[1]   But the best efforts of the young lions in their native lair are sometimes eclipsed elsewhere.   Not long ago I noticed in a provincial paper a good instance of the manner in which a statement may be beaten out. What the reporter had to say was that at the meeting which he attended there were speeches

[1] It is curious that the same word has passed into the language to express two precisely opposite conditions of style.   For the word " Telegraphese " the *New English Dictionary* gives these meanings : (1) The concise and elliptical style in which telegrams are worded.   (2) An elaborate or inflated style, such as was attributed to leading articles in the *Daily Telegraph* newspaper.

and music. The stereotyped formula for that statement is : " The programme consisted of speeches interspersed with vocal and instrumental music," which, as journalese goes, may be considered almost concise. My reporter meant to improve upon the formula, and this is how he did it :

The programme of the evening was alike interesting and instructive, consisting of music and oratory, music that unlocks the depths of the human heart and bears away the soul captive to visions of higher things than the jingle of the money-changer's gold; and oratory that crystallises these emotions into spoken articulated words, and gives a concrete appreciation of the facts of the day where there had previously been only an abstract sense of altruism. Both music and oratory were of a high character. The tone of the meeting was appreciative while the musicians charmed it, and enthusiastic when the orators appealed to it.

That young man almost deserved the additional eighteenpence, or whatever sum it was, that his long-winded ingenuity was worth to him, especially if (as I like to think) he was at the same time enjoying a joke at the expense of his editor. But this kind of stuff is not peculiar to journalism. Are there no sesquipedalian orators or precious litterateurs ? And I remember an Oxford lecture by Ruskin in which he laughed at himself and said that people no longer thought him a fine writer, because now if he thought some one's

house was on fire he only said, " Sir, your house
is on fire," whereas formerly he used to say,
" Sir, the abode in which you probably passed
the delightful days of your youth is in imminent
danger of inflammation." The style of the
paper with the largest circulation to-day is less
Corinthian than was that of its predecessors,
and the war tends to restrict verbosity in the
press generally. " Smaller Papers, Shorter Paragraphs " is a standing heading, for which relief
many thanks have, I hope, been given.

Let modern journalism bear its proper share
of the blame, but it is not the only, and perhaps
no longer now the worst, sinner. It is a delusion
to suppose that the descriptive reporters are the
only people who do violence to the majesty of
English undefiled. Professor Quiller-Couch, in
his admirable lectures " On the Art of Writing,"
has shown from a wide range of examples how
often English is superseded by Jargon. The
recent growth of bureaucracy is responsible for
much corruption of the language, and a writer
in the *Times* has turned the tables on those who
scoff at journalese by asking them to consider
" officialese," with its pomposity of phrase and
its wretched clichés. Journalese with all its
faults is for the most part at least intelligible.
Can as much be said for the language which is
used by the various Controllers ? Here is a
sample :

Where the year ending September 30, 1914, is adopted by a brewer for the purpose of computing standard barrelage, and the brewer proves to the Commissioners that he has closed any brewery and it has not since been used as a brewery, so much of any beer so brewed at the closed brewery as the Commissioners think just in the circumstances shall be deemed to be beer brewed at the brewer's brewery.

A journalist suggested that the real purpose of this Order was that its recital might be set by the police as a new "drunk or sober" test. Here is another Order fearfully and wonderfully worded :

As from the dates hereafter mentioned the price of coal sold or offered for sale at the pit's mouth directly or indirectly by the owner of the mine or on his behalf for use in the United Kingdom shall be a price exceeding by nine shillings in the case of mines in the South Wales and Monmouthshire and Forest of Dean districts and six shillings and sixpence in other cases or such lower sum as may be fixed by the Controller of Coal Mines in any particular case the price of coal of the same description, sold in similar quantities, and under similar conditions affecting the sale at the pit's mouth at the same coal mine on the corresponding date (or as near thereto as, having regard to the course of business, may be practicable) in the twelve months ended the thirtieth day of June nineteen hundred and fourteen.

Who can wonder that an editor, on being asked to print this Order for the enlightenment of the public, headed it " A Cryptic Message," and

appended a note saying, " We fear we cannot
undertake to interpret it for our readers"?   There
is military officialese also, as perpetrated, for
instance, in the official War Bulletins.   I am not
now thinking of these documents from the point
of view of their relation to facts, though when
the time comes an interesting study might be
made by comparing the bulletins of the several
belligerents in respect of their use of euphemism,
meiosis, exaggeration, *suppressio veri* and *sug-
gestio falsi*.   I do not think that the British
bulletins would have anything to fear from such
a comparison, but at present I am thinking only
of style.   In their sobriety and restraint the
bulletins of the British commanders have been
good, but their English has sometimes been at
fault.   For instance, we were told one day that
" A further 77 prisoners have been brought in."
This is a phrase founded on French, but it is
not English.

The modern journalists, then, are not the only
jargoneers.   Yet Mr. Hardy was not ill-advised
in pointing his plea for pure English to journalists
in particular.   It is they who have the greatest
opportunity to do well and who at the same time
are under the strongest temptation to do ill.
" Next to the man who knows how wisely to
form the manners of men and to rule them at
home and in war," Milton held in honour " the
man who strives to establish the method and

habit of speaking and writing received from a
good age of the nation, and, as it were, to fortify
the same with a kind of wall, the daring to overleap
which let a law only short of that of Romulus
be used to prevent." [1]   It is the journalists who
hold or breach this fort.   They write more than
other men.   They are more read than other
writers.   Millions of people read nothing except
what the journalists write.   At the same time,
in no calling is the pursuit of excellence more
arduous than in journalism.   In many respects,
as I have shown, the necessary conditions in which
the journalist has to turn out his tale of bricks
or thrash his straw are adverse to it.   Again,
the temptation to be slovenly and slipshod is
great owing to the obviously evanescent nature
of the journalist's output.   There was a dinner
some years ago when competition among the
London evening papers was beginning to be
very keen, and one of them had recently increased
its size.   The late Mr. Harry Cust had made
one of his sparkling after-dinner speeches, and
as it was a dinner of the Omar Khayyám Club,
a rival editor turned to Mr. Cust and said :

> Each morn twelve pages brings, you say ;
> Yes, but where goes the page of yesterday ?

I expect that there are times when even the most
conscientious journalist has thought with relief

[1] Quoted by Lord Morley in his *Studies in Literature*, p. 224.

of the quick oblivion which awaits his labours. But this is to sink into the weak-mindedness spoken of by the poet.[1] There is nothing which a journalist should cultivate more scrupulously than the craftsman's conscience, and there is no better training in this than the study of good literature. There has been much talk among journalists about a qualifying test, and schools of journalism have been founded, especially in America, where, from the point of view here discussed, they are not less needed than elsewhere. In any such school these words by John Bright should be written up for all to read, mark, learn, and inwardly digest. " If my manner of speaking is good," he wrote when an old man, " it may have become so from reading what is good." And again : " It is a good thing to use few words and the best words, which are those which are simple and forcible, with no needless use of adjectives, too many of which spoil speaking and writing. To assist in attaining to a practice like this, the reading of good books—I mean well-written books—is helpful, so that the eye and the ear and the mind may become familiar with good language." The habit of good literature,

---

[1] And oh, when nature sinks, as oft she may,
    Through long-lived pressure of obscure distress,
    Still to be strenuous for the bright reward,
    And in the soul admit of no decay,
    Brook no continuance of weak-mindedness ;
    Great is the glory, for the strife is hard.

the cultivation of a literary conscience, may easily lend some light to hours of obscure drudgery. Much of the work of the journalist is humble and insignificant. He has, it is true, his golden opportunities sometimes, which make up for the more numerous hours of obscure drudgery— opportunities to strike some blow for a cause in which he believes, to help in righting a wrong, to form and not merely to follow public opinion, to nerve, it may even be, a nation's purpose. This is an aspect of journalism, however, outside my present scope ; but even in the humdrum hours there may be the craftsman's pleasure and credit in doing the job as well as a man can and as the conditions of the case admit.   In reviewing, one may read and try to understand more or less of the book which he criticises.   Every leading article may be more or less pointed, and more or less fair.   An interview may reproduce more or less of what the victim said.   A report may give more or less of the speaker's real points. A " news story " may be more or less veracious. Even a headline and a contents bill may be less or more misleading.   And above all, anything and everything which a journalist writes may less or more defile the fount of pure English. The writer, however humble may be his sphere, who has some knowledge and appreciation of good literature, may always keep an ideal before him.   He will be capable, in Mr. Hardy's words, of " that grin of delight which William Morris assured us comes over the real artist either in letters or in any other forms of art at a close approximation to, if not an exact achievement of, his ideal."

VI

WORDS AND THE WAR

NATIONS write their autobiographies, it has been said, in three manuscripts—the book of their deeds, the book of their words, and the book of their art. The British Empire is writing its history to-day in the deeds of its sons on land, at sea, and in the air. What expression will be given to these deeds by art or literature remains to be seen, though *The Muse in Arms* has shown some worthy first-fruits ; but meanwhile records of the great war are being impressed every day, often unconsciously and unobserved, upon the palimpsest of our language. " New occasions teach " new words as well as " new duties." A page of history may be summed in a new word or phrase, or (as is hardly less significant) in the altered use of an old one. The new horrors of the war are told in such words as *gassed, tear-shells, shell-shock, barbed-wire disease* [1];

---

[1] This last term occurs in the Agreement between the British and German Governments on the Treatment of Prisoners, July 1917 (*Parliamentary Paper*, Cd. 8590). It means a form of nervous breakdown. For an amusing misconception, see Lord Newton's account, in the House of Lords (April 24, 1918) of his negotiations with the Turks.

its heroisms in the story of those who went *over the top*. What record of common effort and Homeric manhood on the part of the *A*ustralian and *N*ew Zealand *A*rmy *C*orps will be enshrined for ever in *Anzac* and *Anzac beach* ! What an instance of the tragic irony of history is contained in the recorded use of the phrase *the steam-roller* [1] to signify the supposed irresistible advance of the Russian hosts ! What a chapter in the history of the woman's movement is told in the terms, as strange as the story they tell—the *Waacs* and the *Wrens* ! [2] Nor is it only in the field of military action that the tremendous times in which we live are being recorded in the use of words. Archbishop Trench in his fascinating little book *On the Study of Words* introduced one of his chapters with the lines of Keats :

> some watcher of the skies,
> When a new planet swims into his ken.

" The feeling wherewith we watch the rise above the horizon of words, destined it may be to shine for ever as luminaries in the moral and intellectual

---

[1] " The immense legions of Russia are continuing their unconquerable advance " (*Times*, leader, August 25, 1914). " Our task is stonewalling, and that of the Russians is *steamrolling*" (*Times*, " Our Military Correspondent," August 29, 1914).

[2] See articles in the *Times*—of November 19, 1917, on the Women's Army Auxiliary Corps: " The men call them 'the Waacs' (pronounced Wack), and the women have accepted the title " ; and of January 9, 1918, on " Women for the Navy : Rank and Rating in the Wrens " : " Though the uniforms are not yet quite ready, women desiring to offer their services to the *W*omen's *R*oyal *N*aval *S*ervice (the Wrens) can do so at once."

heaven above us, will not be very different from his." Of the growth of new words and phrases in this aspect also the present war furnishes examples.

Every change in military conditions is reflected in a changed use of words. Mr. Lloyd George has often said that the present is a war of guns. This is not the whole truth (for, though the guns prepare the way, it is still the infantry who drive home), but the statement is yet largely true. It may already be traced in the language. Hitherto the word *heavy* in its special military use has been applied to the cavalry, as in Tennyson's " Charge of the Heavy Brigade." When Thackeray in *Pendennis* wrote of " the band of the Heavies playing at Brighton," he referred to the Household Cavalry; and when, in *Charles O'Malley*, Lever said, " We'd better call out the heavies," he meant the Dragoons; but when a correspondent at the present front says that "we are waiting for *the heavies* to come up," he means the heavy guns.

The war of guns is also a war of trenches, and much of its story is connected with the word *dug-out*. " Dug-outs I have known " was the title of a lively article " by a Subaltern " who " classed dug-outs under four headings : palatial, bearable, purgatorial, and Boche " (*Westminster Gazette*, July 14, 1917). The word is not new. The Dictionary has a passage to illustrate it of

the year 1881 : " Instead of dug-outs in the
prairies, he found the farmers living in large,
handsome frame houses." The next edition
will have to add some account of the luxurious
dug-outs in the German lines ; perhaps also, if
the bombardment of London from the air con-
tinues, of other places of cover. " Dive for your
dug-out is a pretty safe maxim in London," so
an officer on leave from the front wrote in the
Times in an account of the raid on July 7, adding,
" Remember always there are the bullets and
splinters of your own shrapnel, and the *duds*
that fall without bursting." *Duds* is an old word
with a new meaning. From rags and tatters,
it came to be applied contemptuously to soft,
worthless fellows, and now to shells that do not
go off, as above.

In another sense the term " dug-out " will
record for future generations an important aspect
of Britain's military effort. Here is a quotation
which will do as well as another to illustrate the
use of the term as applied to a retired officer who
is taken from his retreat to resume active duty :

In the old days of the war the Travelling Medical
Board consisted of a R.A.M.C. regular Lieutenant-
Colonel (usually a dug-out), a regular Lieutenant-Colonel
of a combatant unit (usually a dug-out), and a R.A.M.C.
Lieutenant or Captain (a civilian turned soldier), the
first-named being President.[1]

---

[1] *New Statesman*, June 30, 1917.

It is an expressive term, conveying the gentle note of contempt which is discernible in the passage just quoted. The word is not included in the *Oxford Dictionary* (D volume, dated 1897), nor yet in the Addenda of September 1914. The new use must have been invented by some young man still rejoicing in his strength and in fulness of professional employment. It is a variant of *Dug-up*, which term was, if I remember aright, often applied to some veteran called up to complete a side in cricket. *Dug-out* does some injustice to the spirit of men who willingly offered themselves, and when the history of the war is written the term will be one of honour. A professor of history has already rescued it from contempt. He points out that, when Lord Kitchener's plans were made known, the German newspapers were confident that the New Army either would never materialise for sheer lack of cadres, or that if it did the men would be useless from want of training by competent officers; and then he goes on to say this: " Sarcasm has occasionally been lavished on the *dug-outs*, but they did much to save the situation. There were a certain number of commissions given to ineligibles ; there were a certain number of incompetent dug-outs placed in command of units which they failed to train or discipline up to the standard of the majority. Nevertheless, granting the existence of these exceptions, the great feat was yet accomplished." [1]

No class of word-coinages is more interesting than those which apply the names of persons or places as the names of things. There is no surer evidence—unless it is to be found in the signs of public-houses—of the great place filled by a man in popular fame than that his name should acquire this secondary immortality in the mouths of men. Sometimes the name is connected with a deed or a peculiarity of the hero ; sometimes the greater his fame, the more trivial the thing named after him. *Cavour* became the name of a cigar, *Gladstone* of a travelling-bag. This last coinage was merely a trick in giving a popular name to a trade novelty. One would like to think that it was suggested by the statesman's famous phrase about Turkish " bag and baggage," but Mr. Fisher, of the Strand, was selling " Gladstone bags " at an earlier date. On the other hand, Gladstone's Budget of 1860, reducing the Customs duties on light wines, caused his name to be given to cheap claret, as in this schoolmaster's version of an epigram :

> Tucca, what makes you mix your port
> With gladstone of the viler sort ? . . . .
> Your friends perchance deserve to die,
> But why your precious wine—yes, why ?

---

[1] Professor Oman in a Victoria League pamphlet entitled " Britain's Part in the War," 1917.

Such atrocity is not peculiar to the days of Martial, for in the Dictionary, under "Gladstone," there is this quotation from the *Daily Telegraph* : "The finest Château - Laffitte was introduced alongside the most rasping Gladstonian." *Bobby* and *peeler* were so named, as everybody knows, from Sir Robert Peel's institution of the Metropolitan Police. The ancestor of all *broughams* was " an odd little sort of garden chair " in which the Lord Chancellor used to drive about. Great commanders have been similarly used. The mighty name of *Napoleon* was given to a game of cards as well as to the gold piece of his coinage. *Wellington* (as also Napoleon again) became the name of a boot ; *Garibaldi* of a lady's blouse— of any colour, though originally of the hue of his red shirts. The present war will preserve at least one great name in a worthier connection. *Kitchener's army*, *Kitchener boys*, the *Kitchener crowd*, $K1$, $K2$, and the like terms, passing into popular use, will be standing memorial of his military insight and the magnetic attraction of his name.[1]

The names of places also often become the names of things, and of this process previous wars have furnished examples. When a new aniline dye was discovered in 1859, it was named after a battle that had just been fought, *magenta*.

---

[1] *The First Hundred Thousand, being the Unofficial Chronicle of a Unit of $K1$,* was the title of the excellent book by "Ian Hay," and " When $K1$ does its bit " of an article in the *Cornhill Magazine,* January 1918.

The man who so named it may have had no secondary thought in his mind ; but, if so, he coined better than he knew in associating a crimson stain with a fiercely contested battle. Our chemists are said to be busy in such researches now, and the battles of the present war may perhaps be turned to like purpose. In a different connection we hear a good deal of officers, militant and medical, being *stellenbosched*. The Afrikander term came into current use here during the Boer War ; Stellenbosch was formerly the district to which officers who had failed in Kaffir wars were relegated, by way of being superseded without formal disgrace. In the present war there have been too many of such cities and districts of refuge for any one of them to oust " stellenbosch."

To name weapons or other contrivances after their inventors is an obvious source of new words : *Browning*, *Maxim*, *Nordenfeldt*, *Zeppelin* are familiar examples. The war has already brought into the language the *Lewis*, the *Mills*, and the *Stokes*, though it remains to be seen whether the names will come into use thus by themselves without the addition of " gun " in the first case, " bomb " in the second, and " trench mortar " in the third. It was not till 1852 that the term *shrapnel* was officially adopted, though General Henry Shrapnel invented the thing during the Peninsular War. H.M. Landships have too many inventors for any one of them to give his name to the things; besides, they had already been called *tanks*, secretively—a good instance of the use of language to conceal thoughts. The dictionary-makers will have to wait a while for the official names of other new contrivances which the war may have brought forth. For the present *Dora* would forbid. Was it in the City or the Law Courts that this shorthand for the *D*efence *o*f the *R*ealm *A*ct was coined?

The names given by the soldiers to various kinds of shells illustrate many different ways in which new words are coined. Some are what the philologists call onomatopœic: the name corresponds, that is, to the sound of the thing. *Whizz-bang* and *pip-squeak* are good instances. Others are founded upon a humorous association of ideas, often connected with the prize-ring or the stage. During an air raid on London a soldier back on leave from the front was invited by an old lady to take cover in her house. " Don't you worry, ma'am," he said, " one of them bombs is not half as bad as a *Jack Johnson*." [1] The black pugilist's name has been playfully applied to the formidable blows struck by big black shells. " These are the real *Jack Johnsons*, or *coal scuttles*, which make a hole big enough to bury a platoon." [2] Why are anti-aircraft guns

[1] *Lloyd's Weekly News*, July 8, 1917.
[2] Philip Gibbs, *The Battles of the Somme*, p. 139.

called *Archies* ?   The reference may be to a
song — so I have been told — that was in
vogue at the beginning of the war, " Archibald !   Certainly not ! "   The "certainly not"
was, rightly or wrongly, attributed to the infant
efforts of the guns in question, and the name
now survives to illustrate (in an inverted way)
the principle also well known to philologists
of *lucus a non lucendo*.   Another group of names
given by the men to guns and shells has a different
kind of home association.   *Plum puddings* as
a name for bombs and *sausages* for observation
balloons require no explanation.   In another
set of names there is a touch of comic poetry.
The deep gruff voice of the 15-incher has caused
it to be christened *Grandmother*, and then by
analogy the 12 - inchers became *Aunties*.   *Pill-
box*, for the enemy's concrete machine-gun em-
placement, is another instance of wrapping up
a death-dealing contrivance in a cover of domestic
humour.   In their choice of words, as in their
songs and in their everyday philosophy, the
British soldiers are of one mind with the sergeant
who, sitting in a trench knee-deep in water,
explained to one of the press correspondents,
" You know, sir, it doesn't do to take this war
seriously." [1]

" Mathematics must not want words," said
De Morgan, " because Cicero did not know

---

[1] Philip Gibbs, *The Battles of the Somme*, p. 3.

the differential calculus," and the new art of aeronautics, or aviation, has introduced a large number of new words—though, to be sure, many of them are derived from the language spoken by Cicero. If any one regrets that Greek has also been called in to make new words, he should remember that the legend of Icarus is Greek, not Anglo-Saxon. It is interesting, by the way, to note that the earliest recorded definition (1753) of *aeronautics* was " the pretended art of sailing a vessel through the air." On the whole, the words which have been coined to keep pace with the development of the art have been well formed, such as *biplane*, *monoplane*, *aerodrome* (on the analogy of hippodrome). *Aerobatics* for " stunts " in the air was suggested by acrobat— wrongly of course from the purist's point of view (for the athletic note in acrobat resides in the first part of the word, not in the second) ; but the formation of new words on false analogies is a process familiar in philology. Many of the new words are consonant also with the spirit of motion in the air. *Volplane*, for instance, seems by its very sound to suggest a gliding descent. Flying is essentially a young man's art, and the boys love to talk in a slang of their own. Here is a piece of recorded conversation :

First " *Hun.*" " Did you see old Cole's zoom on a quirk this morning ? "

Second " *Hun.*" " No ; what happened ? "

First " *Hun.*"   " Oh, nothing to write home about . . . stalled his 'bus and pancaked thirty feet . . . crashed completely . . . put a vertical gust up me . . . just as I was starting my solo flip in a rumpty ! "

This is typical of the conversation to be heard on any aerodrome where two or more flying pupils may be gathered together.

Cryptic, decidedly, to the uninitiated : the reader who wants a crib will find it in the *Daily Mail* of July 19, 1917.   Not every piece of this airman's slang is likely to pass into regular currency, but *zoom* at least deserves to live.   It is, I suppose, onomatopœic, but at any rate it is a capital example of what are called comprehensive words—of words, that is (like circle or isothermal), which are economical and sum up a whole sentence of definition.   *Zoom*, we are told, describes " the action of an aeroplane which, while flying level, is hauled up abruptly and made to fly for a few moments at a dangerously sharp angle—sometimes the only means of avoiding an obstacle when flying low."   The same writer explains another excellent word :

Streamline in aerodynamics means briefly the direction taken by particles of air on striking a moving body, but it also refers to the peculiar shape of many component parts of an aeroplane, designed expressly to give the minimum of air resistance.   In this connection the jaunty headgear of the Royal Flying Corps is known as a streamline cap.

Who was the inventor of " Tommy " as a name for the typical private soldier in the British Army ?   History does not record.   The clerk who in 1815 used " Thomas Atkins " in the specimen forms in the King's Regulations little foresaw that his casual thought would give a name for ever to the fighting man—" Ambassador from Britain's crown And type of all her race." In the present war there have been some deliberate attempts at similar coinages.   Will the name *Tony* stick to the Portuguese soldier ?   On the chance that it may, let the lexicographers note this report from Somewhere in France :

The cordiality of the relationship between the British soldiers and the Portuguese may be taken as finally cemented by the fact that the latter now have a nickname. They are " Antonio," which is already being shortened to " Tony," a fit counterpart to " Tommy," showing that the rapprochement is consecrated and complete.[1]

What will the American private be called ? According to the New York *Sun*, the question was settled before he landed in Europe : " his name must be *Teddy* " :

" Sammy " does not seem to fit the typical adventurous American fighting man.   There is, however, a name that symbolises the true American fighting spirit.   Preparedness, militancy against militarism, the " punch," the Big Stick—Teddy ![2]

---

[1] *Daily News*, June 29, 1917.   [2] *Times*, June 30, 1917.

But deliberate efforts to coin words with a purpose do not always, or often, succeed.   Clever people propose, but the common people decide ; and while the New York *Sun* was suggesting a particular advertisement for Mr. Roosevelt, the French people had adopted the generic Uncle Sam.   An English correspondent, describing the arrival of the first American contingent at " A Port in France," records as follows :

> There was quite a discussion on board every ship of the convoy as to what the American soldier should call himself.   It was generally agreed that the old name of the Regular infantryman, *Doughboy*, would fail to carry any conviction, and in casting around for a name it was found that *Sammy* was the only nickname worthy to rank with our *Tommy* and the French *Poilu*.   The choice has found an unsolicited testimonial in the unanimity with which the inhabitants of this port address all unknown Americans as *Sammee*.[1]

The origin of war words and phrases can sometimes be given with reasonable precision, but one is inclined in other cases to wish that a professor of language were attached to the General Staff at the front in order to fix the winged words as they fly from mouth to mouth, to pin down the first use, to discover beyond cavil the real significance.   How tantalising, for instance, in its indefinite   result was the

[1] *Times*, July 2.   Mr. *Punch* also suggested the name : see his issues of June 13 and August 1, 1917.

discussion which occupied the correspondence columns of the *Times* towards the beginning of the war on the question why the soldiers used the phrase *going west* for death ! Were the men talking poetry without knowing it ? Did their purpose hold, with Tennyson's Ulysses,

> To sail beyond the sunset, and the baths
> Of all the western stars, until I die ?

Or, with Wordsworth, did

> Stepping westward seem to be
> A kind of heavenly destiny ?

Or, on the other hand, to plunge from these heights to plainest prose, was the " Subaltern " right who traced the phrase back to some operations at Aldershot a few years ago when " a Staff officer, complete with eye-glass, galloped past the battalion to which I have the honour to belong, and, in a very high-pitched and fruity voice, shouted to the commanding officer, ' Tell the general that I have gone west.' . . . Ever since then the men have made use of the expression to denote passing away. An officer's servant will regretfully inform his master that his bath water has gone west, *i.e.* that he has kicked it over. A man will mourn that his proficiency pay has gone west, after having failed to make the necessary score. As was natural, the expression was used with reference to casualties in the present campaign. It has spread to other units, and is now universal." This matter-of-fact explanation may be correct as far as it applies to the particular unit to which the subaltern refers, but the students of poetry and folklore who intervened in the discussion need not on that account retire. Why did the phrase become " universal " ? and why, for that matter, does some such meaning attach to *going west* (as Professor Gollancz showed) in many different times and places ? We need not assume that every soldier who uses the phrase is a poet or a folklorist, but the influence of poetry and tradition is often unconscious, and the words of the *Times* in summing up the discussion may be allowed to stand : " It would seem that behind this phrase there lingers some primeval tradition, founded perhaps on sun-worship or on the instinctive feeling that beyond the sunset is the land of darkness and the shadow of death." [1]

Philology, not folklore, was at hand to explain the word *Blighty*, used both as substantive and adjective. No phrases are now more familiar than *back to Blighty*, *a Blighty wound*, *a Blighty boy* (*i.e.* a casualty serious enough for transference to a base hospital). There is a newspaper so called, and Sir Arthur Conan Doyle has used the word in verse:

> But I'll tell 'em in Blighty, wherever I be,
> How the Guards came through.[2]

---

[1] *Times*, leading article, January 12, 1915. Professor Gollancz's letter was in the issue of January 8 ; the Subaltern's, in that of January 11.

[2] *Times*, June 23 1917.

Until Anglo-Indians came forward to explain, every one was puzzled to understand why the home country should be called by so unkind a name. In India, we are told, " wilayat "—the government, or province, of a *wali*—has come to mean a foreign country, and especially England. In Hindustani patois the word became " bilati," and this was readily corrupted by British soldiers in India to *blighty*. No doubt the association of " blight," " blighted," commends it to the cheerful irony of the British soldier.

Adoption has in all ages and tongues been a fruitful source of new words. Our close alliance with the French has naturally added French war-words to English use, and there are some which have already become well acclimatised. The *Bosches* (or Boches) is the common appellative, especially at the front, for the enemy, and the adjectival form (*e.g.* " Boche dug-outs," as cited above) is also frequent. The French word came into slang use, I believe, before the present war. Was it a corruption of the second part of *Allobroge*, which the French dictionaries define as " Homme grossier " ? Whatever be its origin, the word is expressive, and sticks. There is enough of antipathy and contempt in it, with a touch of Gallic humour which is absent from the *Huns, Hun, Hunnish* of English newspapers.[1]

[1] " More than fourteen hundred years ago Attila and his Huns came to Châlons on the Marne, and were forced to retreat to the Rhine after

There is righteous indignation, however, in the latter terms, and the German Emperor himself is responsible for them.[1] There was once a powerful German tribe who gave themselves the proud name of the *franks* or the free. A chapter in the rise and fall of national ideals is latent in the fortunes of that word and its derivatives, and in the modern application of Huns.

Another French war-word which seems likely to be adopted is *camouflage*. The idea of protective mimicry in war is old, and the invention of a single word to express it meets a felt need. " Auto-canon et ses servants *camouflés* forment une masse indistincte que ne peuvent découvrir les aviateurs ennemis." [2] " The King saw all the latest Protean tricks for concealing, or, as we all say now, for *camouflaging*, guns, snipers, observers, and all machines and implements of

---

tremendous slaughter.   On the same ground the forces of the monarch who has styled himself the modern Attila are meeting a like fate" (*Times*, leader, September 14, 1914).   A king of Prussia had been likened to Attila before William II.'s Chinese allocution ; see Trevelyan's *Life of Macaulay*, ch. vii.   It has been pointed out in the press that long before the Emperor's day Campbell wrote in " Hohenlinden " of " furious Frank and fiery Hun " ; and this passage in a letter of Byron's, from Ravenna, August 31, 1820, has been recalled : " O Jerusalem, Jerusalem ! the Huns are on the Po ; but if once they pass it on their march to Naples, all Italy will rise behind them : the Dogs, the Wolves, may they perish like the Host of Sennacherib ! " But in both these cases the Huns were Austrian.

[1] See his allocution on the occasion of the Boxer rising, July 1900 : " Quarter will not be given.   Whoever falls into your hands is forfeit to you ; just as a thousand years ago the Huns under Attila made a name for themselves which is still mighty in tradition and story."

[2] *L'Illustration*, July 7, 1917.

war." [1]   The verb *camoufler* and the noun *camouflage* are derived from *camouflet*, which is defined
by Littré as " fumée épaisse qu'on souffle mali-
cieusement dans le nez avec un cornet de papier."
Thence the word came to be applied figuratively
to any affront, and in previous wars to a particular
device in military mining.

From France, 'too, come some new words
which have been coined to describe certain phases
of the enemy's " offensive behind the lines."
M. Clemenceau, in a speech in the Senate in
July 1917, described the *defeatist* campaign
carried on in his country through enemy machina-
tions in which a principal part was alleged to have
been played by Bolo Pasha.   The word *Boloism*
was thereupon coined, and Mr. Lloyd George
gave it an official imprimatur.   " Beware," he
said, " of people who try to sow dissension,
distrust, suspicion, disunion.   The enemy, beaten
on most of the battlefields, is organising with
deadly care and ingenuity an offensive behind
the lines.   I know what I am talking about.
See what has happened in France—they discovered it in time—and look out for Boloism in
all its shapes and forms.   It is the latest and most
formidable weapon in the German armoury." [2]

Some adoptions of foreign words have a
different origin.   *Fas est et ab hoste doceri*, and

---

[1] *Manchester Guardian*, July 16, 1917.
[2] Speech at the Albert Hall, *Times*, October 23, 1917.

in a few cases it has been found well to borrow from the Germans, but with differences which are subtle and characteristic.   There was a picture in *Punch* of a wall in a village reclaimed from the enemy on which the familiar inscription " Gott strafe England " had been chalked.   A Highland soldier comes up to it and, with a twinkle, crosses through the word " England " and writes above it " Scotland."   If any German could ever appreciate all the quiet fun and national spirit implied in this picture, he might be able to understand also the exact nuance with which the British soldiers speak of things being " quiet at the front, sir, except just for the morning (or evening) *hate*," and the tone in which the word *strafe* and *strafing* are passing into conversational use in this country.   In something of the same spirit the sneer attributed to the German Emperor has been adopted, and our Old Army bears proudly upon its banners the title, in popular parlance, of the *Old Contemptibles*.

The food crisis has caused the Germans to coin an excellent word—*Hamstertante*.   The word is untranslatable, says the writer of a lively article in the *Times*,[1] who paraphrases it as " Auntie-who-gets-food-on-the-sly."   But hamster is an English word as well as a German—" A species of rodent," says the Dictionary, " which has cheek-pouches in which it carries the grain with

1 " Everyday Life in Berlin," by a Neutral, in the *Times*, January 28, 1918.

which it stores its burrows." " Fortunately for England," says an old book on natural history, "the hamster is not indigenous within the precincts of the island." But cases in the police-courts now tell a different tale, and *Hamsteraunties* would not be a bad word for a certain class of *food-hoarders*.

The political discussions in foreign countries have during this war introduced some new words into our newspapers, as, for instance, *trialism* (the policy of converting the Dual Monarchy into a Triple, Austro-Hungarian-Bohemian), and, from Russia, Maximalist (or Bolshevist). Mr. Arthur Henderson was blamed in the *Times* (August 1, 1917) for visiting Paris " in company with Mr. Ramsay MacDonald and the four Russian *Maximalist* delegates." Another newspaper had explained the term : " *Leninism* is a doctrine of long standing, which had a numerous following among Russian Social Democrats many years before this war. Its adherents are commonly called *Maximalists*, because they hold that any conditions which render a political revolution possible must be equally favourable to the attainment of the ' maximum,' a social revolution." [1]

It is not only the combatant who has originated

---

[1] *Nation*, July 28, 1917. For a discussion of the origin of the term *Bolshevik* (= the biggest, or *whole-hogger*) see letters by Dr. Hagberg Wright and Mr. J. Y. MacAlister in the *Times Literary Supplement*, Feb. 7 and 21, 1918.

war-words. What volumes of polemic are likely
to grow up around the letters *C.O.*, no longer
denoting Commanding Officer only, but applied
also to that very different person, the *Conscientious
Objector* ! The C.O.'s (new style) are not
popular persons, but there is something that
sounds almost endearing in the other term for
them—the *conchies*. This term, however, when
I last noted it,[1] was still in the half-way house
of inverted commas. It is only when these are
dropped that a new word can be regarded as
adopted into the family of a language. A
certificate of exemption may be given to an
applicant, says the Military Service Act, " on
the ground of a *conscientious objection* to the
undertaking of combatant service." Parliament,
in its prudence, gave no definition. I do not
envy any future dictionary-maker who may feel
bound to collate a definition, if he can, from the
proceedings of the Tribunals. A generic name,
Cuthbert, has been given to supposed shirkers or
" slackers " who are exempted in another way—
by taking refuge, to wit, in *funkholes*. These
are coinages which the *Evening News* has made
familiar ; but " *Cuthbert* in his *creep-hole* " would
have sounded just as well, or better, and an old
English word might thereby have been restored

---

[1] In a *Times* leading article of December 29, 1917 : " He gives such a
good account of the 'conchies' that we are rather at a loss to understand
why so many of them are kept at unproductive employment at Dartmoor
and elsewhere."

to currency. " A poor shifting excuse," says a
book of 1681, " a miserable come-off, a very
creep-hole." Another new usage which will
require some explanation in dictionaries of the
future is *the comb*, meaning the extraction of men
from other employments for the Army. The
word was plied with great frequency on the day
(April 9) fixed for the introduction of a further
Military Service Bill in 1918. " Now," said the
Pall Mall Gazette, " that the older men are to
be called up, it is imperative that the Government Departments should at once comb out the
young *indispensables* whom they have been
harbouring." The older men, said the *Westminster Gazette*, " are not asking jealously and
suspiciously whether all the young men have
been taken first, whether ' the comb ' has been
effectively plied in the Government Departments." The *Westminster*, it will be noted,
half apologised for adopting the not very nice,
though expressive, word by putting it in inverted
commas ; but later in the day the Prime Minister
gave it the sanction of parliamentary usage,
introducing also another new phrase. " We
must call upon the Civil Service," he said, " to
do more, and a *clean cut* of young fit men must
be made. It is proposed that no fit men below
the age of 25 should be retained. We *comb out*
beyond that." The " clean cut " had previously
been used, as politicians will remember, to denote

the total exclusion of Ulster counties from the sphere of the Home Rule Bill.

The political issues raised by a war, the diplomatic expedients adopted in a peace, are also the occasions of new words or of new senses for old ones. Thus it was the peace which followed the Crimean War that brought the terms *neutralise, neutralisation* into vogue in the sense of making a place neutral in time of war. " The Black Sea is neutralised," said the eleventh article of the Treaty of Paris (1856), and this was, I think, the first use of the word in that sense, though "neutral" and " neutrality" were of much older currency in the same connection. Belgium, for instance, was created " an independent and perfectly neutral State " by treaties of 1831–32 and 1839. Such treaties cease to be binding, the German Foreign Secretary explained to the British Ambassador in August 1914, when military necessity which knows no other law is involved. The phrase which has been used to express this and other forms of the German national creed has brought another word into world-wide currency. The point of departure was Mr. Asquith's historic declaration of our war aims. " We shall never sheathe the sword, which we have not lightly drawn, until Belgium recovers in full measure all, and more than all, that she has sacrificed, until France is adequately secured against the menace of aggression, until the rights of the smaller nationalities of Europe are placed upon an unassailable foundation, and until the military domination of Prussia is wholly and finally destroyed" (Guildhall, November 9, 1914). Mr. Asquith is a master of compression, but his definition of the fourth of these aims has been abbreviated yet further in hundreds of speeches, leading articles, and books into " the destruction of Prussian *militarism*." The word is now on every one's tongue, as in a speech by the Prime Minister in which he spoke of " the aggressive and arrogant spirit of *Prussian militarism* " (Glasgow, June 29, 1917); and in an earlier speech by the French Premier of the day : " We want the restitution of the lost provinces and the crushing of *Prussian militarism*, for the peace of the world is irreconcilable with its bloody caprices" (April 13, 1915). Or, again, in Mr. Balfour's speech at the Guildhall when he said that " the United States saw with an impartiality perhaps impossible to us what *German militarism* really meant, not only for those who were actually fighting it at the moment, but for every free community." [1] The world is at war in order, on the one side, to destroy " militarism." What precisely does the word mean ? Its history as given in the *Oxford Dictionary* is interesting.

[1] *Times*, July 14, 1917.

The first recorded use of the French word in English is in a translation from Garibaldi. He spoke of " an army, bright in glory, yet untainted with that disease of modern times, known under the sinister name of *militarism*." [1] Four years later comes the prophetic remark : " Prussian officialism is supreme, and Prussian militarism as well."   Next, under the date 1891, we are given this passage : " Industrialism as opposed to militarism is now the central idea of the New World."   And there the Dictionary leaves it. An after-the-war edition will have to carry the matter further, drawing out the full and exact meaning of the word by later illustrations and distinctions.   *Militarism* is to be distinguished first, in the spirit of Garibaldi's phrase, from military force.   The hope that this war will end war is associated in all practical minds with the idea of military force, which shall be held in re-serve as a sanction of the decrees of some League of Nations.   What Wordsworth wrote in 1816 is still applicable : " The nation would err grievously if she suffered the abuse which other states have made of military power to prevent her from perceiving that no people ever was, or can be, independent, free, or secure, much less great, in any application of the word, without martial propensities, and an assiduous cultivation of military virtues."   This side of the case may

---

[1] *Daily Telegraph*, April 28, 1864.

be illustrated by reference to a new group of words which have been brought into currency during the present war. Just as the Crimean War gave us a *peace-at-any-price* party, so this war has given us *pacifism* and *pacifists*—words of unscholarly formation, but very commonly used. Pacifism is defined in the *Concise Oxford Dictionary* (an indispensable supplement, as yet, to the larger work) as " the doctrine that the abolition of war is both desirable and possible." In a sense we are all pacifists now, but if aggressive war is hereafter to be made difficult or impossible, it can only be done by bringing superior military force to bear down German force now, and (as already said) by organising force in reserve for the future. The point was partly made in a remark by Mr. Holman, the Premier of New South Wales, which has the advantage for a lexicographer of including two of the words now under discussion : " I am a *Pacifist*. But if ever there were an inopportune moment for Pacifist propaganda it is now, when we need the most highly perfected military organisation to save us from the very *militarism* which these gentlemen condemn." [1] If, then, the condemnation of militarism does not exclude the idea of using military force, what is the idea to which militarism is essentially opposed ? The quotation given above, which opposes it to

[1] *Morning Post*, June 14, 1917.

industrialism, does not comprise the whole matter. Here is a recent passage which serves as well as any account that I have seen in so few words to explain the two opposed ideas : " Our idea was, and is, that latent force ought to be able to conserve peace.   The German idea is that nothing but militant force can achieve this purpose.   That is militarism, and that is what we are up against. So long as militarism exists the German definition of International Law as trash is strictly correct." [1] The word *international* was coined by Jeremy Bentham in 1780, and Archbishop Trench, writing in 1855, found it " difficult to understand how we could have managed so long to do without it."   But the word has been long in advance of the thing in any really effective sense.   The word *nationalism* came into use fifty years later than Bentham's " international," but it had a potent idea behind it.   Philosophic historians have sometimes characterised the nineteenth century as the age of nationalism.   If the twentieth century is to be the age of internationalism, a condition precedent is the destruction of Prussian militarism.

The peace, when it comes, will keep dictionary-makers busy.   Who can say what precise definitions will be forthcoming of such formulas as *No annexations*, *No indemnities*, and the *Right of Self-determination* ?   Already the negotiations

---

[1] *New Witness*, June 14, 1917.

at Brest-Litovsk have raised the question, When is an annexation not an annexation ? How will the line be drawn between *indemnity* and *reparation* ? As for the Right of Self-determination, the latter word, as the *Oxford Dictionary* shows, comes from metaphysical and theological writers, and the subtleties which gathered round it at Brest-Litovsk were in keeping with its origins.

Meanwhile, as the phrase " Prussian militarism " involves fundamental questions of international politics, so there is another war-word which cuts straight down to first principles in economics. I omitted to make note of the first appearance of *profiteering* ; but by the time it had caught on, the *Spectator* was to the fore with one of its earnest articles, to point out, more in sorrow than in anger, the wickedness of politicians in using words without stopping to consider precisely what they mean (June 16, 1917). The Prime Minister took up the challenge in a speech to which the *Times* gave the heading, " Mr. Lloyd George on Profiteering." Here is the passage which will be the *locus classicus* for definition of the new word :

The country is entitled to ask from the Government that they will not permit the burdens of the country to be increased by what is called profiteering. Although I have been criticised for using that word, I believe on the whole it is a rather good one. It is profit-eer-ing

as distinguished from profiting.   Profiting is fair recompense for services rendered either in production or dis-
tribution ; profiteering is an extravagant recompense given
for services rendered.   I believe that unfair in peace.   In
war it is an outrage.[1]

Mr. Lloyd George's distinction is lacking in
precision, as we shall see, but this does not
invalidate his usage of the new word.   New
words often follow close analysis, but sometimes
they may usefully anticipate and prompt it.
The popular instinct was right in feeling that a
new word was wanted here to mark a departure
in moral and economic ideas from the good old
rule, the simple plan,

> That they should take who have the power,
> And they should keep who can.

The actual word coined to meet this advance is
well formed.   There was indeed already an old
word *profiter*, to which (if one may judge from
the passages cited in the Dictionary) a slightly
derogatory tone was attached ; but the suffix *eer*
emphasises the sneer.   Some words ending in
eer are, it is true, void of offence, but in many
there is always a contemptuous implication.   No
one feels flattered by being called a " sonneteer "
or a " pamphleteer."   The suffix stamps him
with the suggestion of fatal facility or incontinence.
And so it is meant to be with the " profiteer,"

[1] *Times*, July 2, 1917.

and the essential service rendered by the new word is the stigma which it carries with it. Of course much hard and clear thinking will be required before the stigma is translated into law or executive order. Dr. Shadwell has usefully pointed out that "the word *profiteering* is applied indiscriminately to two distinct processes : (1) Making money in a favourable market for which the seller is not responsible ; (2) manipulating the market and artificially raising prices in order to make money. The latter is a cause of high prices, the former a consequence. The distinction," he adds, " is not merely verbal ; it entails moral, legal, and practical differences. The second sort of profiteering is criminal [? should be made criminal] ; it can be peremptorily stopped and heavily punished without doing any harm at all. The first is not criminal [? is not immoral], and interference is apt to entail the serious consequence of drying up supplies."[1] The distinction thus drawn is real and important, and hereafter it may be expressed by some other new words, but meanwhile the discussion is not ended—perhaps it is only beginning. The Prime Minister, it will have been noted, in defining the new word, drew a distinction between a " fair " and an " extravagant " [unfair] recompense. But what is " fair " ? Mr. Luxmoore (who, if I am not mistaken, was

---

[1] *Times*, June 6, 1917.

a member of Ruskin's Guild of St. George)
paraphrased *Unto this Last* and answered thus
the question which is involved in Mr. Lloyd
George's definition : " The duty of the seller is
to supply the public with that which is needed
and good for the public as cheaply as he can,
taking only such profit for himself as is proportionate to the labour spent by him and by his
workmen for that end, and proportionate means
such as will support them in their rank of life
with due provision for old age. The less work
he does, the less gain he deserves. Anything
beyond that gain is profiteering." [1] Economics
are to be moralised, it seems. The profiter is
to be invited to consider the old question, What
shall it profit a man if he shall gain the whole
world and lose his own soul ? Such are the far-
reaching discussions to which attention is likely
to be called by the vogue of the new word *profiteer*.

In another sphere the war has suggested the
need of a new word, which, however, has not
yet been found. What is the British Empire of
the future to be called ? General Smuts propounded the question in his speech in the Royal
Gallery on May 16, 1917. The Empire is not
an Empire. It is a combination of a Kingdom,
an Empire, self-governing Dominions, and Crown
Colonies. " You can see," said General Smuts,
" that no political ideas which we have evolved

[1] *Times*, June 21, 1917.

in the past will apply to this world which is comprised in the British Empire, and any name we have yet found for this group is insufficient. The man who will find a proper name for this system will, I think, do real service to the Empire." The search is likely to be long. Nothing that has hitherto been suggested will do. That the old nomenclature was insufficient was recognised when Edward VII. succeeded to the throne. On his coinage, as on that of his successor, the Sovereign is styled " Britt. Omn. Rex," and by Act of Parliament he is declared to be, besides Emperor of India, King not only of Great Britain and Ireland, but also of " the British dominions beyond the seas."   All this, though it recognises the difficulty propounded by General Smuts, gives no solution of it.   There is an agglomeration of titles but no concise substitution.   At one time " The British *Commonwealth* " was suggested, but (apart from other possible objections) the word Commonwealth has now been appropriated by Australia.   General Smuts himself suggested, for part at least of the British system, the name " The British Commonwealth of Nations," but that (besides being only partially applicable) is too long. The connecting link of the whole system is the Crown, and this fact may suggest that " The British *Realm* " would do ; but perhaps the associations of realm are too distinctively English :

> This royal throne of kings, this sceptred isle, . . .
> This blessed plot, this earth, this realm, this England.

After all, will it be so very hard a fate if we are driven to keep the term " British Empire " to denote the collection of States which in one way or another pay allegiance to a common Sovereign ? " An Empire," said Burke, " is the aggregate of many States under one common head." The terms Empire, Imperial, have an etymological meaning which does not fit all parts of the British system, and some historical associations which do not accord with its principles. But we need not be the slaves of phrases. Words alter their meaning as the things which they express alter. Nor are all the associations of Empire such as need make even a Russian Maximalist ashamed. Here is the ideal of the Roman Empire as drawn by the last of the Latin poets, himself, by the way, an Egyptian :

> She, she alone, has taken the conquered to her bosom, and has made men to be of one household with one name, herself their mother, not their lord, and has called her vassals citizens, and has linked far places in a bond of love. . . .

" We are not a State," says General Smuts, " but a community of States and nations. We are far greater than any Empire which has ever existed." Yes, but why should not the word " Empire " be left to gather a new meaning from the case of an Empire with a diversity greater, and a freedom larger, than any which Rome knew ?

VII

A STUDY IN SUPERLATIVES

THE superlative degree accords ill, I suppose,
with what is called judicious criticism. Excellence in art and literature is relative rather than
absolute, and to say that such or such a work is the
best, the greatest, or the most moving, requires
to be qualified and guarded in many relations
before the saying can be brought to any strict
test. A great living English man of letters was
once asked to give the best passages in English
literature. He did as he was asked, but took
the precaution of quoting Scripture : " There is
one glory of the sun, and another glory of the
moon, and another glory of the stars : for one
star differeth from another star in glory." For
like reasons, orders of merit and comparative
tables are deprecated by severe judges of literature. " We are not called upon," says Lord
Morley in his essay on Wordsworth, " to place
great men of his stamp as if they were collegians
in a class-list."

We are not called upon, but at times we all

do it; and though the superlative degree may
be discountenanced by the more austere judges,
yet there is something to be said in favour of
good lovers and good haters in literature.   For
one thing, a positive and absolute judgment has
the great merit of being arresting or challenging.
You read a qualified or carefully hedged estimate
with a correspondingly languid interest, and do
not take the trouble, perhaps, to test and examine
it for yourself; but when a writer who is entitled
to respect tells you that such or such a piece is
indisputably the best in the world, then if you
know the piece already your attention is at once
challenged, or if you do not know it you are forced
to refer to it forthwith.   It is this which makes
Swinburne's prose writings, for all their faults,
so full of interest and stimulus.   For instance,
when we read of a certain piece that it is " so
much the noblest of sacred poems in our language
that there is none which comes near it enough to
stand second," that it is " a hymn touched as
with the fire and bathed as in the light of sun-
beams, tuned as to chords and cadences of refluent
sea-music beyond reach of harp and organ, large
echoes of the serene and sonorous tides of heaven,"
who can avoid being roused to curiosity or pro-
voked to dissent ?   Tennyson said that a good
hymn is the most difficult thing in the world
to write, as in it you have to be both commonplace and poetical.   He liked Heber's " Holy,

N

Holy, Holy " better than most ; " it is in a fine
metre, too." But the reader will not find Swinburne's piece in Heber or George Herbert, nor,
so far as I know, in any Sacred Treasury or Book
of Church Hymns. It is the third part of
Christina Rossetti's *Old and New Year's Ditties* :

Passing away, saith the World, passing away.

If any second piece is to be found worthy to rank
with this, it must be sought in the same poet ;
and, according to Dante Rossetti, her " Advent "
hymn was once pronounced by Swinburne to be
" the noblest of all her poems." Passages from
this poem, which, though very beautiful, is less
haunting in melody than the other, were sung,
I remember, at the first part of her burial service
in Woburn Square. It is, by the way, a disgrace
of long standing to the English Church that,
with so great a wealth of religious poetry at choice,
so much doggerel should be used in places where
they sing. Swinburne, in another essay, cited,
not indeed another poem, but a few lines by a
very different poet, as worthy to stand beside
Miss Rossetti. " It cannot be denied," he says,
" that Herrick's sacred verse at its worst is as
offensive as his secular verse at its worst; nor
can it be denied that no severer sentence of condemnation can be passed upon any poet's work.
But neither Herbert nor Crashaw could have
bettered such a divinely beautiful triplet as this :

> We see Him come, and know Him ours,
> Who with His sunshine and His showers
> Turns all the patient ground to flowers.[1]

That is worthy of Miss Rossetti herself: and praise of such work can go no higher." Ruskin is another writer who deals freely in arresting superlatives. When we read that a certain passage is "the noblest group of words ever uttered by man," one turns the page with lively curiosity to find them. His reference was to the epitaph of Simonides on the Spartans who fell at Thermopylae.[2] For "the most vile sentence in the literature of any country or time," one might be sure that Ruskin would go to the political economists.[3]

The personal touch is one of the charming things in writers who are not afraid of the superlative degree. In an Author's Note to the new

---

[1] *Noble Numbers*, 96.

[2] Often translated ; never yet better than by Cicero :

> Dic hospes Spartae nos te hic vidisse jacentes
> Dum sanctis patriae legibus obsequimur ;

and by Bowles :

> Go tell the Spartans, thou that passest by,
> That here, obedient to their laws, we lie.

The epitaph was thus adapted by Edmund Garrett for English use :

> Tell England, you that pass our monument,
> Men who died serving Her rest here, content.

[3] " As no one will deny that Man possesses carnivorous teeth, or that all animals that possess them are more or less predatory, it is unnecessary to argue *a priori* that a predatory instinct . . . is one of the conditions of Man's nature and consequently of all arrangements of civilised society." The sentence was found in the *Transactions of the Social Science Congress* ; the date, 1860.

edition of his Works, Mr. Conrad says that he is " a great foe to favouritism," both personal and literary, but the remark may safely be taken as made half at least in irony, for it serves as introduction to an express permission to think *Lord Jim* his best book. You cannot know a man intimately without knowing his likes and dislikes. *Noscitur a sociis.* A man is known by the company he keeps in his reading, by the authors he loves, by his preferences and his aversions. A well-loved writer cites this from Thoreau as " the noblest and most useful passage I remember to have read in any modern author " : " It takes two to speak truth—one to speak and another to hear." The same writer tells us that to his thinking " the noblest passage in one of the noblest books of this century is where the old pope glories in the trial, nay, in the partial fall and but imperfect triumph of the younger hero." [1] Does not the avowal of these preferences throw light on the persuasive sympathy and the manly note which are the secret of the charm of Robert Louis Stevenson ? What a good introduction it is to the quality of the author of *Erewhon* when he begins the most charming of his books with this avowal : " Most men will readily admit that the two poets who have the greatest hold over Englishmen are Handel and Shakespeare." Or, again, to take an instance in a different sort, what

---

[1] See Book X. 1183 *seq.* of *The Ring and the Book.*

a light it throws on the limitations of Macaulay that, writing in 1850, he " could not remember that any better poetry had been published since his *Lays* appeared " in 1842.   The interval had seen the appearance of Tennyson's *Poems*, *The Princess* and *In Memoriam*, and of Browning's *Pippa Passes* and *Dramatic Lyrics*.

So, again, with discussions about the best books or the greatest writers, and with attempts to draw up lists of merit : such exercises are partly futile, but they are pleasant.   *Idem velle et idem nolle* is a bond of friendship, whilst differences about Shakespeare and the musical glasses give a pleasant spice to literary table-talk.   Sometimes the game is played openly for pleasure and no excuses are made.   For instance, in Lord Carlisle's *Journal* it is recorded as the most natural and delightful thing in the world that The Club sat for hours discussing the proper order in which to place great writers or famous books :

May 4.—Dined with the Club.   Very pleasant, though select.   Something led to my reminding Lord Aberdeen that we both put *Macbeth* first of Shakespeare's great plays.   Lord Lansdowne quite concurred.   Macaulay thinks it may be a little owing to our recollections of Mrs. Siddons.   He is much inclined to rank them thus : *Othello, Lear, Macbeth, Hamlet.*

Macaulay played a strong hand at such things, and no breakfast at the Albany was complete without its class list.   Here is the record of one :

November 29. — Breakfasted with Macaulay. He thinks that, though the last eight books of *Paradise Lost* contain incomparable beauties, Milton's fame would have stood higher if only the first four had been preserved. He would then have been placed above Homer.

Elsewhere Macaulay " cannot conceive how any person of the least pretension to taste " can doubt that the proper order is Homer, Aeschylus, Milton ; but on this occasion he forgot Dante, whom at another time he placed first of all " artists who have operated on the imagination by means of words," and Shakespeare, whose primacy was to be taken, I suppose, without saying ; for at another meeting of The Club we read : " Macaulay gave a list of six poets, whom he places above all others, in the order of his preference : Shakespeare, Homer, Dante, Aeschylus, Milton, Sophocles. Milman on the whole acquiesced. I fought some battle for Virgil coming before Sophocles, but ' What,' said Macaulay, ' did Virgil ever write like the *Philoctetes* ? ' He would place Lucretius and Ariosto before Virgil." Lord Morley has given us a different list, and admits only four names to it. " The greatest poets," he says, " reflect beside all else the broad-bosomed haven of a perfect and positive faith, in which mankind has for some space found shelter, unsuspicious of the new and distant way-farings that are ever in store. To this band of

sacred bards few are called, while perhaps not
more than four high names would fill the list
of the chosen : Dante, the poet of Catholicism ;
Shakespeare, of Feudalism ; Milton, of Protestant-
ism ; Goethe, of that new faith which is as
yet without any universally recognised label,
but whose heaven is an ever-closer harmony
between the consciousness of man and all the
natural forces of the universe, whose liturgy is
culture, and whose deity is a certain high com-
posure of the human heart." Considering the
long periphrasis drawn up in order to include
Goethe, one may wonder that no *ism* was found
to entitle Homer to a place among the band
of sacred bards.

On re-reading Trevelyan's *Life of Macaulay*,
in which innumerable *obiter dicta* in this sort are
recorded, I felt quite reconciled to the part I had
played in my journalistic days by inveigling
various persons of greater or less distinction to
take up Lord Avebury's challenge and draw up
for the amusement of the readers of the *Pall
Mall Gazette* rival lists of " The Best Hundred
Books." Other men, while not averse from this
kind of pastime, indulge in it only after excuse
or throw the responsibility on the ladies. It was
thus that Mr. Gladstone once enticed Lord
Morley. " By the way," said Mr. Gladstone,
" ladies nowadays keep question-books, and
among other things ask their friends for the

finest line in poetry"; after which exordium
the two friends seem to have settled down quite
comfortably to a study in superlatives, discussing,
after the best line in poetry, who is the greatest
Scot, and placing historians in order of merit.

I suppose no two persons ever chose the same
line as the finest in all poetry. Mr. Gladstone
was divided between three. "Perhaps," he
said, "the most glorious is Milton's," but Lord
Morley did not remember which it was, suggesting that a reader "might do worse than turn
over Milton in search for the finest line." If
he wants a short cut to an answer which would
pass muster he may turn to an appendix in the
Life of Tennyson, where some of that poet's
favourite lines in Milton are collected and
annotated. Mr. Gladstone went on: "Or else
Wordsworth's 'Or hear old Triton blow his
wreathed horn.' Yet what so splendid as Pene-
lope's not rejoicing the heart of anybody less
than Odysseus:

μηδέ τι χείρονος ἀνδρὸς εὐφραίνοιμι νόημα."

It is worth noting that Tennyson also was inclined to go to Wordsworth for the finest line.
The line in "Tintern Abbey"—

Whose dwelling is the light of setting suns—

is, he said, "almost the grandest in the English
language, giving the sense of the abiding in the
transient." Lord Morley gives, not as the finest,

but as " the most melting and melodious single verse in all the exercises of our English tongue," this from *Macbeth* :

> After life's fitful fever he sleeps well.

To select the best passages in verse and prose was a task set by a magazine-editor to various well-known people some years ago. Among those who responded, and whose preferences are best worth knowing, were Matthew Arnold, Thomas Hardy, George Meredith, Swinburne, John Addington Symonds, and Frederic Myers. Their selected pieces covered a wide range. " There was a pope," wrote Lord Acton once to Mrs. Drew, " who said that fifty books would include every good idea in the world. Literature has doubled since then, and one would have to take a hundred. How interesting it would be to get that question answered by one's most intelligent acquaintances. . . . There would be a surprising agreement." It was not found to be so when lists of the Best Hundred Books came to be drawn up, and in the case of the later " symposium " on the best passages there was again little agreement. There was, however, some confusion from a doubt whether the Bible and Shakespeare were or were not to be taken for granted as containing many of the best passages in the world. Leaving them out, I note that only one writer appeared in more than one of the

sets of passages selected by the six men of letters
above mentioned.   Arnold included in his selections the address of Zeus to the horses of Achilles
—a passage from the seventeenth *Iliad* which he
translated in his Lectures on Homer.   Meredith
gave the twenty-fourth *Iliad* as containing " the
highest reaches in poetry " ; Symonds selected
a passage from the eighteenth *Iliad*, and Myers
one from the eleventh *Odyssey*.   Arnold for his
second piece of poetry chose the stanza from
the saddest of the Odes of Horace, which is thus
rendered by Conington :

> Your land, your house, your lovely bride
>   Must lose you ; of your cherish'd trees
> None to its fleeting master's side
>   Will cleave, but those sad cypresses.

Is this Ode the best to be found in Horace ?
Perhaps for pathos it is, and Ruskin somewhere
notes the same stanza as specially memorable.
But if one be in a different mood, will any of the
Odes seem better than the fifth of the third book
—the one which makes so fine a thing of the story
of Regulus ?   If we may judge from an excellent
chapter in *A Diversity of Creatures*, it is Mr.
Kipling's favourite.   For his specimens of the
best prose, Arnold took a passage by Bossuet on
St. Paul, which is translated in *Essays in Criticism*,
and Burke's panegyric on Howard, the phil-
anthropist.   Mr. Hardy's pieces of poetry came
from Shelley (whose " Lament " he called " the

most beautiful of English lyrics ") and (with apologies for " so old-fashioned a taste ") from *Childe Harold* (the description of the Lake of Geneva, Canto iii. 85-87).   In prose he selected two passages from Carlyle—the comparison of the growth of the earth to the growth of an oak in the *French Revolution* and the description of night in a city in *Sartor Resartus*.   Meredith's selections, which were many, included pieces by Keats, Coleridge (" Kubla Khan "), and Tennyson (" Œnone ") ; and in prose, Charlotte Brontë's description of the actress Rachel as Vashti in the twenty-third chapter of *Villette*.   Swinburne chose passages from the *Agamemnon* of Aeschylus and from Dante's *Inferno*.   Frederic Myers included passages from Virgil in his list, selecting, characteristically, the praise of a country life from the second *Georgic* (475 *seq.*) and the famous passage from the sixth *Aeneid* (724-751), in which the poet expounds the doctrines of one great spirit and of reincarnation.   No one selected the five lines from the eighth Eclogue which Voltaire pronounced " the finest in Virgil " and Macaulay " the finest in the Latin language " :

Saepibus in nostris parvam te roscida mala—
Dux ego vester eram—vidi cum matre legentem :
Alter ab undecimo tum me iam acceperat annus,
Iam fragilis poteram ab terra contingere ramos :
Ut vidi, ut perii, ut me malus abstulit error !
Incipe Maenalios. . . .

Amongst the translations Calverley's is the best :

> Within our orchard-walls I saw thee first,
> A wee child with her mother—(I was sent
> To guide you)—gathering apples wet with dew.
> Ten years and one I scarce had numbered then ;
> Could scarce on tiptoe reach the brittle boughs.
> I saw, I fell, I was myself no more !
> Begin, my flute, a song of Arcady.

In awarding superlatives to poets, how much is to be held back on the score of lack of originality ? Virgil borrowed this picture of a country boy's love at first sight from Theocritus. I again quote Calverley's version :

> I loved thee, maiden, when thou cam'st long since,
> To pluck the hyacinth-blossom on the fell,
> Thou and thy mother, piloted by me.
> I saw thee, see thee still, from that day forth
> For ever ; but 'tis naught, ay naught, to thee.

It will be noticed that the prettiest touch in Virgil's lines—

> Could scarce on tiptoe reach the brittle boughs—

is Virgil's own. If the selection had to be not of a passage but of a single line, what would it be ? Probably most people would agree with Professor Tyrrell who gave as " the best line in Latin poetry " Virgil's

> Sunt lacrimae rerum et mentem mortalia tangunt.

In a lord of language such as Virgil, the question

of his best thing may be pursued from line to
word :

All the charm of all the Muses often flowering in a lonely
   word.

Tennyson himself selected for instance of what
he meant the epithet applied to the golden bough
in the sixth *Aeneid*—"*cunctantem* ramum." Professor Tyrrell, in his delightful book on *Latin
Poetry*, has given other and, I think, better instances. The feeblest line in Virgil is, according
to Mr. Myers, in the tenth *Aeneid* :

> Sed non et Troilus heros
> Dicta parat contra, iaculum nam torquet in hostem—

" a passage which suggests a modern exercise
painfully achieved by a schoolboy and inspired
by a gradus." " The very worst line in Latin
poetry " was, according to Professor Tyrrell,
achieved by Statius when he apostrophised the
condition of childlessness as " to be avoided by
every effort " (*Orbitas omni fugienda nisu*).

No one ever yet agreed entirely with anybody else's golden treasury of elegant extracts.
There would seem more chance of agreement
when the field of choice is more restricted. An
exercise in this sort which has amused men of
letters is to place the five great Odes of Keats
in order of merit. I count them as five, because
the " Ode to Indolence " is by consent of all
good judges an inferior performance ; and that

" To Maia," which might have ranked with the others, is only a fragment.   The Poet Laureate, in his *Critical Essay on Keats*, has placed the five in order and given his reasons.   The Cambridge Professor of English Literature, in one of his pleasant causeries, " From a Cornish Window," has examined the examination work by Mr. Bridges, and finding it faulty, has brought out a Tripos List of his own, degrading one candidate, " Autumn," from first to fourth, and changing the places of all the others.   And all the while, unnoticed by the other examiners, a greater than they had, by a nice discrimination of superlatives, given a first to each of the Odes.   " Perhaps," says Mr. Swinburne, " the two nearest to absolute perfection, to the triumphant achievement and accomplishment of the very utmost beauty possible to human words, may be that to ' Autumn ' and that on a ' Grecian Urn ' ;   the most radiant, fervent, and musical is that to a ' Nightingale ' ; the most pictorial and perhaps the tenderest in its ardour of passionate fancy is that to ' Psyche ' ; the subtlest in sweetness of thought and feeling is that on ' Melancholy.' "   It does not appear in what order the poet would have placed the Odes if he had been pressed to give competitive marks.   It is clear, from the different order given by Mr. Bridges and Professor Quiller-Couch respectively, that they attach different weight to the various points in which a poem may excel.   Mr. Bridges thinks most of perfection of form, and gives a bad mark to a piece which contains any fault.   Judging the Odes by this standard, he places the " Autumn " first and the " Grecian Urn " last.   That the " Autumn " is without flaw is common ground with all lovers of poetry.   That it is possible to find flaws in the " Grecian Urn " must be admitted because the Poet Laureate and the Professor have found them, though it will have been noticed that this Ode, which Mr. Bridges puts furthest from attaining to perfection, is placed by Swinburne with the " Autumn " as nearest to it.   George Meredith, too, named, among his favourite pieces in English literature, first the " Grecian Urn," and next the " Autumn."   What, then, is perfection in poetry ? what is the test of " the very utmost beauty possible to human words " ? Professor Quiller-Couch counts as one element in it the power of exciting what he calls " the Great Thrill "—" the sudden shiver, the awed surprise of the magic of poetry."   Absence of flaw, orderly sequence, the expression in beautiful words of a true and beautiful idea : these of themselves do not necessarily convey the thrill of which " Q " speaks.   It must be felt, and nobody can answer for another ; but for my part I am more thrilled by the second and third stanzas of the " Grecian Urn " than by anything in the " Autumn."   In this quality the " Grecian Urn "

seems to me second only to the " Nightingale."
It may, I think, safely be said that a vote of the
best judges would place the " Nightingale " at
the head of the list.   Mr. Bridges, though he
places " Autumn " first, yet admits to the " Nightingale " that he " could not name any English
poem of the same length which contains so much
beauty as this ode."   Professor Quiller - Couch
places it first.   Tennyson used to recite lines from
the same ode as examples of " the innermost soul
of poetry."   And Swinburne, though he does
not give it the palm for perfection, yet says elsewhere that " the ' Ode to a Nightingale ' is one
of the final masterpieces of human work in all
time and for all ages." [1]   As for the other Odes,
every one may place them in what order he will;
or, if he prefer, he may apply to these great works
of poetry what William Blake said : " There is
no competition among great artists.   None is
first in the Kingdom of Heaven."   The game
of examining the five Odes has at any rate the
advantage of making the players refresh their
memory of pieces of which it has been said that
" greater lyrical poetry the world may have seen
than any that is in these, lovelier it surely has
never seen nor ever can it possibly see."

[1] In yet another place, having occasion to mention single poems by
Keats, Swinburne selects neither the "Nightingale" nor the "Autumn"
but the "Psyche" or the "Grecian Urn" as "poems which for perfect
apprehension and execution of all attainable in their own sphere would weigh
down all the world of poetry."

To enlarge the question and ask, Which is the best ode in the English language ? were to open up a very wide field.   The term " ode " is large and variously defined.   Odes may be classified, for instance, either according as they are in regular or irregular measures, or according to their motive and subject ; and when we are told that such and such an ode is the best, the finest, or the noblest, we are not much the wiser unless we are told also what is the exact field of comparison.   But though the question is thus perhaps futile, it has often been put and answered ; but with one exception no two answers that I can recall are found to agree.   Macaulay pronounced " Alexander's Feast " to be " the noblest ode in our language," and herein he had at least one other person ͵to agree with him—namely, Dryden himself, who is reported to have confirmed a young man's compliment by saying, " A nobler ode never was produced nor ever will be."   Dr. Johnson, on the other hand, though not displacing Dryden, said that his poem on Mrs. Anne Killigrew was " undoubtedly the noblest ode that our language ever has produced." Those who disagree with the doctor may turn for support to an incidental passage in Matthew Arnold's essay on Gray.   To Dryden a very high place must surely be assigned among the writers of English irregular odes, but the first place is given by a modern critic to a later poet.

o

Wordsworth's " Ode on Intimations of Immortality " is, says Mr. Watts - Dunton, " the
finest irregular ode in the language ; for, although
Coleridge's ' Ode to the Departing Year ' excels it in Pindaric fire, it is below Wordsworth's
masterpiece in almost every other quality save
rhythm."   Shelley said that the finest ode in the
language was a different piece by Coleridge—
the " Ode to France," but that is in regular
measure.   As I have said, we must know what
is being compared.   According to Hallam,
Milton's " Ode on the Nativity " is " the finest
in the English language.   A grandeur, a simplicity, a breadth of manner, an imagination at
once elevated and restrained by the subject, reign
throughout it.   If Pindar is a model of lyric
poetry, it would be hard to name any other ode
so truly Pindaric ; but more has naturally been
derived from the Scriptures."   So far at least
as regular odes are concerned, is it reasonably
possible to dispute Hallam's judgment ?   Among
modern odes in irregular measure, is any finer
than Tennyson's " On the Death of the Duke
of Wellington " ?   The fortunes of this now
famous piece have been remarkable.   At the
time of publication the critics received it with
almost universal depreciation ; but a friendly
poet wrote to Tennyson to say how greatly he
admired it, and added a prediction : " I believe,"
said Sir Henry Taylor, " that many hundreds

of thousands in future times will feel about it as I do, or with a yet stronger and deeper feeling; and I am sure that every one will feel about it according to his capacity of feeling what is great and true." The author of *Philip van Artevelde* was right. The poem is now recognised as one of Tennyson's masterpieces, and there are passages in it which have passed into the common memory and inspiration of the race. But it is easy to see why the first reception of the ode was different. The public look to a popular poet to give what they have already learnt to admire in him. In form and substance the ode was unconventional; it was un-Tennysonian. But in losing the Tennysonian smoothness, it found the heroic note. I have often thought that these lines from the passage about the way to glory may be applied to the poem itself:

> He shall find the stubborn thistle bursting
> Into glossy purples, which outredden
> All voluptuous garden-roses.

Which is Tennyson's best poem ? The question would be incapable of reasonable discussion without preliminary agreement on many points. I suppose that *In Memoriam* is generally regarded as his masterpiece; but for purposes of comparison with other pieces, is *In Memoriam* to be taken as one poem or as a hundred and thirty-three ? And is *The Princess* to be taken as a single piece, or may the wonderful songs be

treated separately ? Such questions are not
worth pursuing, but some individual preferences
which I have noted shall here be recorded,
because they suggest an interesting reflection.
Every one knows the " Stanzas " (as they were
originally called) beginning :

> Oh that 'twere possible
> After long grief and pain,
> To find the arms of my true love
> Round me once again !

Swinburne called this " the poem of deepest
charm and fullest delight of pathos and melody
ever written even by Mr. Tennyson." [1]   Lord
Curzon, in recording [2] a day spent with Tennyson, has told us that the poet read the following
as " the most beautiful lines which he had written,
and among what he hoped would be regarded as
the most beautiful lines in English poetry " :

> Myriads of rivulets hurrying thro' the lawn,
> The moan of doves in immemorial elms,
> And murmuring of innumerable bees.

These are the last lines of the " small, sweet
Idyl " in the seventh canto of *The Princess*, and
about this piece the poet's son (confirming Lord
Curzon) says : " For *simple* rhythm and vowel
music my father considered his ' Come down,
O maid, from yonder mountain height,' written
in Switzerland (chiefly at Lauterbrunnen and

---

[1] In the *Academy*, January 29, 1876.
[2] *Times*, October 29, 1909.

Grindelwald) and descriptive of the waste Alpine heights and gorges, and of the sweet, rich valleys below, as amongst his *most successful work*." Ruskin was of the same opinion. He instanced " the piece of Alp in *The Princess* " as one of " the most wonderful things in all poetry." But another writer, entitled to speak both as poet and critic, has singled out a very different piece as Tennyson's " most perfect poem." " Surely," said Frederic Myers, " the ode ' To Virgil,' read with due lightening of certain trochaic accents in the latter half of each line, touches the high-water mark of English song. Apart from the specific allusions, almost every phrase recalls and rivals some intimate magic, some incommunicable fire. . . . We are here among the things that shall endure. It may be that our English primacy in poetry, now some four centuries old, is drawing to its close. It may be that the art must pass ere long to younger races, with fresher idioms and a new outlook on this ancient world. But whatever else shall pass from us, Tennyson shall remain." Now the pieces above noted are widely different in metre, in mode, in subject. That three good judges should each select a different one as the poet's most successful work is a tribute to the range and variety of Tennyson's genius. And there is another point. Of the three pieces, the " Stanzas " were first published in 1835, the

" Alpine Idyl " in 1847, and the " Virgil " in 1885.
There have been poets who wrote fine things
at as early an age, and others who continued to
write at as great an age.   But Keats and Shelley
died young.   And, on the other hand, Wordsworth's best work was all done between the
ages of twenty-eight and thirty-eight (1798–
1808);   nobody would select as Browning's
best anything of later date than *The Ring and the
Book*, published when he was fifty-six ; and Mr.
Gosse has written a book to show that Swinburne's
fount of inspiration gave out when he was removed by Mr. Watts-Dunton from the society
of other friends and led in strings to The Pines
at the age of forty-two.   Is there any other case
than this of Tennyson in the history of English
literature, where it may be a question of reasonable discussion whether a poet's best piece was
written at the age of twenty-six, of thirty-eight,
or of seventy-six ?

Who are the greatest English men of letters ?
The question is answered very conspicuously
in the reading-room of the British Museum.
When the dome was redecorated some years ago,
it was decided to place a name in letters of gold
beneath each of the twenty windows.   The
names in historical order are these : Chaucer,
Caxton, Tindale, Spenser, Shakespeare, Bacon,
Milton, Locke, Addison, Swift, Pope, Gibbon,
Wordsworth, Scott, Byron, Carlyle, Macaulay,

Tennyson, Browning—and the twentieth place is for the present left vacant, being partly hidden by a clock.   Is this to give some twentieth-century genius a chance ?   Or is there a subtler intent in placing a timepiece over a nameless scroll ?   I have sometimes thought so when the light grows faint in the dome beneath which so many once famous works and records are stored :

Thronging through the cloud-rift, whose are they, the faces
   Faint revealed yet sure divined, the famous ones of old ?
"What," they smile, "our names, our deeds so soon erases
   Time upon his tablet where Life's glory lies enrolled ? "

However this may be, I suppose that no list of the sort was ever more canvassed than this. Innumerable students, as they sit and wait for their books, must have looked up to the dome and been challenged to criticism.   Are the Elizabethans sufficiently represented ?   Is the eighteenth century over-represented ?   Should Dr. Johnson have been left out ?   And if Lord Morley were a Trustee of the Museum at the time, what did he think of the omission of Burke ? " The supreme writer of the eighteenth century," said De Quincey of him.   " Our greatest English prose writer," said Matthew Arnold.   And are both Tennyson and Browning rightly included in a list which finds no room for Keats or Shelley ?

Which is the best novel that ever was written ? Two dealers in superlatives have answered the question—differently, but with equal assurance.

" I am going through *Don Quixote* again, and admire it more than ever. It is certainly the best novel in the world, beyond all comparison." " The best novel in the world is *The Vicar of Wakefield.*" It is easy to see why Macaulay did not give the palm to Goldsmith nor Ruskin to Cervantes. Macaulay greatly admired *The Vicar*, predicting that its fame would last as long as our language, and nothing ever annoyed him more than a slip of the pen whereby for three months, between the appearance of one number of the *Edinburgh Review* and the next, he had presented himself before the world as a critic who thought *The Vicar* one of Goldsmith's worst books.[1]   But he was a voracious reader of novels, whose ambition was to make history as interesting as any of them, and he could not pardon the lack of probability and consistency in Goldsmith's story. And Ruskin, though he loved *Don Quixote* and knew it almost by heart from boyhood, had reasons of his own, as a tilter at windmills, for coming to think it " the most mischievous book ever written." " It was always *throughout real* chivalry to me ; and it is precisely

[1] The essay on Warren Hastings, as it originally appeared, contains this passage : " More eminent men than Mr. Gleig have written nearly as ill as he, when they have stooped to similar drudgery. It would be unjust to estimate Goldsmith by *The Vicar of Wakefield*, or Scott by *The Life of Napoleon.*" For *The Vicar of Wakefield* Macaulay meant to put *The History of Greece*, but neither in writing nor in correcting the proof did he notice what he had actually said. This deserves a note in a study of superlatives as the most unaccountable slip of the pen ever perpetrated by a man of letters.

because the most touching valour and tenderness
are rendered vain by madness, and because, thus
vain, they are made a subject of laughter to vulgar
and shallow persons, and because *all* true chivalry
is thus by implication accused of madness and
involved in shame, that I call the book so deadly."
Macaulay died too soon to know, and Ruskin
had too much horror of the morbid taint to love,
a third novel which may dispute the primacy
with the two already named. "The greatest
work of fiction ever created or conceived is," said
Mr. Swinburne, "*Les Misérables*." Others would
probably put in a plea for a novel by Scott, but
they would disagree in selecting it. Those who
have loved him most find the greatest difficulty
in deciding which of his novels is the best.
Edward FitzGerald used to say that one of the
sorrows of old age was the thought that he might
never live to have this Waverley novel or that
read to him again, and he felt the same in the
case of each of his favourites in turn. Ruskin,
who was another devoted lover of Scott, was
constantly drawing up lists of the novels in order
of preference, but no two of his lists agree.
Seven novels, however, appear in all his lists,
namely : *Waverley, Guy Mannering, Antiquary,
Old Mortality, Heart of Midlothian, Abbot,* and
Redgauntlet. If he had been forced to choose
one as the very best, he would, I think, have
named *Heart of Midlothian.* Tennyson preferred

Old Mortality.   Bulwer Lytton is said to have given first place to the one which Ruskin liked least—*The Bride of Lammermoor*.

Macaulay, in placing *Don Quixote* first of all novels beyond compare, was faithless for the moment in his allegiance to Jane Austen. In the essay on Madame D'Arblay, he names Jane Austen as second only to Shakespeare in the delineation of character, and in his diary of a later date there is this entry :

Home and finished *Persuasion*.   I have now read over again all Miss Austen's novels.   Charming they are ; but I found a little more to criticise than formerly.   Yet there are in the world no compositions which approach nearer to perfection.

For those readers who have found the taste for Jane Austen difficult to acquire, I hasten to add a contrary opinion. " I know it's very wrong," said Charlotte Brontë, " but the fact is I can't read them. They have not got story enough in them to engage my attention. I don't want my blood curdled, but I like it stirred. Miss Austen strikes me as milk-and-watery, and, to say truth, as dull." And here is an avowal of Edward FitzGerald to like effect :

I cannot get on with Books about the Daily Life which I find rather insufferable in practice about me. I never could read Miss Austen, nor (later) the famous George Eliot.   Give me People, Places, and Things which I don't and can't see ; Antiquaries, Jeanie Deans,

Dalgettys, &c. . . . As to Thackeray's, they are terrible; I really look at them on the shelf, and am half afraid to touch them.   He, you know, could go deeper into the Springs of Common Action than these Ladies : wonderful he is, but not delightful, which one thirsts for as one gets old and dry.

Tennyson, more catholic than his friend, could enjoy Miss Austen and Thackeray as well as Scott.   " Delicious " was the word he applied to the novels which Old Fitz found " not Delightful," and as for the others, he almost agreed with Macaulay.   " The realism and Life-likeness of Miss Austen's Dramatis Personae come nearest," he said, " to Shakespeare," adding, however, that Shakespeare is " a sun to which Jane Austen, tho' a bright and true little world, is but an asteroid."   Decidedly there is room for wide differences of taste in the world of novels. Does Miss Yonge's *Heir of Redclyffe* still find readers ?   It was eagerly read by Lord Raglan and other officers during the Crimean War, and it exercised a dominating fascination, we are told, over William Morris and his set at Oxford. Canon Dixon, the poet, in mentioning this book as the first which seemed to him greatly to influence Morris, pronounced it, after nearly half a century's reflection and experience, to be " unquestionably one of the finest books in the world."   It is one of the advantages of a study of such superlatives that it may confirm us all

in the courage of our real likes or dislikes. We
can none of us be more heterodox than was Dr.
Johnson sometimes, as in his animadversions on
Milton and Gray ; or more perverse than Matthew
Arnold, as in his freakish saying that Shelley
would be remembered more for his prose than as
a poet ; or more limited than Macaulay, who
could see little to praise in Dickens and Wordsworth.

Who is the greatest historian ? The question
is more manageable, for the field of reasonable
choice is restricted. The Father of History
may perhaps be left out, unless indeed we accept
Browning's standard :

> Give these, I exhort you, their guerdon and glory
>   For daring so much, before they well did it.
> The first of the new, in our race's story,
>   Beats the last of the old ; 'tis no idle quiddit.

But let us put Herodotus aside with a different
superlative. By common consent he is " one of
the most delightful story - tellers " (Jebb); his
history is " the most delightful of all story-
books " (Harrison [1]). The choice of the world's
greatest historian then lies between the greatest
of the Greek historians, the greatest of the Roman,
and the greatest of the English. Each of these

[1] But there is another claimant for this latter superlative. "When
asked the question which all literary people have been asking each other
since the days of Pisistratus, Fox replied, 'I would not say I would rather
have written the *Odyssey*, but I know that I would rather read it. I believe
it to be the first tale in the world.' "

writers predicted enduring fame for his work,
and each claim has been endorsed by posterity.
Thucydides composed his history " not as the
exploit of an hour but as a possession for all
time."   The confidence of Tacitus that the glory
of Agricola would endure in after ages has been
justified by the genius of the historian.   And
Gibbon, when he wrote the last lines of his last
page, rejoiced not only at the recovery of his
freedom, but also at the establishment of his
fame.   Which of these three is the greatest ?
The answer must partly depend on the view which
is taken of the subjects with which they severally
deal.   If a man holds with Richard Cobden
that " one copy of the *Times* contains more useful
information than the whole of the historical
books of Thucydides," or with Robert Lowe[1]
that a good colliery accident throws the battle
of Marathon into the shade, then Tacitus and
Gibbon start with a great advantage, though even
so it might be the more admired in Thucydides
that he should have made so much, in force of
dramatic presentment and in profundity of observation, out of events so small in scale.   With
those, on the other hand, who rate the glory
that was Greece as high as the grandeur that was
Rome, and still more with those who find in the

---

[1] Who, however, was probably poking fun at the Civil Engineers at whose
Institute it was that, on a convivial occasion, he delivered the notorious
speech from which I am quoting.

main theme of Thucydides one of the world's great tragedies,[1] the three historians may be held to start on equal terms so far as the dignity of their themes is concerned.   Three modern writers of repute (and two of them writers of famous histories) have answered the question now before us, and each gives a different answer with equal positiveness.   " It is no personal paradox," says Mr. Frederic Harrison, " but the judgment of all competent men that the *Decline and Fall* of Gibbon is the most perfect historical composition that exists in any language."   But Mr. Harrison forgot, when he wrote this sentence as the spokesman of all competent men, that a few pages before in the same essay on *Some Great Books of History*, he had himself pronounced the work of Thucydides to be " perhaps the greatest of all histories." Macaulay was of the same opinion, minus the " perhaps "—a word not found in his dictionary. " This day," he wrote in 1835, " I finished Thucydides after reading him with inexpressible interest and admiration.   He is the greatest

---

[1] " It seems to me now," wrote Ruskin in his Autobiography, " as if I had known Thucydides as I knew Homer (Pope's) since I could spell.   But the fact was that for a youth who had so little Greek to bless himself with at seventeen to know every syllable of his Thucydides at half-past eighteen meant some steady sitting at it.   The perfect honesty of the Greek soldier, his high breeding, his political insight, and the scorn of construction with which he knotted his meaning into a rhythmic strength that writhed and wrought every way at once, all interested me intensely in him as a writer ; while his subject, the central tragedy of all the world, the suicide of Greece, was felt by me with a sympathy in which the best powers of my heart and brain were brought up to their fullest, for my years."

historian that ever lived." "I am still of the same mind," he wrote a year later. "I do assure you," he said in a letter, "that there is no prose composition in the world, not even the *De Corona*, which I place so high as the seventh book of Thucydides. It is the *ne plus ultra* of human art." And he went on to say how delighted he was to find in Gray's letters this query to Wharton : "The retreat from Syracuse—is it or is it not the finest thing you ever read in your life?" Jowett also was of Macaulay's opinion. Mr. Froude, on the other hand, seems to have given the palm to the Roman historian. "The greatest man," he says, "who has as yet given himself to the recording of human affairs is, beyond question, Cornelius Tacitus. Alone in Tacitus a serene calmness of insight was compatible with intensity of feeling." And Mr. Harrison's Master, Auguste Comte, called Tacitus "incomparable," and placed him in the Positivist Calendar next to Socrates on account of his profound insight into human nature. There is thus good authority, it will be seen, for any choice one may make between the three greatest historians. One thing, it is worth noting, is common to all of them. Each was a scientific historian according to the lights of his day, but each was also aware that history belongs to literature as well as to science. The style of Thucydides, as every schoolboy knows to his

pain, is involved and difficult ; but, as Professor
Jebb has said, no writer has " grander bursts
of rugged eloquence " and few have equalled
his sense of tragic circumstance.   The Roman
historian was a more conscious artist, and Tacitean
brevity has become proverbial.   Tacitus is incomparable, because for one thing he is untranslatable.   The style of Gibbon, though
mannered to the verge of pomposity, is remarkable for sustained weight and vigour.   Each
was in his different way a literary artist.   Which
of the three does the reader prefer ?   The
answer will finally depend in some measure, I
imagine, on individual taste and on the moral
judgment which governs our sympathies.   Lord
Acton is sometimes supposed to be a dispassion-
ate historian, but he is always passing moral
judgments.   " Excepting Froude," he wrote,
" I think Carlyle the most detestable of historians.
The doctrine of heroes, the doctrine that will is
above law, comes next in atrocity to the doctrine
that the flag covers the goods, that the cause
justifies its agents, which is what Froude lives
for."   From this point of view, a good case may
be made for Macaulay's favourite among our
Three.   Tacitus, says one of the best of his
translators, took an unhopeful and cynical view
of human nature.   The work of Gibbon, says
one of his biographers, is more fitted to inspire
admiration than love or sympathy.   " His cheek

rarely flushes in enthusiasm for a good cause.
The tragedy of human life never seems to touch
him, no glimpse of the infinite ever calms and
raises the reader of his pages.   Like nearly all
the men of his day, he was of the earth earthy."
In Thucydides, Professor Jebb finds " that greatness which is given by sustained intensity of noble
thought and feeling."

One more question : it has often worried
unoffending people—especially those in " situations," as the Duke of Wellington put it, " much
exposed to authors."   If in a moment of presumption I should send this little book about books
to a friend, it may worry him, and so I will give
an answer.   What is the best and neatest way of
acknowledging an unwelcome presentation-copy ?
The one indispensable thing is of course to ac-
knowledge it promptly before you can possibly
be expected to have read the book.   Disraeli's
formula, " I shall lose no time in reading your
valuable book," has often been quoted and, with
variations, adopted.   It is clever ; but, unless
the vanity of an author has given him the skin
of a rhinoceros, the ambiguity of the phrase is
likely to prick.   For perfection of politeness one
must turn to France, and an exquisite example is
given in Trevelyan's *Life of Macaulay*.   Zachary
Macaulay was in the habit of sending (sometimes
with the postage only in part prepaid) copies of
Blue-books and periodicals about the slave-trade

P

to his Parisian friends, one of whom, M. Dumont, wrote :

MON CHER AMI—Je ne laisserai pas partir Mr. Inglis sans le charger de quelques lignes pour vous, afin de vous remercier du *Christian Observer* que vous avez eu la bonté de m'envoyer. Vous savez que j'ai *a great taste for it*; mais il faut avouer une triste vérité, c'est que je manque absolument de loisir pour le lire. Ne m'en envoyez plus, car je me sens peiné d'avoir sous les yeux de si bonnes choses dont je n'ai pas le temps de me nourrir.

VIII

THE POETRY OF A PAINTER

When I was editing Ruskin's Works I was allowed to inspect the eleven tin boxes in which a large part of the Turner Bequest to the nation had for fifty years been buried in the cellars of the National Gallery, and at the time I gave some account of their contents.[1] Mr. Thornbury, whose *Life of Turner* has some claims to be considered the worst-contrived biography in the language, had seen these treasures, but he made inadequate use of them.   The note-books, sketchbooks, and bundles of drawings ought to have been used as the foundation of the *Life*, and the labours of Mr. Finberg (which, it may be hoped, will be continued) have already shown, what important results may thus be obtained.[2]   Mr.

---

[1] In the Introduction to the Turner volume (xiii.) in the Library Edition of Ruskin's Works, published in 1904 ; and in an illustrated volume, *Hidden Treasures at the National Gallery*, published by the *Pall Mall Gazette* in 1905.

[2] See his admirable *Inventory of the Drawings of the Turner Bequest*, 2 vols., 1909 ; his *Turner's Sketches and Drawings*, 1910 ; and an account of *Turner's "Isle of Wight" Sketch-Book* in the First Annual Volume of the Walpole Society, 1912.   See also the Third and Sixth Volumes.

Thornbury was content to treat this biographical
material in a casual manner, and the impression
he gave of the note - books was that they are
a hopeless muddle - jumble.   Such impression
accords with the idea which Mr. Hamerton also
conveyed that Turner was an ill-educated illiterate.
Sir Walter Armstrong has done something to
correct this idea, and the note-books themselves
disprove it, though, as will be shown in the
present paper, they throw a most curious light
on the artist's limitations.   What Ruskin's father
said on examining Turner's house on the day
after his death must occur to every one who goes
through the boxes in which so much of the
artist's work in life was buried : " The industry
of the man was as great as his genius," and the
industry had method in it.   Before setting out
on a sketching tour he carefully read up his route,
often getting some travelled friend to prepare an
itinerary for him, not only marking what towns
had good inns, but making notes of picturesque
places or effects of which he had heard or read.
Then the artist equipped himself with sketch-
books of all sorts and sizes.   Some are small
enough to go into a waistcoat pocket, and are
filled with rough scrawls and hieroglyphics, such
as were made perhaps in the coach.   Sometimes
the thumb-nails are of exquisite delicacy and
firmness; as, for instance, in two or three little
books containing bits of architecture and sculpture

done in Rome. Then come the larger sketch-
books, used when the artist was settled at his
inn ; these contain sometimes pencil - sketches
of great delicacy, carried far to completion, and
sometimes bolder and rougher outlines, to serve
as memoranda of the leading lines in a composition. The books had for the most part been
labelled by the painter, as thus : " 79. Skies,"
" 84. Studies for Pictures, Copies of Wilson,"
" 18. Studies in the Louvre "—the book last
mentioned contains some careful copies on a small
scale of pictures in that collection, and is of further
interest as including critiques on some of them.
Turner's memory was prodigious, but he had
aids to it. Whatever was the work he was engaged upon at the time, he was able to refer to
his numbered note-books, where every kind of
material from nature was stored. The quantity
of such material which his industry had accumu-
lated is enormous.

Industry in another sort also is revealed by
the note-books. From the literary point of view,
Turner was a diligent reader and self-educator.
There are lessons in French. There are notes
of historical and literary associations with places
where he was sketching. There are extracts
from books which he had been reading—among
others from the *Treatise on the Art of Painting*
by Gerard de Lairesse, with whom Browning
" parleyed." There are critical remarks on

painters and theories of art. As Professor of
Perspective at the Academy, Turner was a failure
so far as his public lectures were concerned. His
delivery was bad, his grammar was doubtful, and
he had not the skill to make a difficult subject
attractive ; but it has been shown that he wrote
and rewrote his lectures with great pains, and
that he made himself widely acquainted with
the literature of the subject.[1] In the sketch-
books at the National Gallery, the notes and
jottings of all sorts are sometimes carefully
written, correct, and consecutive. At other
times, carelessly spelt and written, they are
unintelligible to any one except to their writer.
Above all, the note-books are full of verses,
sometimes copied from books or broadsheets,
more often of Turner's own composition. He
would make as many beginnings or studies or
versions of a poem as of a picture or drawing.
" His sketch-books," says Mr. Finberg, " contain
on the whole even more poetry than drawings."
The poetry, such as it is, of so great a painter
as Turner deserves some study and suggests
questions of far-reaching interest.

Turner knew good poetry when he read it.
" He was well read in the poets," said Lupton,

[1] See an article by Mr. D. S. MacColl on " Turner's Lectures at the
Academy " in the *Burlington Magazine*, vol. xii. p. 343, and two articles by
Mr. W. T. Whitley on " Turner as a Lecturer " in the same magazine,
vol. xxii. pp. 202, 255.

the engraver. "He was fond of talking of
poetry," said a friend; and another reported that
he was "a great theatre-goer at one time and was
indistinctly voluble on Shakespeare." His taste
was shown when in 1798 the Royal Academy
allowed mottoes to be inserted in its catalogues.
Turner's first quotation was to his picture of
"Morning on the Coniston Fells," exhibited in
that year (now No. 461, National Gallery), and
was taken from the fifth book of *Paradise Lost*:

> Ye Mists and Exhalations, that now rise
> From hill or steaming lake, dusky or grey,
> Till the sun paint your fleecy skirts with gold,
> In honour to the World's great Author rise.

"There was a strange ominousness," says Ruskin,
"as there is about much that great men do, in
the choice of these lines. They express his
peculiar mission as distinguished from other
landscapists; they show how his mind was set
from the first on rendering atmospheric effects."
In the same and in immediately following years
the object of his quotations was again to empha-
sise the atmospheric effects which he sought
to interpret. The best mottoes were still from
Milton, as this for "Twilight at Harlech Castle":

> Now came still evening on and Twilight grey
> Had in her sober livery all things clad.
>   . . . Hesperus, that led
> The starry host, rode brightest, till the Moon
> Rising in clouded majesty unveil'd her peerless light.

Here Turner took liberty with his text, tele-
scoping into one line of irregular length these
two :

> Rising in clouded majesty, at length
> Apparent queen, unveiled her peerless light.

A passage from the sixth book was used to
illustrate " The Battle of the Nile " :

> Immediate in a flame,
> But soon obscured with smoke, all Heaven appeared,
> From those deep-throated engines belched, whose roar
> Embowelled with outrageous noise the air,
> And all her entrails tore, disgorging foul
> Their devilish glut, chained thunderbolts and hail
> Of iron globes.

But the source from which at this period
Turner drew most of his quotations was Thomson's *Seasons*. In the Academy Exhibition of
1798, four of his pictures had quotations from
that poem. Thomson is now, I suppose, little
read,[1] but Mr. Seccombe reminds us that for a
hundred years, lasting until the vogue of Tennyson, Thomson was the favourite poet of the
British public. Turner was under the spell,
and made many attempts to express his admiration in verses of his own. Thomson's cottage
was in Kew Foot Lane, and from it he often
walked over to visit " Mr. Pope," we are told,
at Twickenham. Pope's famous villa, with its

---

[1] Oscar Wilde once divided books into three classes : (1) Books to read,
(2) Books to re-read, and (3) Books not to read at all. Thomson's *Seasons*
headed the list under his third class.

grotto and its weeping willow, was demolished
in 1807, and Turner, who himself had a house
at this time at Twickenham, was very angry.
Indignation wanted to make verses, but they
would not come into any coherent or sustained
shape.   Here from various note-books are some
of Turner's attempts to link the fame of Thomson
and of Pope in an " Invocation of Thames to the
Seasons upon the Demolition of Pope's House " :

> To Twickenham bowers that . . .
> In humble guise should . . . assume
> My self-reared willow, or the grotto's gloom,
> 'Twould be my pride to hold from further scorn
> A remnant of his . . . which once the bank adorn . . .
> If then my ardent love of thee is said with truth,
> . . . the demolition of thy house, forsooth,
> Broke through the trammels, and you, my rhyme,
> Roll into being since that fatal time.

The Baroness Howe, whose agents destroyed the
house and stubbed up the trees, was more successful in demolition than Turner in building a rhyme
of poetical revenge.   But he tried again and again :

> O Seasons Fair, bedeck the shrine
> Of him who made the Seasons shine.
>
> .   .   .   .   .
>
> O Seasons Fair, guard Thomson's Shrine.
> He sung the charms of Season's prime.
> With watery-may his bays entwine,
> While Phebus o'er our Vallies shine.
> High then the Coral shell yet fill
> With distant Thames' translucent rill,
> With Memory sweet and thrush's thrill,
> Yet his lyre with Summer breezes fill.

Akenside, Ossian, Scott, and Byron were all successively laid under contribution by Turner to illustrate his pictures—Byron many times: the great picture, exhibited in 1832 (now No. 516 in the National Gallery), is proof of his sympathy with the genius of the author of Childe Harold's Pilgrimage. "The loveliest result of Turner's art, in the central period of it, was," says Ruskin, "an effort to express on a single canvas the meaning of that poem. . . . While he only illustrated here and there a detached passage from other poets, he endeavoured, as far as in him lay, to delineate the whole mind of Byron."

It is interesting to remember that while he was thus delineating the mind of Byron, there was a poet who, as it were, had been illustrating Turner's painting, though the poet had never seen the pictures nor did the painter know the poems. The Turner of poetry is Shelley. In both there is a strain of pensive melancholy joined to a sense of the material beauty of the universe which finds expression in a love of iridescence, colour-depth, and soft mystery. The vast landscapes of Turner's later manner, melting into indefinite distance, recall many a passage in Shelley's *Prometheus* where the spirits of the mind

> Voyage, cloudlike and unpent,
> Through the boundless element.

Turner painted "Queen Mab's Grotto" and referred in the Academy Catalogue to *A Midsummer Night's Dream*, though the line he quoted is not to be found there. . But in the realisation of his dream Turner's grotto is that of Shelley's Queen Mab rather than of Shakespeare's. The details are different, but the general effect of the picture resembles Shelley's description of Mab's palace :

> If solitude hath ever led thy steps
>   To the wild ocean's echoing shore,
>   And thou hast lingered there,
>
>   .   .   .   .   .
>
> When those far clouds of feathery gold,
>   Shaded with deepest purple, gleam
>   Like islands on a dark blue sea ;
> Then has thy fancy soared above the earth,
>   And furled its wearied wing
>   Within the Fairy's fane.
>
>   Yet not the golden islands
>   Gleaming in yon flood of light,
>   Nor the feathery curtains
>   Stretching o'er the sun's bright couch,
>   Nor the burnished ocean waves
>   Paving that gorgeous dome,
>   So fair, so wonderful a sight
> As Mab's ethereal palace could afford.

In Turner's " Cephalus and Procris " Ruskin notes the sympathy of the faint rays that are just drawing back and dying between the trunks of the far-off forest with the ebbing life of the nymph. There is just the same touch in Shelley's description of the death of the poet in *Alastor* :

Now upon the jaggèd hills
It rests, and still as the divided frame
Of the vast meteor sunk, the Poet's blood,
That ever beat in mystic sympathy
With nature's ebb and flow, grew feebler still ;
And when two lessening points of light alone
Gleamed through the darkness, the alternate gasp
Of his faint respiration scarce did stir
The stagnate night. . . .

In the picture of Venice called " Shylock " Turner
has arranged the clouds of the upper sky in masses
of mingling light, every part and atom sympathis-
ing in that continuous expression of slow movement which Shelley has so beautifully touched :

Underneath the young grey dawn,
And multitudes of dense, white, fleecy clouds
Were wandering in thick flocks along the mountains,
Shepherded by the slow unwilling wind.[1]

How essentially Turnerian is this passage from
the second act of *Prometheus* :

The point of one white star is quivering still,
Deep in the orange light of widening dawn,
Beyond the purple mountains.   Through a chasm
Of wind-divided mist the darker lake
Reflects it : now it fades : it gleams again
As the waves fall, and as the burning threads
Of woven cloud unravel in pale air :
'Tis lost ! and through yon peaks of cloudlike snow
The roseate sunlight quivers.

Ruskin in a famous passage has described the
mingling of tones in Turner's " Téméraire " ;

[1] *Prometheus*, ii. 147.

it might be taken, if one did not know the reference, for a prose version of some scene in Shelley which is luminous and radiant while yet it is

> Dim and dank and grey,
> Like a storm-extinguished day,
> Travelled o'er by dying gleams.

Or, again, take this passage from *Julian and Maddalo* :

> Half the sky
> Was roofed with clouds of rich emblazonry,
> Dark purple at the zenith, which still grew
> Down the steep west into a wondrous hue
> Brighter than burning gold.

The colouring is that of many a sky of Turner's. The quest of the poet in *Alastor* pursuing an ideal beauty might be taken for a summary of the painter's artistic life :

> Nature's most secret steps
> He like her shadow has pursued, where'er
> The red volcano overcanopies
> Its fields of snow and pinnacles of ice
> With burning smoke, or where . . .
> . . . the starry domes
> Of diamond and of gold expand above
> Numberless and immeasurable halls,
> Frequent with crystal column, and clear shrines
> Of pearl, and thrones radiant with chrysolite—

with this for the end, so true of the painter's latest experiments :

> He eagerly pursues
> Beyond the realms of dream that fleeting shade ;
> He overleaps the bounds.

The parallelism in all this is strangely close.
And yet not so strange if there be truth in the
fancies of those who believe that a compelling
spirit of the time works to like ends in different
minds. Dates are here significant. *Alastor* was
published in 1816, *Prometheus* in 1820, and
Julian and Maddalo (written in 1818) in 1824.
The time coincides with that of the transition to
Turner's second and more aerial period. And,
curiously, the editors of the poet and the painter
severally give a closely corresponding account
of the circumstances which inspired their work
at the time. Mrs. Shelley, in explaining the
new notes heard in *Alastor*, says this : " As soon
as the peace of 1814 had opened the Continent,
Shelley went abroad. He visited some of the
more magnificent scenes of Switzerland, and
returned to England from Lucerne by the Reuss
and the Rhine. The river-navigation enchanted
him." And Ruskin, in explaining Turner's
transition from grey to colour, puts it down to
the foreign tour of 1819 or 1820 : " When he
first travelled on the Continent he was comparatively a young student ; not yet able to draw
form as he wanted, he was forced to give all his
thoughts and strength to this primary object.
But now he was free to receive other impressions ;
the time was come for perfecting his art, and the
first sunset which he saw on the Rhine taught
him that all previous landscape art was vain

an'd valueless . . . and a new dawn rose over the rocks of the Siebengebirge."

In addition to quotations from British poets, Turner drew for his mottoes or references upon Virgil, Ovid, Callimachus, and Homer. In this field he often indulged in a characteristic love of mystification. He liked to put people off the true scent. Alternately he pretended to less and to more borrowing from classical sources than was in fact the case. He was at a dinner-party where his glorious picture of " Ulysses deriding Polyphemus " was the theme of some idle talk. " Come, now," said Turner, " I bet you don't know where I took the subject from." " From the *Odyssey*, of course," replied his fellow-guest. " *Odyssey*," grunted Turner, bursting into a chuckle; " not a bit of it ! I took it from Tom Dibdin. Don't you know the lines :

> He ate his mutton, drank his wine,
>   And then he poked his eye out ? "

On the other hand, in exhibiting the " Apollo and the Python " at the Academy in 1811 he printed these lines, ascribing them to " Hymn of Callimachus " :

> Envenom'd by thy darts, the monster coil'd,
> Portentous, horrible, and vast, his snake-like form :
> Rent the huge portal of the rocky den,
> And in the throes of death, he tore
> His many wounds in one, while earth
> Absorbing blacken'd with his gore.

There is a passage about the contest with the
Python in the *Hymn to Apollo*, but the lines
which Turner fathered upon Callimachus do
not come from him. They were put together,
as Mr. Monkhouse showed, from descriptions
of two of Ovid's dragons—the Python in the
first book of the *Metamorphoses* and the Dragon
destroyed by Cadmus in the third book. " The
jumble is just the mixture of Ovid, Milton,
Thomson, Pope, out of which Turner formed
his poetical style." With Ovid's *Metamorphoses*
he was thoroughly familiar, and doubtless he
had a Classical Dictionary at his elbow. It has
often been suggested that he had no mythological
meanings in his classical compositions, for that
his only source of inspiration was probably
Lemprière. Even if such were the case, the
criticism shows a lack of acquaintance with that
entertaining Dictionary, for Lemprière nearly
always adds to his bald and frank recital of the
myths an interpretation—according to his lights
—of their natural and moral meaning.

Turner had, then, a considerable knowledge
of the poets, and a deep interest at second hand
in classical literature ; but the more he read and
the more his art of painting developed, the greater
became his desire to find poetical expression in
poetry of his own making. When the " Views
in the Southern Coast of England " were in
preparation, he desired to write the letterpress

as well as make the drawings. His first essay
was described by Combe, the editor, in a letter
to Cooke, the engraver and publisher, as " the
most extraordinary composition he had ever read.
It is impossible for me to correct it, for in some
parts I do not understand it." Whether it was
in prose or verse does not appear, and Turner's
prose was often even more unintelligible than
his verse. The essay, whatever it was, did not
appear ; but he continued to write verses as he
travelled round the coast making drawings, and
many passages in the longest and most sustained
of his metrical attempts are clearly taken from
his drawings, unless indeed the two processes
went on together. For instance, in the beautiful
drawing of Poole we may see both the deep
worn road and the groaning waggon of the
following lines :

> A sandy heath, whose deep worn road
> Sustains the groaning waggon's ponderous load ;
> This branches southwards at the point of Thule,
> Forms the harbour of the town of Poole.

Another passage in the same piece describes
the drawing of Corfe Castle :

> Southward of this indentured strand
> The ruins of Corfe's ruined turrets stand,
> Between two lofty downs, whose shelving side
> The deep foundations for her towers supplied.

The drawing of Lulworth Cove is easily recognised
in the following lines :

Q

> For Nature jealous has allowed no breaks
> Of streams or valleys sloping save but one,
> And there she still presents a breast of stone :
> Above are downs where press [? browse] the nibbling
>   sheep ;
> Below, the seamews full possession keep.

Allusions to many other places which Turner
then visited will be recognised, says Mr. Rawlinson, in the long poem which was found written in
his sketch-books of the tour. " Strange and disjointed as this is, in common with the numerous
other poetical effusions which Turner continued
to produce to the end of his life, it is not devoid
of merit, and there are passages in which may
be seen, despite the awkward diction, the same
vein of romantic imagination which found a
happier expression through the medium of his
brush." Mr. Rawlinson does not point us to
the passages, and it is not easy to find them.
Here, however, are some lines which succeed
at least in testifying to Turner's sympathy with
the heroic in Roman story. He is describing
a Roman camp and a fort on the coast :

> Oh ! powerful beings, hail ! whose stubborn soul
> Even o'er itself to urge . . . self-control.
> Thus Regulus, whom every torture did await,
> Denied himself admittance at the gate
> Because a captive to proud Carthage power,
> But his fierce soul would not the Romans lower.
> Not wife or children dear, or self, could hold
> A moment's parley,—love made him bold,

Love of his country ; for not aught beside
He loved,—but for that love he died.
The same inflexibility of will
Made them to choose the inhospitable hill ;
Without recourse they stood supremely great,
And firmly bid defiance even to fate.
Thus stands aloft this yet encinctured fort,
" The Maiden " called, still of commanding port.
So the famed Jungfrau meets the nether skies
In endless snow untrod, and man denies,
With all his wiles : precipitous or bold,
The same great characters its summits hold :
Thus graves o'er all the guarded area tell
Who fought for its possession, and who fell.

An eye to character is shown occasionally in
the poem, as in this picture drawn at Poole :

One straggling street here constitutes a town ;
Across the gutter here ship-owners frown,
Jingling their money—passengers deride,—
The consequence of misconceived pride ;

or in this sketch of a village school :

Close to the mill-race stands the school,
To urchin dreadful on the dunce's stool :
Behold him placed behind the chair,
In doleful guise twisting his yellow hair,
While the grey matron tells him not to look
At passers-by through doorway, but his book.

Another picture of child life occurs in some
lines written in 1809 during a wet day at a river-
side inn :

Alas, another day is gone,
As useless as it was begun ;

The crimson'd streak of early morn
Check'd the sweet lark that o'er the corn
Fluttered her wings at twilight grey. . . .
Not so the cottar's children at the door,
Rich in content, tho' Nature made them poor,
Standing in threshold emulous to catch
The pendant drop from off the dripping thatch—
The daring boy——Thus Britain's early race—
To feel the heaviest drop upon his face,
Or heedless of the storm o'er his abode
Launches his paper boat across the road
Where the deep gullies which his father's cart
Made in their progress to the mart,
Full to the brim, deluged by the rain,
They prove to him a channel to the main
Guiding his vessel down the stream,
The pangs of hunger vanish like a dream.

" Thus Britain's early race " : the passage recalls
Turner's famous picture (No. 498, National
Gallery) of " Dido building Carthage," in which
the principal incident in the foreground is a group
of children sailing toy boats, expressive of the
ruling passion which was to be the source of
future greatness. In the halting verses, as in
the accomplished drawings and pictures, Turner's
landscape is always humanised. He was of the
school to which Byron and Ruskin belonged,
and held that what gives to natural scenes their
highest power of appeal is association with the
life, the labour, and the art of man. Any analysis
of a series of works by Turner—such as Ruskin's
of the " Liber Studiorum " or Mr. Hamerton's

of the " Rivers of France "—brings out this
point, and we may trace it throughout the poem.
" The meshy nets " by Thames' side " bespeak
the owner poor." The changes of the moon
are emblematic of human fates :

> Oft changes on the moon the gleam of joy
> So fair, so gay, assumes a gloom and woe,
> And prince and peasant feel alike the blow.

The sight of a coastguard station sets him to
imagine a story of courtship and seduction.
The sight of a quarry causes him to picture the
summer and the winter labours of the workmen.
His constant sympathy with those who go down
to the sea in ships and occupy their business in
great waters appears as frequently in these verses
as in his pictures, though in the former with many
a lapse into bathos. Here and there in the poem
there are single lines, and more rarely two consecutive lines, which are really successful in
expression.

> Hill after hill incessant cheats the eye

is a good imitation of Pope.

> The scudding clouds distil a constant dew.

> Where massy fragments seem disjoined to play
> With sportive sea-nymphs in the face of day.

> Beneath the western waves the marshes lie.

> Even to the sandy frailty of the main.

> But thought created by the ardent mind
> Proves oft as changing as the changing wind.

These are good lines, but Turner was never able
to keep at one level for more than a line or two.
He lacked not only the literary instinct, but that
power of logical coherence—*ordo concatenatioque
rerum*—which is required for sustained composition.   Had he some consciousness of this?
Here are some lines from another note-book :

> Vacancy most fair but yesterday
> O'er these pure leaves maintained her sway
> Until the pen did immolate.
> But with a stain inviolate
> The spotless innocence retreats
> From every leaf as fancy beats
> Pure like the stream that pours
> From April's cloud the driving shower.
> Hope still accompanies and sighs—
> Hope that with ever-sparkling eyes
> Looks on the yellow melting skies,
> Yet still with anxious pleasing care
> Makes ⎱ every leaf appear more fair.
> Thinks ⎰
> Delusion sweet thus tempts us on
> Till all the leaves are like to one ;
> Yet Hope looks back as heretofore
> And smiling seems to say encore.

This was a fair copy, for it is in ink, and the
author has appended the note, " Written at
Purley [near Pangbourne] on the Thame.   Rainy
morning—no fishing."   There seems to be a
humorous sense in these lines that his poetical
pastime was but idle ink-spilling after all.

Hope, however, continued to say encore.   In

the Academy Catalogue of 1812, Turner first
inserted lines from a " MS. poem, Fallacies of
Hope," and from time to time, down to 1850,
mottoes for his pictures were attributed to the
same source. Sometimes, when his literary invention gave out, he appended to the title a bare
reference to the same imaginary work—thus in
part, no doubt, piquing curiosity, but also, I
cannot doubt, desiring to indicate that the pictures in question had a place in some general
scheme. The mottoes from the " Fallacies of
Hope " were applied to pictures of many different
subjects, but especially to those of Carthage,
Rome, and Venice. Of Carthage he thought
perhaps as typical of the vain pursuit of wealth ;
of Rome, of the vain pursuit of power ; and of
Venice, of the vain pursuit of beauty. The
earliest of his pictures from the story of Carthage
was the " Hannibal crossing the Alps," exhibited
in 1812 (No. 490 in the National Gallery). The
idea was suggested to him partly by a picture of
the same subject by Cozens, partly by a storm
at Farnley. " He was absorbed," said Mr.
Fawkes, " he was entranced. He was making
notes of form and colour on the back of a letter.
I proposed some better drawing-block, but he
said it did very well. Presently the storm
passed, and he finished. ' There,' said he,
' Hawkey, in two years you will see this again.
and call it " Hannibal crossing the Alps." ' "   As

the picture took shape, Turner wrote these lines, having reference to the pillage of Saguntum in 219 B.C. and Hannibal's expedition into Italy in the following year :

> Craft, treachery, and fraud,—Salassian force
> Hung on the fainting rear ; then plunder seized
> The victor and the captive,—Saguntum's spoil
> Alike became their prey ; still the chief advanced,
> Looked on the sun with hope, low, broad, and wan,
> While the fierce archer of the downward year
> Stains Italy's blanched barrier with storms.
> In vain each pass, ensanguined deep with dead,
> Or rocky fragments, wide destruction rolled.
> Still on Campania's fertile plains he thought,
> But the loud breeze sobbed, Capua's joys beware.

In these lines, as one of his biographers remarks, Turner came nearest to good poetry. The conception is fine, and Sagittarius is well introduced. The lines which he wrote for his picture of " The Decline of the Carthaginian Empire " (No. 499) are also not devoid of merit :

> At Hope's delusive smile
> The chieftain's safety and the mother's pride
> Were to the insidious conqueror's grasp resigned ;
> While o'er the western waves th' ensanguined sun,
> In gathering haze, a stormy signal spread,
> And set portentous.

The lines written for " Caligula's Palace and Bridge " (No. 512) point the moral which he had in his mind :

> What now remains of all the mighty bridge
> Which made the Lucrine Lake an inner pool,
> Caligula, but massive fragments, left
> As monuments of doubt and ruined hopes,
> Yet gleaming in the morning's ray, that tell
> How Baiae's shore was loved in times gone by.

The references to the " Fallacies of Hope " in the case of the Venetian pictures were generally references only, perhaps because Turner felt that he saw Venice with Byron's eye and was afraid of putting the MS. poem in comparison with *Childe Harold*:

> In Venice, Tasso's echoes are no more,
> And silent rows the songless gondolier ;
> Her palaces are crumbling to the shore,
> And music meets not always now the ear ;
> Those days are gone—but Beauty still is here.
> States fall, arts fade—but Nature doth not die,
> Nor yet forget how Venice once was dear,
> The pleasant place of all festivity,
> The revel of the earth, the masque of Italy.

The lines well fit the later Venetian pictures by Turner—ghost-like dreams, "themselves so beautiful and so frail, wrecks of all that they once were —twilight of twilight."   If other written passages are wanted to fit his Venices of the " Going to the Ball " and " Returning from the Ball," they may be found in Browning's verse or Ruskin's prose :

> What, they lived once thus at Venice where the merchants
>   were the kings,
> Where St. Mark's is, where the Doges used to wed the sea
>   with rings ? . . .

Balls and masks begun at midnight, burning ever to midday,
When they made up fresh adventures for the morrow, do
  you say ? . . .

Dream-like and dim, but glorious, the unnumbered palaces lift their shafts out of the hollow sea—pale ranks of motionless flames—their mighty towers sent up to heaven like tongues of more eager fire—their grey domes looming vast and dark, like eclipsed worlds—their sculptured arabesques and purple marble fading farther and fainter, league beyond league, lost in the light of distance.

Sometimes Turner aimed only at a line or two of verse which should fit the obvious note or subject of the picture. Such is the case of some alternative lines which occur in one of his sketchbooks :

> Where is the star which shone at eve . . .
> The gleaming star of eve. . . .
> The first pale star of Eve ere Twilight comes.

The last line is the best, and Mr. Finberg is probably right in connecting it with the lovely picture called " The Evening Star " which is among the buried Turners first exhibited in 1906 (No. 1991). More often the object of the painter's " long - sought lines " [1] seems to have been to suggest to the spectator an under meaning. The critics treated the attempts as definitions of

---

[1] See the motto for "The Garreteer's Petition," exhibited in 1809 :

> Aid me, ye powers ! Oh, bid my thoughts to roll
> In quick succession, animate my soul ;
> Descend, my muse, and every thought refine,
> And finish well my long, my long-sought line.

the obscure by the more obscure. The picture
of " The Exile and the Rock Limpet " was
exhibited with these lines from the " Fallacies
of Hope " :

> Ah ! thy tent-formed shell is like
> A soldier's bivouac, alone
> Amidst a sea of blood. . . .
> But you can join your comrades.

The picture (No. 529) represents Napoleon on
the shore of St. Helena at sunset, watching a
solitary shell. The picture was ridiculed by
Thackeray and parodied thus in *Punch* :

225. The Duke of Wellington and the Shrimp
(Seringapatam, early morning)—

> And can it be, thou hideous imp,
> That life is, ah ! how brief, and glory but a shrimp.

The chaff was tolerable, but in this instance the
clue given by Turner's lines was both needed
and intelligible. Ruskin records how Turner
" tried hard one day for a quarter of an hour to
make me guess what he was doing in the picture
of Napoleon, before it had been exhibited, giving
me hint after hint in a rough way ; but I could not
guess, and he would not tell me." The disciple
had to wait like the rest of the world for revelation
through the MS. poem, and this made the rough
smooth enough. Napoleon was figured as seeing
a resemblance in a limpet's shell to a tent, and the
second thought was that even this poor wave-

washed disc had power and liberty now denied to *him*. There was more excuse for the King of Bavaria who failed to understand Turner's picture of the "·Opening of the Walhalla." The picture—painted in honour of the Temple of Art, containing marble busts of eminent Germans, which had been opened on the Danube near Regensburg—was thus described in the Academy Catalogue :

> L'honneur au Roi de Bavare
> Who rode on thy relentless car, fallacious Hope ?
> He, though scathed at Ratisbon, poured on
> The tide of war o'er all thy plain, Bavare,
> Like the swollen Danube to the gates of Wien.
> But peace returns—the morning ray
> Beams on the Valhalla, reared to science and the arts
> And men renowned of German fatherland.

Turner, it is said, sent the picture as a present to King Ludwig, but the King, unable to make anything of it, returned the gift. Another Fallacy of Hope ! The wags of the press continued to ridicule alike the pictures and the verses. Here is what *Punch* said of one of the dream-like visions of Venice described above :

We had almost forgotten Mr. J. M. W. Turner, R.A., and his celebrated MS. poem, the " Fallacies of Hope," to which he constantly refers us " as in former years "; but on this occasion he has obliged us by simply mentioning the title of the poem without troubling us with an extract . . . We will quote for him :

Oh, what a scene!   Can this be Venice?   No,
And yet methinks it is—because I see,
Amid the lumps of yellow, red, and blue,
Something that looks like a Venetian spire.
That dash of orange in the background there
Bespeaks 'tis morning.   And that little boat
(Almost the colour of tomato sauce)
Proclaims them now returning from the ball :
This is my picture I would fain convey.
I hope I do.   Alas! what FALLACY.

But the old man continued to quote from his imagined masterpiece till the end.   Here are some of the latest verses :

(For " The Fountain of Fallacy ") :

Its rainbow dew diffused fell on each anxious lip,
Working wild fantasy, imagining ;
First, Science, in the immeasurable
          Abyss of thought,
Measured her orbit slumbering.

(For " Light and Colour : The Morning after the Deluge ") :

The Ark stood firm on Ararat : the returning sun
Exhaled earth's humid bubbles, and emulous of light,
Reflected her lost forms, each in prismatic guise
Hope's harbinger, ephemeral as the summer fly
Which rises, flits, expands and dies.

(For " The Departure of the Fleet ") :

The orient moon shone on the departing fleet,
Nemesis invoked, the priest held the poisoned cup.

This picture (No. 554, National Gallery) was the last exhibited in Turner's lifetime.

Two things stand out from a survey of Turner's poetry : the persistence of his effort to write verse and the persistent failure of it. His biographers have not always dealt very satisfactorily with this phase of his life's work. Mr. Thornbury was content to make fun of the poems, emphasising the disjointedness, the frequent bathos, and the bad spelling. Mr. Hamerton drew the conclusion that after all we need not take off our hats to Turner, for that, though he painted better than most others, yet we most of us could, if we tried, turn out a better copy of verses than he ever did. As if mediocrity in one art put us on a level with genius in another ! There are deeper questions to be considered. First, what was the motive which compelled a consummate master in one art to strive so continually after expression in another ?

Most men are governed by various motives, and in this case something should be ascribed to Turner's obstinate pride and constant ambition ; perhaps something, also, to mere love of mystification. He was shy, sensitive, and secretive. He was ill-favoured in appearance. " If they saw my portrait," he said, " they would not believe that my pictures were mine." Of humble origin, and destitute of the graces, he was not content with his repute as an artist. He liked to flatter himself with the thought that a time would come when he would be recognised as a

" literary gentleman."   He kept men waiting—
so he may have thought—for a surprise when the
MS. poem so often paraded in the Academy
Catalogues should at last be given to an admir-
ing world.   It may have been one of Turner's
Fallacies of Hope that fame as a poet would come
to him as the reward of diligence.

All this may have been, but there must also
have been another and a more compelling motive
behind his constant endeavour to link his work
as a painter with expression in a different sort.
Browning in the most perfect of his poems has
some lines which suggest a wider application
than he there gives to them :

> What of Rafael's sonnets, Dante's picture ?
> This : no artist lives and loves, that longs not
> Once, and only once, and for one only,
> (Ah, the prize !) to find his love a language
> Fit and fair and simple and sufficient—
> Using nature that's an art to others,
> Not, this one time, art that's turned his nature.
> Ay, of all the artists living, loving,
> None but would forgo his proper dowry,—
> Does he paint ? he fain would write a poem,—
> Does he write ? he fain would paint a picture,
> Put to proof art alien to the artist's,
> Once, and only once, and for one only,
> So to be the man and leave the artist,
> Gain the man's joy, miss the artist's sorrow.

Turner missed the man's joy (ah, the loss and
the pity of it !) : he found no woman of sympathetic soul to love him, and sought pleasure

and companionship elsewhere. But the instinct
of self-expression, the craving to escape the
artist's sorrow, which Browning goes on to explain, were strong within him. In the exercise
of his proper art he was open to criticism often
unsympathetic or misunderstanding. Shallow
critics have fastened on a saying attributed to
Turner that " Ruskin read into his pictures
things which he himself did not know were
there,"[1] and have concluded therefrom that
nothing more was in the pictures than everybody
could see. It is very doubtful whether Turner
ever did make that remark, but if he did it would
prove nothing. The creators seldom accept
what the critics and commentators say about
them. When Tennyson was asked what he
meant by a passage in an early poem, he felt
inclined to answer with Goethe, " You probably
know better than I do, being young ";[2] and
Browning would assuredly have been a silent
member of the Browning Society. It does not
follow that Tennyson's passage was sound
signifying nothing, or that many of Browning's
works do not require much unravelling. Turner,
in conversation about his works, was " silent as
a granite crest," except when he turned the talk
down with a jest. Yet the works meant more

---

[1] The saying first appeared in the *Literary Gazette* of January 3, 1852.
For a discussion of its authenticity see my note at vol. vi. p. 275 of the
Library Edition of Ruskin's Works.

[2] Lord Morley's *Recollections*, ii. 69.

to him than they were always able to tell, and he wanted to be his own interpreter. " What is the use of them except together ? " was one of his most revealing sayings. He turned to poetry in the hope of finding a medium " that should all-express " him.

The hope was fallacious. He stands on his attainment as a painter : that alone, one life allowed him. He was told that the American purchaser of " The Slave Ship " thought the picture indistinct. " You should tell him," he replied, " that indistinctness is my forte." Indistinctness or worse is the characteristic of his poetry. And here the forte is a fatal fault. He lacked both the logical faculty and the feeling for beauty, and even for coherence, in words. In one of the sketch-books Turner copied out this passage from Lord Holland's *Life of Lope Felix de Vega* :

> The chief object of Poetry is to delineate strongly the characters and passions of Mankind, to paint the appearances of Nature and to describe their effects to our imagination. To accomplish these ends the versification must be smooth, the language pure and impressive, the images just, natural, and appropriate.

He had the imagination of a poet ; his images were sometimes fine and appropriate, but his thoughts travelled faster than his command of language could follow. Some lines at the beginning of the " Southern Coast " poem are here significant. He invokes Providence to aid him so that " Perception and reasoning, *action's slow*

R

ally," may expand the thoughts that in the mind
unawakened lie and enable them to pour forth in
a steady current, not with headlong force.[1]   The
artist's hand obeyed the eye with instant action
in drawing, but the reasoning required in writing
was a slow and a feeble ally.   He tried and tried,
but he made no appeal to literary friends to lick
his rude efforts into shape.   " We have done
our best," wrote a friend to Michelangelo, " to
alter some things in your sonnet, but not to set
it right, since there was not much wanting.
Now that it is changed or put in order, according
as the kindness of your nature wished, the result
will be more due to your own judgment than to
ours, since you have the true conception of the
subject in your mind."   Turner often had a
conception of a poetical passage in his mind, and
many a piece might have been passable if he had
had a Luigi del Riccio at hand to mend the lines.

Passable perhaps, and valuable as notes upon
his pictures, but no more.   There is no trace in
his poetical essays of any magic such as he com-
manded in painting.   These things come of grace
and not by observation, and to Turner was
denied the double gift which belonged to Blake
and Rossetti.   It is still to Turner's paintings
and later drawings that we must turn to find
his poetry.   He never succeeded in explaining

---

[1] I here adopt some emendations which Mr. Monkhouse made in the
text printed by Mr. Thornbury.

them, and like other great works of art in whatever sort they will convey different impressions to
different minds. " He himself told me," wrote
his friend, the late Rev. W. Kingsley, " that he
did not like looking at his own work 'because the
realisation was always immeasurably below the
conception,' and again, to use his own words,
' he considered it his duty to *record*' certain
things he had seen ; and so in these late Swiss
drawings he felt that he could only imperfectly
record the effects of nature, but he did his best
with all his acquired knowledge and power to
tell what he had seen. There is so much in these
drawings that each requires many pages to describe
the idas expressed. One quality, that of colour,
must surely be felt by every one whose colour-
sense is not dead. . . . But for the rendering of
natural facts and for the poetry, it is hopeless
for any one to criticise them who has not in
some degree the mental penetration and grasp of
Turner, and an imagination almost as vivid."

The persistence of so consummate a painter
as Turner in attempting to find adequate self-
expression in verse suggests another remark.
Goethe first among modern writers brought home
to the minds of men the conception of art as a
genus under which poetry, painting, and the rest
were to be classified and distinguished. Lessing
in his famed *Laocoön* defined the several spheres
of sculpture and poetry, and Matthew Arnold

in his " Epilogue to Lessing " tried to see " what
painting is, what poetry." Yet it is notice-
able, says Mr. Pater, that " in its special mode
of handling its given material, each art may be
observed to pass into the condition of some other
art by what German critics term an *Anders-
streben*—a partial alienation from its own limitations, by which the arts are able, not indeed to
supply the place of each other, but reciprocally
to lend each other new forces." And hence the
question has been raised whether there is any one
among the arts which is the type and measure of
them all, and if so, which it is. The question
has been much disputed,[1] and colours the practice
and theories of modern schools. According to
Mr. Pater, all art aspires towards the condition
of music, and Whistler did much to popularise
this theory by the musical terms which he adapted
to his pictures. " I can't thank you too much,"
he wrote to Mr. Leyland, " for the name Noc-
turne as the title for my moonlights. You have
no idea what an irritation it proves to the critics
and consequent pleasure to me : besides, it is
really so charming, and does so poetically say all
I want to say and no more than I wish." Where
the motive was the combination of two or more
dominants, the picture was called a " harmony "
or an " arrangement " ; where a single colour

[1] As, for instance, by Mr. Pater in the essay on " The School of Giorgione "
added to later editions of *Studies in the Renaissance* ; and by Mr. Symonds in
the second volume of his *Essays, Speculative and Suggestive.*

was to give the ground-tone, it was a " note."
If any one is inclined to push Whistler's theory
too far, he should observe, I may remark in
passing, the significant use of the words *so
poetically* in the letter to Mr. Leyland.   For the
rival theory is that all forms of art tend to pass
into the condition of poetry, and takes poetry
as the standard whereby to judge them.   Turner,
it is clear, leaned to this latter view.   On the
technical side many of his pictures and drawings
were studies in colour, but in his mind and
intention they were generally much else, and
the something else belonged to the domain of
the poets.   He painted his impressions, and
those impressions were largely coloured by
thoughts on the fates and fortunes of men and
states.   The medium in which he possessed
mastery was not always well suited to convey
the large and vague ideas which filled his mind.
He had, as we have seen, a deep sense of the
fates of Carthage, but Rossetti with his double
gift wisely chose poetry for his ideas of " The
Burden of Nineveh."   Turner tried poetry, and
failed to supplement his series of pictures by
verse.   His *Anders-streben* was towards poetry ;
but, in order to hold the balance even between
the two theories, I will borrow a figure from one
of his biographers : the poetry in his pictures
is able, " *like music*, to start vibrations according
to the sensibility of each who hears."

IX

THE SECOND THOUGHTS
OF POETS

I was looking the other day over some old school
and college texts of the classics in which on the
interleaved pages various readings were studiously
noted and discussed—in preparation for the
dread day on which the question might be put :
" Which reading do you prefer ? State your
reasons." Such questions, with the annotated
editions of the classics on which they are based,
relate to a stage in the history of scholarship
now drawing to a close. When Latin and Greek
literature was reborn, the texts of it " teemed
with every fault that could spring from a scribe's
ignorance of grammar, metre, and sense." Professor Jebb puts the case by a modern parallel :
" Suppose a piece of very bad English handwriting, full of erasures and corrections, sent to
be printed at a foreign press." The classical
texts were as full of blunders as would have been
a foreign printer's first proof of a passage written
by Dean Stanley or Mr. Andrew Lang. The

correction of such blunders, the restoration of certainly corrupt texts to comparative and probable purity, called for enormous labour on the part of successive generations of scholars.   Casaubon compared his toil in acquiring a connected knowledge of ancient life and manners to the labours of penal servitude, and this perhaps explains the bad temper of rival commentators. But the task of emendation needed something more than labour.   Boyle, who had good reasons for making light of such work, dismissed it as "next after anagrams and acrostics the lowest diversion a man can betake himself to."   Bentley, with more justice, spoke of " a certain divining tact and inspiration—a faculty which can be acquired by no constancy of toil or length of life, but comes solely by the gift of nature and the happy star."   The exercise of this gift in fortunate moments must often have lightened toil. How keen must have been Bentley's delight when it came to him in a flash that the meaning of a certain epigram of Callimachus had been missed owing to a wrong reading !   Hitherto it had been taken to say : " Eudemus dedicated to the Samothracian gods that ship in which, after crossing a smooth sea, he escaped from great storms of the Danai."   One letter only was changed by Bentley,[1] and the true meaning was revealed as

---

[1] Reading ἐπέσθων for ἐπελθὼν, the last word of the first line.   The epigram is vi. 301 in the *Anthology*.

" Eudemus dedicated to the Samothracian gods
that salt-cellar from which he ate frugal salt until
he escaped from the troublous waves of usury."
Eudemus was not an adventurous mariner, but
a needy person who had literally adopted the
advice of the Greek sage, " Borrow from thyself
by reducing thy diet "—a maxim which might
have been used by the Food Controller and the
War Savings Committee.

The invention of printing has put out of date
this kind of acrostic reading, though Bentley,
to be sure, was slow to accept the fact.   With the
text of Shakespeare, playwrights, editors, and
commentators have been legitimately employed ;
but Bentley, in order to give himself a free hand
in attacking the text of Milton, invented the
theory that the blind poet's proofs were read by
a purblind editor.   To Bentley's emendations of
Milton one may apply what Professor Bywater
used to say, with a mock heroic lowering of
the voice, in dismissing a certain reading of
Madvig, " But it is too horrible."   Modern
poets are not exempt, it is true, from printers'
or editors' errors.   There was Shelley, for instance, who wrote with a running pen or pencil,
and often in the open air, leaving blanks to be
filled up afterwards and making interlineations
or erasures as fast as he wrote.   Trelawny, who
caught him at it in a wood, says that the MS.
of the verses, " To Jane, with a Guitar " (Ariel to

Miranda), " might have been taken for a sketch of a marsh overgrown with bulrushes, and the blots for wild ducks." Many of his works were printed in England without submission of the proofs to him in Italy, whilst in the case of his posthumous poems there was great difficulty in deciphering manuscripts in which a page of writing, with " words one upon the other, over and over in tiers," would often yield only two or three available lines. The text of Shelley was thus sometimes as corrupt as that of the classics, and many scholars (Swinburne among them) have been at work with corrections and conjectures upon it. But this was an exceptional case, and in most modern poetry the misprints are few and obvious, though often vexatious enough to the poet. He was a very devil of a printer who took liberties with one of Tennyson's favourite epithets, and made Ida in *The Princess* to be " Follow'd up by a hundred *hairy* does." It was wicked, too, to make Guinevere pass from her monastery " To where beyond these *vices* there is peace." But even if the poet had not lived to correct his printer, the restoration of the true reading in such cases would require no acute exercise of ingenuity. There is, however, another field in which the old question, " Which reading do you prefer ? " may in the case of modern poetry be asked and considered with pleasure and instruction. Poets often have second thoughts, and some live to see second or more editions. The study of various readings may then have an interest for others than bibliographers or " entomologists of criticism." It is no longer a question of choice between various guesses by scholars or pedants at what a poet might, could, would, or should have written ; the choice is between two or more versions all of which he did write. The study thus becomes an exercise in taste with the poet himself for master.

Such study at once reveals that many of the happiest thoughts of poets, many of the words and phrases which might seem most inspired or " inevitable," were, in fact, second thoughts. In the beautiful opening of *Hyperion*, grey-haired Saturn is placed

> Far from the fiery noon, and *eve's one star*.

The italicised phrase is often quoted among poetical gems, but Keats's first thought was more commonplace :

> Far from the fiery noon, and evening.

Shelley's recollection of a spring day in the pine forest near Pisa has these lines :

> The whispering waves were half asleep,
>   The clouds were gone to play,
> And on the bosom of the deep
>   The smile of Heaven lay.

The image of the smile of Heaven on the bosom
of the deep has been much admired, but in the
piece as first printed the third of the lines above
quoted was different :

> And on the woods and on the deep.

In Tennyson's " Palace of Art " is this :

> One seem'd all dark and red—a tract of sand,
>> And some one pacing there alone,
> Who paced for ever in a glimmering land,
>> Lit with a low large moon.

It is one of the best vignettes in the poem, but
the order of the lines, the fulness of alliterative
effect, the imaginative touch of the third line,
were all second thoughts. The stanza as first
printed was less perfect :

> Some were all dark and red, a glimmering land
>> Lit with a low round moon,
> Among brown rocks a man upon the sand
>> Went weeping all alone.

One of the most famous of all poems in
the English language is full of second thoughts.
Mr. Traill in his monograph on Coleridge says
of *The Ancient Mariner* that it was marked by
various notes not elsewhere characteristic of
Coleridge's poetry, and amongst others by " complete equality of execution and an unerring sense
of artistic propriety." He does not tell us of
which version he was thinking—the original as
printed in *Lyrical Ballads* in 1798, or the poem

as revised in successive editions.[1] It is the final version of 1817 with which most people are familiar, but Derwent and Sara Coleridge, in editing their father's poems, reprinted the original version as well, and it is most instructive to compare the two. Coleridge, the critic, was very frank and severe in his treatment of Coleridge, the poet.[2] "My poems have been rightly charged," he said in his Preface to their second edition, "with a profusion of double-epithets and a general turgidness. I have pruned the double-epithets with no sparing hand, and used my best efforts to tame the swell and glitter both of thought and diction." This was not treatment which *The Ancient Mariner* required, for it was conspicuously free from the blemishes in many of the poet's early works, but in other ways the ballad was subjected to equally trenchant revision. Coleridge himself clearly did not think that the piece was marked from the first by complete equality of execution or unerring sense of artistic propriety. He took things out, he put things in, and he made very numerous minor alterations. The revisions fall into three groups. He altered the archaic style throughout; he omitted some grisly passages; and, thirdly, other alterations were introduced with the object either of making the progress of the story clearer or of improving

[1] The stages of revision may be traced in Mr. E. H. Coleridge's Variorum Edition (1912) of the Poetical Works.

[2] Some instances will be found in a different connection below, p. 315.

sound and sense. The revisions of the first
two kinds were suggested by artistic propriety ;
those of the third kind added polish to the
execution. It will be convenient to glance at the
revisions in this order, but the groups are not
mutually exclusive. In making an alteration for
one purpose, a poet often finds that a further
felicity is added unto him. The " ancyent
Marinere " of the first edition became afterwards
" an ancient Mariner " ; and similarly throughout
the poem all archaisms of spelling or language
were removed. " Ne " (for " nor "), " Ee,"
" een " (for " eye," " eyes "), " withouten " (for
" without "), and various archaic words such as
" aventure " and " eldritch " disappeared in the
revised version, with incidental improvement,
it seems to me, in the beauty of the verses. For
instance, take this stanza of the original version :

> One after one, by the horned moon
>   (Listen, O stranger to me),
> Each turned his face with a ghastly pang,
>   And curs'd me with his ee.

The revised version was this :

> One after one, by the star-dogg'd Moon,
>   Too quick for groan or sigh,
> Each turn'd his face with a ghastly pang,
>   And cursed me with his eye.

The primary object of the revision was, in accordance with the general scheme, to get rid of " ee " ;
but in doing this the poet was able to remove

the second line, which was a weak one, and he also substituted for the conventional epithet of the moon, " horned," one which is original and striking.   One other example in this sort must suffice.   In the original there is this verse :

> And in its time the spell was snapt,
>   And I could move my een ;
> I look'd far-forth, but little saw
>   Of what might else be seen.

In getting rid of " een," the poet rewrote the verse thus :

> And now this spell was snapt ; once more
>   I viewed the ocean green,
> And look'd far forth, yet little saw
>   Of what had else been seen.

Apart from the question of " een," the second line seems to me a great improvement.   The removal of the archaic style of the original version was dictated, I cannot doubt, by a sense of artistic propriety.   The note of the piece is simplicity and directness.   The use of what has been called " Wardour Street English " may be permissible in imitations or echoes of ancient ballad poetry, but the purpose which the poets set before them in *Lyrical Ballads*—Coleridge in the use of the supernatural, Wordsworth in that of everyday life—was directness of appeal, and any trace of affectation was thus felt to be a blot upon the first version of *The Ancient Mariner*.

About the next group of alterations which

the poet made upon second thoughts, opinion
may more reasonably be divided.   The third
part, which contains the account of the Spectre-
ship, was very largely rewritten.   In the original
there is this description of Death as well as of his
" pheere," Life-in-Death :

> His bones were black with many a crack,
>   All black and bare I ween ;
> Jet black and bare, save where with rust
> Of mouldy damps and charnel crust
>   They're patch'd with purple and green.

This verse was omitted upon revision, with many
consequential alterations.   One of these was an
altered description of the woman :

> *Her* lips are red, *her* looks are free,
>   *Her* locks are yellow as gold ;
> Her skin is white as leprosy,
> And she is far liker Death than he ;
>   Her flesh makes the still air cold.

Such was the first version.   Upon revision it
became :

> Her lips were red, her looks were free,
>   Her locks were yellow as gold ;
> Her skin was as white as leprosy,
> The nightmare life-in-death was she,
>   Who thicks man's blood with cold.

The last two lines had to be altered because the
description of Death had been cut out, but the
alteration makes the sense clearer by naming
Death's companion, who had been unnamed in

the earlier version.   The same desire to remove
the horrible caused the poet to make large alterations in the sixth part, which in the original
contained this description of the dead crew before
the appearance of the seraph-band :

> They lifted up their stiff right arms,
>   They held them strait and tight ;
> And each right arm burnt like a torch,
>   A torch that's borne upright ;
> Their stony eyeballs glitter'd on
>   In the red and smoky light.

Was the omission of this and the earlier passages
an improvement ?   There is something to be said
on each side.   The original *Ancient Mariner* is
even more weird and uncanny than its successor,
and Mr. Derwent Coleridge thought that some
of the glamour had been removed on revision.
He tells us that Macaulay, who read the poem
when a boy at the house of Hannah More, enter-
tained to the last a preference for the original.
On the other side, Mr. Swinburne entirely
commends " the excision of the stanza which
described the Death-mate of the Spectre-woman,
his bones foul with leprous scurf and green
corruption of the grave, in contrast to the red
lips and yellow locks of the fearfuller Nightmare
Life-in-Death.   Keats in like manner cut off
from the ' Ode on Melancholy ' a first stanza
preserved for us by his biographer, who has duly
noted the delicate justice of instinct implied by

the rejection of all ghastly and violent images, however noble and impressive in their violence and ghastliness, from a poem full only of the subtle sorrow born of beauty. The same keen and tender sense of right made Coleridge reject from his work the horrors while retaining the terrors of death." The latter is, I think, the better opinion. The piece in losing some pictures of horror retains enough of the uncanny to hold us all with the mariner's glittering eye.

Of the third class of alterations I must speak more cursorily, for any full account of them would require pages of quotation. For an instance of the alterations made in order to render clearer the connections and transitions in the tale, the reader may be referred to the opening of the third part.   It was very abrupt in the original :

> I saw a something in the sky,
>   No bigger than my fist.
> At first it seem'd a little speck,
>   And then it seem'd a mist—

not only abrupt, but the second line is a little common.   But now see with what admirable art the poet improved matters, filling in the interval between the parts and leading up more effectively to the new apparition :

> There passed a weary time.   Each throat
> Was parch'd, and glazed each eye.
> A weary time, a weary time !
> How glazed each weary eye !

> When looking westward, I beheld
> A something in the sky.
> At first it seem'd a little speck. . . .

The alterations elsewhere in single lines or words
bear out the remark of his editor that " of
Coleridge it may be said, *nihil tetigit quod non
ornavit.*" In retouching he always removed a
blemish or added a beauty. One of the most
admired passages in the poem is that in which
the instantaneous descent of the tropical night
is described :

> The Sun's rim dips ; the stars rush out ;
> At one stride comes the dark.

These are among the lines which were added
upon revision. When the albatross came, " The
Marineres gave it biscuit-worms " ; but on revision the poet altered thus : " It ate the food it
ne'er had eat," which is certainly a more poetical
way of putting it. Next as an example of the
poet's care to avoid excess, note this :

> The many men so beautiful,
> And they all dead did lie.
> And a million million slimy things
> Liv'd on—and so did I.

Upon revision the poet reduced the number of
the slimy things which were seen and despised
to " A thousand thousand." This may seem a
trifling alteration, but the secret of the hold which
the poem has upon the reader is that it is everywhere so precise as to make us accept it like a

ship's log, and Coleridge felt, I think, that any
obvious trace of exaggeration weakened the
effect.   Everybody remembers the line, " Brown
skeletons of leaves that lag," but in the original
it was, " The skeletons, etc."   The substitution
of the word " brown " is a good example of the
poet's careful finish.   I have cited only a very
few of the minor alterations.   A study of them
all might be an excellent lesson in taste.

I am aware that one of the modern poets who
best repays such study has warned us off from it.
" The love of bibliomaniacs for first editions "
filled Tennyson, we are told, " with horror. And
once he said to me," adds his biographer, " ' Why
do they treasure the rubbish I shot from my
full-finish'd cantos ? ' "   " The first editions are
the worst editions."   " For himself many passages in Wordsworth and other poets had been
entirely spoilt by the modern habit of giving every
various reading along with the text "—with much
else to like effect.   It is clear, however, that we
need not take the poet's outburst seriously, for
the author of the *Memoir*—most filial of biographers—gives us ample material of all kinds
for a study of various readings, and, whenever
there is not much on hand, fills a page or two of
the book with copies of verses which his father
had discarded.   And thanks are due to him on
both scores.   What Tennyson left over would

give him a second reputation if the "full-finish'd
cantos" were lost.   Only a very full poet could
have had the heart to strike out of *Locksley Hall*,
for fear that the description of summer isles of
Eden should be thought too long, such beautiful
lines as these :

All about a summer ocean, leagues on leagues of golden calm,
And within melodious waters rolling round the knolls of palm.

As for the different readings in what Tennyson
did give to the public, a study of his revisions
shows how fastidious was the care that he lavished
upon his lines "to make them wealthier in his
readers' eyes."   He reviled the indolent, irre-
sponsible reviewers, but he often profited by
what they said.   It has been charged against the
notorious review in the *Quarterly* of April 1833
that it "checked the publication of any fresh
verse by the poet for nearly ten years," but was
not Horace "the wise adviser of the nine-years-
ponder'd lay "?   Lockhart's article was in large
part as ponderously silly, as brutal, and as unfair
as Tennyson declared, but the reviewer made here
and there a palpable hit, and fastened shrewdly
(and not without humour) on real faults in the
poet's early manner.   The result was seen in the
revisions of 1842 and later years.   I have read the
review with a variorum edition in hand.   With
hardly an exception, every piece or line which
Lockhart had guyed was either suppressed or re-

written.   I remember a lesson at school in which
the art of a stanza in the " Dream of Fair Women "
was explained to us :

> The high masts flicker'd as they lay afloat ;
>   The crowds, the temples, waver'd, and the shore ;
> The bright death quiver'd at the victim's throat ;
>   Touch'd ; and I knew no more.

The alliteration in the first line, the beauty of
the picture, as clear-cut as a cameo in Keats, were
dwelt upon ; and then, in the third line, the
poetic substitution of the effect for the cause
was adduced as an English illustration of some
passage in Sophocles or Virgil which we were
studying.   But all this only came to Tennyson
on revision.   The stanza in the edition of 1833
was this :

> The tall masts quivered as they lay afloat,
>   The temples and the people and the shore,
> One drew a sharp knife thro' my tender throat
>   Slowly,—and nothing more.

" What touching simplicity," Lockhart said,
" what pathetic resignation ; he cut my throat—
' nothing more ' !   One might indeed ask what
more she would have ? "   There was no answer,
but it was not till a revision in 1853 that the
stanza attained its final perfection.   Many other
revisions in this and other of the poems of 1833
were made before their reappearance in 1842.
" I do not wish," Tennyson had written in a letter
which his son dates approximately 1835, " to be

dragged forward again in any shape before the reading public at present, particularly on the score of my old poems, most of which I have so corrected (particularly ' Œnone ') as to make them much less imperfect, which you who are a wise man would own if you had the corrections. I may very possibly send you these some time." We have them now, and a comparison of the opening lines in the two versions may be taken as a sample :

1833.

There is a dale in Ida, lovelier
Than any in old Ionia, beautiful
With emerald slopes of sunny sward, that lean
Above the loud glenriver, which hath worn
A path thro' steepdown granite walls below
Mantled with flowering tendriltwine.   In front
The cedarshadowy valleys open wide.
Far-seen, high over all the God-built wall
And many a snowycolumned range divine,
Mounted with awful sculptures—men and Gods,
The work of Gods—bright on the dark-blue sky
The windy citadel of Ilion
Shone, like the crown of Troas.   Hither came
Mournful Œnone. . . .

1842.

There lies a vale in Ida, lovelier
Than all the valleys of Ionian hills.
The swimming vapour slopes athwart the glen,
Puts forth an arm, and creeps from pine to pine,
And loiters, slowly drawn.   On either hand
The lawns and meadow-ledges midway down

> Hang rich in flowers, and far below them roars
> The long brook falling thro' the clov'n ravine
> In cataract after cataract to the sea.
> Behind the valley topmost Gargarus
> Stands up and takes the morning : but in front
> The gorges, opening wide apart, reveal
> Troas and Ilion's column'd citadel,
> The crown of Troas.
>   Hither came at noon
> Mournful Œnone. . . .

One need not be as wise a man as James Spedding to see how greatly Tennyson improved the piece. The mannerism of too many compound words is gone ; the movement is at once simpler and more stately ; there are new felicities of phrase ; the pictorial effect is heightened. Everywhere in Tennyson's revisions these points may be noticed, as also the attainment of a more flute-like melody, the stripping off of redundancies, the introduction of a higher strain of thought, or of more emotional intensity. There is a good instance in "The Lotos-Eaters." Every one knows the beautiful passage beginning with the line :

> For they lie beside their nectar, and the bolts are hurl'd,

and ending with

> Like a tale of little meaning tho' the words are strong.

But this reminiscence of Lucretius and the whole of the concluding passage in which it is embedded were second thoughts. In the first version the poem ended with a rollicking song :

> Like a dreamy Lotos-eater, a delirious Lotos-eater.

Apart from the new beauties of the substituted passage, the whole poem gained by linking the ideal of the Lotos-eaters with the gods of Epicurus. This second thought was printed in 1842, but Tennyson was busy with the poem at a later date. Up to 1850 there was this line :

> To hear the emerald-colour'd water falling.

But water is emerald not to the ear but to the eye, and the line was altered :

> To watch the emerald-colour'd water falling.

And again a little further on there was this line :

> The Lotos blooms below the flowery peak.

But peaks are not flowery, and in 1850 the line became :

> The Lotos blooms below the barren peak.

Each of these changes is an improvement of the sense, and at the same time in each case the sound gains by a new but not too obtrusive alliteration. The poet was sensitive on this subject. " People sometimes say," he remarked to his son, " how 'studiedly alliterative' Tennyson's verse is. Why, when I spout my lines first, they come out so alliteratively that I have sometimes no end of trouble to get rid of the alliteration." But here was a contrary case, though, as I have noted, the introduction of the alliterations was not the primary object of the revisions.

Another early poem which owes its final form
to many revisions is "The Lady of Shalott." An
hour's study in taste might be given by asking of
almost every stanza in the piece, Which reading
do you prefer?   Here is the first stanza in its
original form :

> On either side the river lie
> Long fields of barley and of rye,
> That clothe the wold and meet the sky ;
> And thro' the field the road runs by
>   To many-tower'd Camelot ;
> The yellow-leaved water lily,
> The green-sheathed daffodilly,
> Tremble in the water chilly,
>   Round about Shalott.

Upon revision the latter lines were thus altered :

> And up and down the people go,
> Gazing where the lilies blow
> Round an island there below,
>   The island of Shalott.

Every one must feel the improvement.   The
note of affectation and a trace of forcing the
rhyme (in " daffodilly " to rhyme with " chilly ")
have gone ; the second version is simpler, more
euphonious, more pictorial.   The next stanza
was greatly improved ; the exquisite second line,

> Little breezes dusk and shiver,

was a second thought.   And thus one might go

through the poem till one reached the last stanza, which originally was this :

> They crossed themselves, their stars they blest,
> Knight, minstrel, abbot, squire and guest,
> There lay a parchment on her breast,
> That puzzled more than all the rest,
>   The well-fed wits at Camelot.
> *The web was woven curiously,*
> *The charm is broken utterly,*
> *Draw near and fear not—this is I,*
>   *The Lady of Shalott.*

The second version was wholly different :

> Who is this ? and what is here ?
> And in the lighted palace near
> Died the sound of royal cheer ;
> And they cross'd themselves for fear,
>   All the knights at Camelot :
> But Lancelot mused a little space ;
> He said, " She has a lovely face ;
> God in his mercy lend her grace,
>   The Lady of Shalott."

There was something eerie in the last four lines of the earlier version which is partly missed in the revision, but the poem gains by the greater emotional intensity, by the note of what the critics call " high seriousness " with which the poem now concludes.

In the case of *In Memoriam* the printed variants are few comparatively to the length of the poem, but it had been in preparation, and probably was often revised in manuscript, during many

years before it was published in 1850.   Here and
there, however, lines were retouched long afterwards.   A verse in the fortieth stanza was this :

> And, doubtless, unto thee is given
>   A life that bears immortal fruit
>   In such great offices as suit
> The full-grown energies of heaven.

The third line now reads :

> In those great offices that suit.

Which reading do you prefer ? and why ?   The
poet himself has stated his reasons.   " I never,"
he said, " put two *ss* together in any verse of
mine," and he instanced the piece which begins,
" You ask me, why, tho' ill at ease " : " My line
is not, as often quoted, ' And freedom broaden*s*
*s*lowly down,' but ' And freedom slowly broadens
down.' "   It was not, however, till 1883 that
Tennyson " kicked the geese out of the boat "
in the line above quoted from *In Memoriam*.

In the variorum editions of the earlier poems
collated by Mr. Churton Collins, and in the
Memoir of the poet by his son, many other instances of revisions equally interesting are noted.
Some were made as late as in 1891.   By a poet
who thus to extreme old age polished and revised
his verses, the first editions naturally might be
dismissed as the worst.   Yet it was not always
or certainly so.   Edward FitzGerald doubted
whether the second version of " The Miller's

Daughter " was altogether an improvement upon
the first.   There are two lines in " Œnone " which
are given in every book of Familiar Quotations :

> Self-reverence, self-knowledge, self-control,
> These three alone lead life to sovereign power.

But in the first edition the second line was
different :

> Are the three hinges of the gates of Life.

Mr. Herbert Paul, backed by the authority of
Lord Coleridge, cannot understand " why Tennyson rejected that noble and simple line " of the
earlier version.   The hinges seem to me to
creak a little, but let every reader decide according to his taste.   " One should be fearful," said
Joubert, " of being wrong in poetry when one
thinks differently from the poets, and in religion
when one thinks differently from the saints."
It is a consolation, in such questions of literary
casuistry as we are here concerned with, to know
that whatever choice we may make a poet was
at one time or another on our side.   There is,
however, one piece by Tennyson with regard to
which it cannot reasonably be held that the first
version was the worst, though a reader may be left
free to think that the third is the best.[1]   Everybody knows " The Charge of the Light Brigade,"

---

[1] As Tennyson (in a different connection) has it :
> Is it so true that second thoughts are best ?
> Not first and third which are a riper first ?

but few probably remember the numerous, exten-
sive, and successive alterations to which it was
subjected before attaining its now familiar form.
Take, for instance, the spirited stanza with which
the piece ends :

> When can their glory fade ?
> O the wild charge they made !
>   All the world wonder'd.
> Honour the charge they made !
> Honour the Light Brigade,
>   Noble six hundred.

So it was written at first, and to this form the poet
finally reverted, and he was certainly right, for
the second version was tame :

> Honour the brave and bold !
> Long shall the tale be told,
> Yes, when our babes are old—
>   How they rode onward.

But in another respect the poet's second thoughts
were still worse. The first version contained
the famous line, " Some one had blunder'd,"
and this appears also, though in an altered setting,
in the third and final version ; but in the meanwhile, when Tennyson revised the piece for inclusion in the *Maud* volume, the line was removed.
Ruskin wrote to protest. " I am very sorry," he
said, "you put the ' Some one had blunder'd '
out of the ' Light Brigade.' It was precisely
the most tragical line in the poem. It is as true

to its history as essential to its tragedy." [1]   The thing is obvious, and the omission was the more strange because the line was originally the keynote of the poem.   " My father's poems were generally based," says his son, " on some single phrase like ' Some one had blunder'd,' and were rolled about, so to speak, in his head, before he wrote them down."   Elsewhere in the *Memoir* we are told, partly, how the keynote came to be struck out : " Some friends of excellent critical judgment prevailed upon him to omit the phrase." If their critical judgment were excellent, it was perverted in this case, we may suppose, by consideration of military or political susceptibilities. " Certain people of importance entered. . . . Then I stopped my painting."

There is no poem which lends itself more easily to a study in taste under the poet's direction than FitzGerald's " golden Eastern lay."   Tennyson knew " no version done in English more divinely

[1] I have heard it objected that to be quite true to history we should read for " Some one had blunder'd," " Every one blunder'd."   But this was said by a student of war and was not meant as a literary criticism, any more than was the famous emendation suggested by Mr. Babbage, the mathematician, in " The Vision of Sin " :

> Every moment dies a man,
> Every moment one is born—

an arrangement which would keep the population in a state of equipoise. Mr. Babbage made the proper calculation and proposed as a second thought for the next edition :

> Every moment dies a man,
> And one and a sixteenth is born.

well," but we are not told which of the three main
versions he preferred. They differ largely, and
the care of pious editors has collated, tabulated,
and even indexed the differences. The first
edition of FitzGerald's *Omar* (1859) contained
only 75 stanzas. The second (1868) contained
110; the order was often changed, and the
verbal alterations were many. The third (1872)
contained 101, and there was again much revision.
The variations between it and the last edition
(1879) are comparatively few. One source of
interest in studying the variations is to note how
the translator dealt in process of revision with his
Persian original, and this is ground which has
been worked over by many scholars; but Fitz-
Gerald's translation (if such it should be called)
is an English classic, and greater interest, as also
less recondite, may be found in tracing the
English poet's search after perfection. "Every
quatrain," said Swinburne, "though it is something so much more than graceful or distinguished
or elegant, is also, one may say, the sublimation
of elegance, the apotheosis of distinction, the
transfiguration of grace." Was the perfection
attained already when FitzGerald first published
his poem, or did his later revision refine it?
Mr. Palgrave says of the earliest version that
the text was "not, perhaps, always altered in
later issues to advantage." This remark seems
over-carefully hedged. There was more than one

later issue ; there were hundreds of alterations, and many re-alterations.   To say that perhaps not each and every alteration was an improvement is to state what nobody would care to deny, but the proposition is of the kind of which Omar said that after hearing them he " came out by the same door wherein he went."   To me it seems that the alterations introduced in the second edition were generally, but not quite always, improvements, and that wherever the text as finally left by FitzGerald differs from earlier versions, it differs, without exception, to advantage. We will take a few of the best, and best-known, quatrains, and the reader shall judge :

First Edition.

Here with a Loaf of Bread beneath the Bough,
A Flask of Wine, a Book of Verse—and Thou
     Beside me singing in the Wilderness—
And Wilderness is Paradise enow.

Final Edition.

A Book of Verses underneath the Bough,
A Jug of Wine, a Loaf of Bread—and Thou
     Beside me singing in the Wilderness—
Oh, Wilderness were Paradise enow !

I do not know what Omar's order would have been, but I am sure that FitzGerald was right in altering Bread—Wine—Verse   to   Verse—Wine—Bread. The music of the lines seems to me to be bettered as well, and the wistful note to be enhanced.   This

latter point may be noticed in a seemingly trivial
alteration in another beautiful quatrain :

> Alas, that Spring should vanish with the Rose !
> That Youth's sweet-scented Manuscript should close !
>   The Nightingale that in the Branches sang,
> Ah, whence, and whither flown again, who knows !

The poet upon final revision altered " Alas "
to " Yet Ah," thereby substituting a more
poignant note for the conventional " Alas," and
at the same time introducing an echo in his last
line.   It is remarkable how much improvement
may be made by the alteration of a single word :

> The Moving Finger writes ; and, having writ,
> Moves on : nor all thy Piety nor Wit
>   Shall lure it back to cancel half a Line,
> Nor all thy Tears wash out a Word of it.

The verse might seem incapable of improvement,
but the poet, before he had done with it, altered
" thy " in the second and fourth lines to " your."
I think that the music gains by the addition of
a vowel-sound, and also that the sense of cosmic
movement is heightened by the substitution of a
more general term for a more particular.   Another
famous quatrain shows a more palpable improvement :

> They say the Lion and the Lizard keep
> The Courts where Jamshyd gloried and drank deep ;
>   And Bahrám, that great Hunter—the Wild Ass
> Stamps o'er his Head, and he lies fast asleep.

One might have thought the quatrain perfect,

but that the poet bettered it by rewriting the
last line :

Stamps o'er his Head, but cannot break his Sleep.

The " crowning stanza," as Swinburne once
called it (quoting the first edition), was much
retouched, and the variations are of interest :

First Edition.

Oh, Thou, who Man of baser Earth didst make,
And who with Eden didst devise the Snake ;
   For all the Sin wherewith the Face of Man
Is blacken'd, Man's Forgiveness give—and take !

Second Edition.

Oh, Thou, who Man of baser Earth didst make,
And e'en with Paradise devise the Snake ;
   For all the Sin the Face of wretched Man
Is black with—Man's Forgiveness give—and take !

The alteration of the second line is perhaps an
improvement as reducing the alliteration of *d*'s.
In revising the third and fourth lines, FitzGerald
thought, we may suppose, of St. Paul's " wretched
man," but the words " Is black with " are not
happy.   The final version is as follows :

Oh, Thou, who Man of baser Earth didst make,
And ev'n with Paradise devise the Snake ;
   For all the Sin wherewith the Face of Man
Is blacken'd—Man's forgiveness give—and take !

Professor Cowell, who was FitzGerald's master
in Persian, told him that the last line was a mis-
translation, " but he never cared to alter it."
Why should he ?   It is the most majestic line

in his poem ; and besides, as Mr. Heron-Allen
has shown, though there is no original in Omar
for this quatrain, there are passages in the *Mantik-
ut-Tair* of Attar which may well have suggested
it, and FitzGerald fused much study of Persian
poetry into his golden Eastern lay. Such was
the case with two notable quatrains which did not
appear in the first edition :

> I sent my Soul through the Invisible,
> Some letter of that After-life to spell :
>   And by and by my Soul return'd to me,
> And answer'd " I myself am Heav'n and Hell."

> Heav'n but the Vision of fulfill'd Desire,
> And Hell the Shadow from a Soul on fire,
>   Cast on the Darkness into which Ourselves,
> So late emerged from, shall so soon expire.

In a letter read at a dinner of the Omar Khayyám
Club, Mr. Swinburne, after recounting his pur-
chase for a penny of a copy of the first edition,
went on to say : " It is the only edition worth
having, as FitzGerald, like the ass of genius
he was, cut out of later editions the crowning
stanza which is the core or kernel of the whole."
This is a hard saying. There are only two stanzas
of the first edition which are not represented in
the later issues ; there are twenty-eight in the
final issue which did not appear in the first.
Are the twenty-eight, including the two just
quoted, worth nothing ? Of the two discarded

stanzas, Mr. Swinburne doubtless was thinking of this :

> But leave the Wise to wrangle, and with me
> The Quarrel of the Universe let be :
> And, in some corner of the Hubbub coucht,
> Make Game of that which makes as much of Thee.

It is certainly difficult to see why this quatrain was cut out. I can only suppose that when FitzGerald rearranged the order of the stanzas and inserted many others he could find no convenient place for this. It is characteristic, but is it the stanza which crowns the poem ? In his *Studies in Prose and Poetry* Mr. Swinburne, as I have already noted, quotes as " the crowning stanza " the one beginning with the line, " Oh, Thou, who Man of baser Earth didst make," and this stanza, as we have seen, was not cut out of later editions. The book-lover has a natural bias in favour of the edition in which he first read a favourite piece. Perhaps this is the real reason why I like best the third edition of FitzGerald's *Omar*. It was given to me during my last term at Winchester by the mother of a school-friend, and, next, it was my book of verse beneath the bough on many a " golden Oxford afternoon." Personal bias apart, however, it is certain that those who know *Omar* in FitzGerald's first edition alone deprive themselves of two sources of interest and enjoyment : they miss the study of the poet's refining work, and they go without

several beautiful quatrains. The question which
edition is now best worth having (I speak of
intrinsic, not of bibliopolic, value) admits of no
debate. It is the " Golden Treasury " edition,
for therein the final version is supplemented both
by an exact reprint of the first and by a collection
of the stanzas which appeared in the second
edition only.

A poem which has vied with FitzGerald's
Omar in popularity is Myers's *St. Paul*. It
appeals to a different audience ; but, apart from
its religious address, the distinctive stanza employed by Myers, the faultless rhythmical cadence
and the sonorous verbal melody have for fifty
years attracted lovers of poetry. The very
defects of the piece, as they may be deemed by a
severe taste—its sometimes metallic ring, its over-
elaboration of phrase—have perhaps assisted its
vogue. Between its appearance in 1867 and the
poet's death in 1901 there were sixteen editions,
and as soon as it passed out of copyright, the
book mart was flooded, as in the case of *Omar*,
with cheap reprints of the first edition. As
FitzGerald, so Frederic Myers constantly retouched his poem, adding at one time or another
twenty-two verses and discarding seventeen of
the original. Some of the new verses, and
especially the six in praise of love, are very
beautiful, but none have quite the same charm

that belonged to those of the original version.
A similar remark applies, I think, to most of the
poet's revisions of lines and words; one sees
why they were made and is forced at times to
recognise their propriety, and yet one regrets
them.   The piece was written for the Seatonian
prize at Cambridge, and failed to win it, but who
has ever heard of the poem which the judges
preferred?   The metre adopted by Myers was
unconventional.   Perhaps, too, the judges failed
to find their conception of St. Paul in the poem.
Many other readers have been in like case—
Ruskin for one.   He was introduced to Myers's
poems by Prince Leopold, and wrote: "The
John Baptist seems to me entirely beautiful and
right in its dream of him.   The *St. Paul* is not
according to my thought," adding with courtly
concession (for the Prince was enamoured of the
piece), "but I am glad to have my thought
changed."   The point is, however, that Myers
was not writing a thesis on Pauline theology
or an historical study of the Apostle's life; he
was writing a poem, and pouring out on a given
subject the emotions and imagination of a poet.
In the chapters of autobiography prefixed to
his posthumous *Fragments of Prose and Poetry*
he tells us, what indeed the poems themselves
sufficiently reveal, that the "*St. Paul* and *St.
John the Baptist*, intensely personal in their
emotion, may serve as a sufficient record of those

years of eager faith." They are the record of the poet's conversion to the Christian faith in its emotional fulness—a conversion which immediately supervened upon a burning Hellenism. " Few men," he tells us in describing his travels in Greece, " can have drunk that departed loveliness into a more passionate heart. It was the life of about the sixth century before Christ, on the isles of the Aegean, which drew me most;— that intensest and almost unconscious bloom of the Hellenic spirit. . . . Gazing on those straits and channels of purple sea, I felt that nowise could I come closer still ; never more intimately than thus could embrace that vanished beauty." It is the fusion of Hellenic beauty with Christian emotion which gives to Myers's *St. Paul* its peculiar charm, as in these often quoted and justly admired verses :

Lo as some bard on isles of the Aegean
    Lovely and eager when the earth was young,
Burning to hurl his heart into a paean,
    Praise of the hero from whose loins he sprung ;—

He, I suppose, with such a care to carry,
    Wandered disconsolate and waited long,
Smiting his breast, wherein the notes would tarry,
    Chiding the slumber of the seed of song :

Then in the sudden glory of a minute
    Airy and excellent the proëm came,
Rending his bosom, for a god was in it,
    Waking the seed, for it had burst in flame.

> So even I athirst for His inspiring,
>   I who have talked with Him forget again ;
> Yes, many days with sobs and with desiring
>   Offer to God a patience and a pain ;
>
> Then thro' the mid complaint of my confession,
>   Then thro' the pang and passion of my prayer,
> Leaps with a start the shock of His possession,
>   Thrills me and touches, and the Lord is there.

These are among the verses which the poet, during his many revisions, never altered. Another beautiful section of the poem is that in which the legend of Damaris [1] gave scope for descriptions of Athens :

> Ay and ere now above the shining city
>   Full of all knowledge and a God unknown
> Stood I and spake, and passion of my pity
>   Drew Him from heaven and showed Him to His own....
>
> Then to their temple Damaris would clamber,
>   High where an idol till the dawn was done
> Bright in a light and eminent in amber
>   Caught the serene surprises of the sun.

So during many editions stood the latter verse— unforgettable—but in the end it was rewritten thus :

> Then to their temple Damaris would clamber,
>   Stood where an idol in the lifted sky
> Bright in a light and eminent in amber
>   Heard not, nor pitied her, nor made reply.

From the verse thus altered, some of the perhaps too obvious cunning of the alliterative choice of words is removed ; the whole effect is rendered

---

[1] Acts xvii. 34.

more severe, and the way is better prepared for
the conversion of Damaris. Yet it is with a pang
that one parts with the exquisite picture of sun-
rise on the Parthenon. " I wish," Ruskin had
written, " the verses were less studiously alliterative, but the verbal art of them is wonderful."
Many of the poet's revisions had the effect, and
perhaps the purpose, of removing alliterations—
sometimes to obvious advantage, where the
alliteration had been otherwise otiose, as, for
instance, in the line :

> John than which man a grander or a greater.

The alteration of " grander " to " sadder " was
in every way an improvement. In other cases
the improvement is doubtful. There is an
instance in the fifth verse of the first canto :

> What was their sweet desire and subtle yearning,
>   Lovers, and ladies whom their song enrols ?
> Faint to the flame which in my breast is burning,
>   Less than the love with which I ache for souls.

Myers—perhaps in deference to a critic [1]—altered
" ladies " to " women," and half the witchery of
the line seems to me to have gone.

Two of the loveliest of modern poems (each
the best-known piece of its author) owe much of
their perfection to second thoughts. There are
good judges who have called *Love in the Valley*

---

[1] George Meredith, in a review of the poem in the *Fortnightly* (Jan.
1868), had cited this stanza as an instance of " lackadaisacal alliteration."

the greatest love poem of its century, and any dull
fool who supposes George Meredith's verse to
be all harsh and crabbed should be made to learn
it by heart for his soul's good.   But when *Love
in the Valley* is exalted to such pride of place, of
which version is it spoken ?   It was written in
1851, and rewritten in 1878.   The better the
judge the greater the likelihood, I think, that the
later version is preferred.   Tennyson, it is true,
was delighted by the earlier, but we are not told
that he knew the later, and I have read somewhere
the remark that the later is " intolerable to any
reader fortunate enough to possess the first
copy."   " Intolerable " shows intolerance ; but
the writer was preening himself on the possession
of a first edition.   In the Collected Edition of
Meredith's Works both versions of the poem are
given, and a pleasant hour may be spent in a
poet's workshop by comparing them.   The
young poet had already in 1851 found the
swinging cadence,[1] but the very first lines

---

[1] A writer in the *Quarterly Review* (July 1902) has suggested that Meredith
may have found a model in the song by George Darley beginning

> Sweet in her green dell the flower of beauty slumbers,
>   Lull'd by the faint breezes sighing through her hair ;
> Sleeps she and hears not the melancholy numbers
>   Breathed to my sad lute 'mid the lonely air.
> Down from the high cliffs the rivulet is teeming
>   To wind round the willow banks that lure him from above :
> O that in tears, from my rocky prison streaming,
>   I too could glide to the bower of my love.

Darley's piece is No. 640 in *The Oxford Book of Verse.*

give instances of maturer artistry in the version
of 1878 :

Under yonder beech-tree $\left\{ {(1851) \text{ standing} \atop (1878) \text{ single}} \right\}$ on the green-sward.

Couched with her arms behind her $\left\{ {(1851) \text{ little} \atop (1878) \text{ golden}} \right\}$ head.

A sensitive ear will feel the revision in each line
to be an improvement, and the pleasanter sound
is wedded to fuller sense. " *Single* on the green-
sward " adds something, and something definite,
to the picture, whereas " standing " was otiose,
and the change of " little " into " golden " gives
colour to the picture. Wherever a stanza of the
first version is retained in the second, there are
retouchings, and each of these gives a new beauty
or removes a blemish. Here is the second stanza
of 1851 :

> Shy as the squirrel and wayward as the swallow ;
>   Swift as the swallow when athwart the western flood
> Circleting the surface he meets his mirrored winglets,—
>   Is that dear one in her maiden bud.
> Shy as the squirrel whose nest is in the pine-tops ;
>   Gentle—ah ! that she were jealous as the dove !
> Full of all the wildness of the woodland creatures,
>   Happy in herself is the maiden that I love !

It is charming, but the fourth and sixth lines are
not up to the level of the rest : the execution is
less perfect, and the sentiment is a little common.
But see how the master in revising the poem
mends matters :

Shy as the squirrel and wayward as the swallow,
  Swift as the swallow along the river's light
Circleting the surface to meet his mirrored winglets,
  Fleeter she seems in her stay than in her flight.
Shy as the squirrel that leaps among the pine-tops,
  Wayward as the swallow overhead at set of sun,
She whom I love is hard to catch and conquer,
  Hard, but O the glory of the winning were she won !

It is exquisite, and, if the earlier version were not
known, one might suppose that the lines came
in their inevitable rightness from a careless rapture
of imagination. And indeed it may be that
to the poet composing in the full maturity of his
powers the alterations of 1878 came inevitably
and not with observation ; but, however this
may have been, the student is free to consider why
the lines were recast, and wherein the improvement
consists. The grammatical construction of the
second and third lines is simplified. The swallow
" along the river's light " is more pictorial than
" athwart the western flood." The weak fourth
line of the original version—weak, among other
reasons, because there is no likeness between
the " maiden bud " and the swallow—is replaced
by a fancy of perfect congruity. The return
to the swallow in the sixth line adds yet more
to the melody and sequence of the whole ; and
as for the alteration at the end, every wise man's
son will know that it is better. But one cannot
have everything, and there is one discarded line
in the earlier version of the stanza—the seventh,

"Full of all the wildness of the woodland creatures"
—which is not willingly forgotten. Presently,
however, as we shall see, the poet gives it back
to us with usury. I pass to the third stanza,[1]
partly for the pleasure of transcribing it, but also
because the revision, though slight, is significant :

> When her mother tends her before the laughing mirror
>   Tying up her laces, looping up her hair,
> Often she thinks, were this wild thing wedded,
>   More love should I have, and much less care.
> When her mother tends her before the lighted mirror,
>   Loosening her laces, combing down her curls,
> Often she thinks, were this wild thing wedded,
>   I should miss but one for many boys and girls.

There are some slight alterations in the fourth and
eighth lines here, but the significant one is in the
fifth, which in the earlier version was " When
her mother tends her before the bashful mirror."
Was the epithet altered only in order to echo the
first line more nearly (" *l*aughing," " *l*ighted ") ?
or was it also (as I suppose) because the epithet
" bashful " was felt to strike a false note, perhaps
as offending against good taste and at any rate
as not in tune with the naïve charm of the rest of
the stanza ? Elsewhere in the earlier version,
pretty though it is, there are lines and phrases
which smack somewhat of the novelette, as where
the lover is smitten with " anguish at the thought,
Should some idle lordling bribe her mind with

---

[1] In the poem of 1851, the *fourth*, for the third stanza was omitted in 1878.

jewels," or where, powerless to speak the ardour
of his passion, he catches her little hand.   Every
jarring note of this kind was removed in the later
version, whilst in the fifteen added stanzas we
are given a succession of exquisite pictures,
" full " themselves " of all the wildness of the
woodland creatures," and redolent of every beauty
of an English country-side :

Heartless she is as the shadow in the meadows
 Flying to the hills on a blue and breezy noon.
No, she is athirst and drinking up her wonder :
 Earth to her is young as the slip of the new moon.
Deals she an unkindness, 'tis but her rapid measure,
 Even as in a dance ; and her smile can heal no less :
Like the swinging May-cloud that pelts the flowers with
  hail-stones
 Off a sunny border, she was made to bruise and bless.

Lovely are the curves of the white owl sweeping
 Wavy in the dusk lit by one large star.
Lone on the fir-branch, his rattle-note unvaried,
 Brooding o'er the gloom, spins the brown eve-jar.
Darker grows the valley, more and more forgetting :
 So were it with me if forgetting could be willed.
Tell the grassy hollow that holds the bubbling well-
  spring,
 Tell it to forget the source that keeps it filled.

  . . . . . .

Soft new beech-leaves, up to beamy April
 Spreading bough on bough a primrose mountain, you
Lucid in the moon, raise lilies to the sky-fields,
 Youngest green transfused in silver shining through :

Fairer than the lily, than the wild white cherry :
   Fair as in image my seraph love appears
Borne to me by dreams when dawn is at my eyelids :
   Fair as in the flesh she swims to me on tears.

Could I find a place to be alone with heaven,
   I would speak my heart out : heaven is my need.
Every woodland tree is flushing like the dogwood,
   Flashing like the whitebeam, swaying like the reed.
Flushing like the dogwood crimson in October ;
   Streaming like the flag-reed south-west blown ;
Flashing as in gusts the sudden-lighted whitebeam :
   All seem to know what is for heaven alone.

The love poem of 1851 was transformed upon revision into the most beautiful of " Poems and Lyrics of the Joy of Earth."

Every lover, and every lover of poetry, knows Rossetti's *Blessed Damozel*, but most readers know it only in one form and have not marked " the noble care," as a brother - poet calls it, " spent in the rejection and rearrangement of whatever was crude or lax in the first cast." The piece was first written for *The Hodgepodge*, a manuscript family magazine, in Rossetti's nineteenth year, and of its original form no copy is extant. Three years later he added four stanzas and printed it in *The Germ* (1850). Six years later it was reprinted, with revisions, in *The Oxford and Cambridge Magazine* (1856). One at least of the revisions then made was suggested by Ruskin. Fourteen years then passed, and the poem, further revised and reduced from twenty-five stanzas to twenty-four, was included in the famous volume of *Poems* (1870). From time to time, as new editions appeared, Rossetti retouched the piece, the edition of 1881 containing his final revision. Which were the stanzas added in *The Germ*? What was "the line," as Rossetti wrote to Allingham, which "Ruskin made me alter"? These questions cannot be answered, but the successive variations in the printed text can be studied, and the poet's letters to his brother sometimes enable us to watch the file at its work. The variations are very numerous, and some of the lines went through several stages of revision before reaching the final perfection. It is noteworthy, however, that wherever the poem is pictorial, wherever the poet is describing something which might be transferred to canvas, he saw it clearly once and for all, found at first the exactly right words, and did not afterwards alter either form or colour. Of the actually painted "Blessed Damozel" there were many versions; the word-painting of her and her company remained unaltered. There are only two exceptions, and they are slight. In the original version the handmaidens sit circle-wise "with bound locks And bosoms coverèd"; in the final version the latter line is altered to "And foreheads garlanded." This is an added touch of colour. In the other case a colour-definition was omitted in exchange for a greater beauty of expression :

Germ.

The blessèd damozel leaned out
　　From the gold bar of Heaven ;
Her blue grave eyes were deeper much
　　Than a deep water, even.

1870 *and after.*

The blessèd damozel leaned out
　　From the gold bar of Heaven ;
Her eyes were deeper than the depth
　　Of waters stilled at even.

A comparison of the texts discloses many added beauties and corrected blemishes, but one example in each sort must here suffice. For example of the former, take the following stanza. It is one of those in which the poet, in intervals of the vision, gives the thoughts of the lover who still dwells on earth :

Germ.

(Alas ! to her wise simple mind
　　These things were all but known
Before : they trembled on her sense,—
　　Her voice had caught their tone.
Alas for lonely Heaven ! Alas
　　For life wrung out alone !)

1870.

(Alas ! we two, we two, thou say'st !
　　Yea, one wast thou with me
That once of old.　But shall God lift
　　To endless unity
The soul whose likeness with thy soul
　　Was but its love for thee ?)

U

Each is beautiful, but the two last lines of the rewritten stanza have a depth of tenderness which is not touched in the earlier version. The stanza which was most often altered by the poet is the seventh ; here, he must have felt, was a blemish to be corrected. A certain quaint simplicity and directness is of the essence of the piece ; but once at least it trembles on the verge of bathos :

(1) *Germ.*

Heard hardly, some of her new friends,
　Playing at holy games,
Spake, gentle-mouth'd, among themselves,
　Their virginal new names.

(6) 1881.

Around her, lovers, newly met
　'Mid deathless love's acclaims,
Spoke evermore among themselves
　Their heart-remembered names.

These are the first and the last versions, but there were several intermediate :

(2) *O. and C. Magazine.*

She scarcely heard her sweet new friends
　Playing at holy games,
Softly they spake among themselves
　Their virginal chaste names.

(3) 1870.

Heard hardly, some of her new friends
　Amid their loving games
Spoke evermore among themselves
　Their virginal chaste names.

(4) 1870 (2nd ed.).
Around her, lovers, newly met
   In joy no sorrow claims,
Spoke evermore among themselves
   Their rapturous new names.

(5) Tauchnitz, 1873.
Around her, lovers, newly met
   'Mid deathless love's acclaims,
Spoke evermore among themselves
   Their rapturous new names.

It is of curious interest to note in these successive
retouchings the poet's doubts and reversions.
" Heard hardly " is not a good phrase ; yet,
after dismissing it in No. 2, Rossetti restored
it in No. 3. By this time the second line had
begun to displease him, but though he altered it,
he still retained the " games." When he was
revising the *Poems* of 1870 for a new edition
(No. 4), he dismissed both " Hardly heard " and
the games, and he altered the last line. The new
first line in No. 4 was a great improvement,
and was not afterwards changed ; but the second
line was rightly felt to be unsatisfactory. It was
altered, greatly for the better, in No. 5. But
even yet the poet had not done with the lines,
and in No. 6 the names of the lovers, which
had been, successively, " virginal new," " virginal
chaste," and " rapturous new," now became
" heart-remembered." A stanza, it seems, may
go through as many stages as may a soul in the

upward path to perfection.   It may be questioned, I think, whether No. 6 is an improvement upon No. 5, but that Nos. 4-6 are improvements upon Nos. 1-3 is certain.   There is only one place in *The Blessed Damozel* where it is difficult to say whether the earlier or the later version is the better:

Germ.

> We two will stand beside that shrine,
>   Occult, withheld, untrod,
> Whose lamps tremble continually
>   With prayer sent up to God ;
> And where each need, reveal'd, expects,
>   Its patient period.

1870.

> We two will stand beside that shrine,
>   Occult, withheld, untrod,
> Whose lamps are stirred continually
>   With prayer sent up to God ;
> And see our prayers, granted, melt
>   Each like a little cloud.

The later imagination is very beautiful, but the cancelled passage is too fine to be forgotten. Perhaps it is best to say with Swinburne that " though a diamond may have supplanted it, a ruby has been plucked out of the golden ring," or to borrow words from another poet and decide that " the leader is fairest, but both are divine."

Rossetti's retouchings were sometimes due to an almost morbid sensitiveness.   In his " Love's Nocturn " he had written :

>   Fair with honourable eyes,
>   Lamps of a pellucid soul—

a beautiful figure; but before it passed from
manuscript to final proof, Browning's *Ring and
the Book* appeared, and in it Rossetti noted the
phrase "lustrous and pellucid soul" applied
by Pompilia to Caponsacchi. "The inevitable
charge of plagiarism struck me at once," he
wrote, "as impending whenever my poem should
be printed," and he robbed himself of a felicitous
phrase; the line as it first stood is much finer
than either of the later variations: "Lamps of
an auspicious soul" (1870), "Lamps of a trans-
lucent soul" (1881). This instance should be
a warning to critics who in all ages have been
over-fond of seasoning their discovery of parallel
passages with suspicion of plagiarism.

Willing though Rossetti was to retouch his
lines in deference to criticism (as his *Family
Letters* abundantly testify), he sometimes held
fast by what he had written. The fine poem
"A Last Confession" begins with a licence in
geography :

>   Our Lombard country-girls along the coast
>   Wear daggers in their garters.

Mr. William Rossetti, in a note to his brother's
poem, remarks that "every one except Dante
Rossetti knows that Lombardy has no coast";
but ignorant, or unrepentant, the poet remained.

There is an amusing instance of the same kind of thing in his address to the Virgin (" Ave ") :

> Far off the trees were as pale wands
> Against the fervid sky : the sea
> Sighed further off eternally
> As human sorrow sighs in sleep.

The poem was under revision, and Mr. William Rossetti protested that these lines would not do: " Nazareth is *quite inland*, about equidistant from the Mediterranean and the Lake of Tiberias : the sea could no more be heard there than in London or Birmingham. I know one may care too much for objections of this sort, yet I think the local mendacity is too glaring." One would like to know what Shakespeare would have said if some one had objected to him that there were no sea-coasts in Bohemia ; but the later poet's reply to the critic is on record. " I fear," wrote Rossetti, " the sea must remain at Nazareth ; you know an old painter would have made no bones if he wanted it for his background."

Not every poet, however, is so robustly impenitent of " local mendacity." There is a curious instance in one of the most unequal, but in part one of the best, of Matthew Arnold's poems, " The Church of Brou " (1853). So the poem is named in the early editions, where it is in three parts. The first tells the story of Margaret of Austria and her husband, Philibert le

Beau, Duke of Savoy; the second describes the
church where the duke and duchess lie buried.
The poet, who had taken his description at second
hand from a rhapsody by Quinet, placed the
church "'mid the Savoy mountain valleys,"
"below the pines," and made "the Alpine
peasants climb up" to it "to pray." But the
Church of Brou, with its splendid tombs, is not
among the mountains; it is on the hard high
road, in the flat and treeless Burgundian plain,
a mile from the railway station of Bourg, between
Mâcon and Ambérieu. The "local mendacity,"
which was great, was pointed out, and what was
to be done? The mountain touches run all
through the poem, but Brou by happy chance is
not mentioned in the third, and crowning, part.
The knife, instead of the file, was used; the first
two parts were cut out, and the third was printed
alone, rechristened "A Tomb among the Mountains" (1877).[1] To be sure, this third part—
with its impetuous rush of inspired imagination—
is a jewel which needs no setting; but presently
Arnold changed his mind again, and in later
editions (1881 onwards) the "Tomb among the
Mountains" reappears as part of "The Church
of Brou." Perhaps he thought that the poetic

[1] "Matthew Arnold told me himself"—so Mr. Oscar Browning wrote
to me—"that the reason why he omitted 'The Church of Brou' from his
Collected Works [1877] was because he found that he had described it
wrongly." It appears from his *Letters* that he passed through Bourg in 1858,
but he did not stop to see the Church.

licence, in matter of geography, was the more justified by the poetic artifice which enhances the effect of the glorious third part by contrast with the tamer introduction. As it thus stands, the conclusion bursts upon the reader with a sense of delighted surprise. Quinet's prose is closely followed, but the poet makes it his own by apt adornment, and no passage in Matthew Arnold is (in Professor Saintsbury's phrase) more full of " star-showers " than that which begins :

> So sleep, for ever sleep, O marble Pair !—

and ends :

> Then, gazing up through the dim pillars high,
> The foliaged marble forest where ye lie,
> *Hush*, ye will say, *it is eternity!*
> *This is the glimmering verge of Heaven, and these*
> *The columns of the heavenly palaces.*
> And in the sweeping of the wind your ear
> The passage of the Angels' wings will hear,
> And on the lichen-crusted leads above
> The rustle of the eternal rain of love.

" The Church of Brou " is not the only case in which Arnold fell into some mistake from not having seen places which he described. When he wrote " Tristram and Iseult " he could not have been to Cornwall, or he would certainly have heard how Tintagel is pronounced. In all his earlier editions he made the word a dactyl, as in :

> To Tȳntăgïl from Ireland bore—
> Keeps his court in Tyntagil—
> The palace towers of Tyntagil—
> Ah no! she is asleep in Tyntagil—

and in other lines. The long syllable is properly
the second, and when this was pointed out to
Arnold he rewrote the lines, as thus :

> From Ireland to Cornwall bore—
> Dwells on loud Tyntagel's hill—
> Tyntagel on its surge-beat hill—
> Ah no! she is asleep in Cornwall now.

The first and the last of these alterations are
somewhat perfunctory. The revision was done,
I think, less in pleasure than as a school task
in correction of false quantities, as sacrifices on
the altar of accuracy. The study of Arnold's
different editions is full of interest, but rather for
his rejections, reinclusions, and rearrangements of
whole pieces than for alterations in particular
lines or words. " The Church of Brou," already
discussed, is one instance of rearrangement. The
treatment, in successive editions, of the lyrics
variously called " Switzerland " and " To Marguerite " is another. Why were the poems at
one time separated ? Were they all written of a
piece ? Are there other lyrics which may be
connected with them ? Who, if any one, was
Marguerite ? She had " sweet eyes of blue " ;
the lady of "Faded Leaves " had " eyes too
expressive to be blue, too lovely to be grey." But

the poet's reticence has never been broken, and we must beware of chatter about Marguerite. How severe was Arnold's standard of self-criticism is shown by the poems which at one time or another he abstained from reprinting. His reasons for rejecting "Empedocles" were given in the famous Preface of 1853. It was sacrificed to a theory, but was revived in 1867 at the petition of Robert Browning. Why "In Utrumque Paratus" and "The New Sirens" should ever have been rejected it is difficult to see; the re-instatement was due in each case to Mr. Swin-burne. That Arnold refrained for thirty years from reprinting the memorial verses called "Haworth Churchyard" was due, as Sir Robert-son Nicoll has shown, to hesitation about his praise of one of the "two gifted women"; the poet waived the point at the suggestion of Dean Boyle, who did not see, we may suppose, why the fine tribute to the genius of Charlotte Brontë should be sacrificed to doubts about Harriet Martineau. Unsparing though Arnold was in rejection, he was less careful in revision. He often attained a perfect felicity, but his ear was far from faultless. He did not alter a line so cacophonous as :

Calm's not life's crown, though calm is well,

or so pedestrian as :

Haunts him that he has not made what he should.

There is, however, one instance in which Arnold revised and improved a piece already well-nigh perfect.   This is " The Scholar-Gipsy "—

> The story of that Oxford scholar poor,
> Of shining parts and quick inventive brain.

The first edition had " Of pregnant parts," and it were needless to dwell on the improvement made by the alteration.   The Scholar left Oxford and joined the gipsies :

> And I, he said, the secret of their art,
> When fully learn'd, will to the world impart :
> But it needs heaven-sent moments for this skill.

The last line is perfect and haunts the memory, but it was a second thought.   The first edition had " But it needs happy moments for this skill "—less happily, because the rhythm needs in that place the weightier sound which " heaven-sent " supplied.   A revision in another stanza has been questioned on the point of sound, and has a curious interest for those who know " the stripling Thames at Bablockhythe."   There the Scholar-Gipsy was met "trailing in the cool stream thy fingers wet "

> As the slow punt swings round.

So Arnold first wrote, and so the line stands in the cheap editions which appeared when the earlier versions of his poems passed out of copyright ; but when the piece was revised for the

" new and complete edition " of 1877, the line had been altered to this :

As the punt's rope chops round.

Each version has been criticised. I remember a letter in the *Westminster Gazette* in which the writer denounced what was really the poet's first version as " the emendation of some twentieth-century fiend who had never heard the old rope chopping." On the other hand, Mr. George Russell includes the revised version among " ineuphonious " lines collected from the poet to show that " where Nature has withheld the ear for music, no labour and no art can supply the want." In this particular case I cannot agree. I think I see why Arnold preferred the second version, and I submit that his preference was sound. The line as first written was pretty, but was too general. It would apply to any ferry where the punt is poled across heading up stream and swinging round to make the other bank. But Arnold, on second thoughts, or perhaps after revisiting the place, remembered that the ferry at Bablockhythe was not of this sort, and decided—true poet that he was—to make his description more particular. The ferry in old days was worked by a rope which " chopped round " a roller on the boat. The line as the poet rewrote it was less smooth in sound, but was in harmony with the thing

described. That he was bent upon enhancing
and particularising the local colour may be in-
ferred from another alteration in the stanza made
at the same time :

> And leaning backward in a pensive dream,
> And fostering in thy lap a heap of flowers
> Pluck'd in shy fields and distant woodland bowers.

So the lines were first printed, but on revision the
generic " woodland " was altered to the place-
name " Wychwood."   A happy emendation in
every way : the word has a witchery in its sound
and for its associations; the introduction of a
place in the northern part of the county adds
point to " distant "; and the country known as
Wychwood Forest is still famous for its rich
variety of beautiful wild flowers and of gipsy
simples.   This alteration may serve as the poet's
answer in advance to one of the most perverse
criticisms ever made by a man of taste.   Dr.
Garnett of the British Museum thought that,
though the charm of Arnold's pieces may be
" enhanced for Oxonians," yet " the numerous
local allusions which endear the poem to those
familiar with the scenery, simply worry when not
understood."   On this amazing deliverance Professor Saintsbury has said some faithful words :
" One may not be an Athenian, and never have
been at Athens, yet be able to enjoy the local
colour of the *Phaedrus*. One may not be an
Italian, and never have been in Italy, yet find

the *Divina Commedia* made not teasing but infinitely vivid and agreeable by Dante's innumerable references to his country, Florentine and
general.   That some keener thrill, some nobler
gust, may arise in the reading of the poem to
those who have actually watched

The line of festal light in Christ Church Hall

from above Hinksey, who know the Fyfield elm
in May, and have trailed their fingers in the
stripling Thames at Bablockhythe, may be
granted.   But in the name of Bandusia and of
Gargarus "—and, as may be interpolated for a
modern instance, of Grantchester—" what offence
can these things give to any worthy wight who
by his ill-luck has not seen them with eyes ? "

Keats, who might have beaten them all, and
whose felicity of phrase was in his best pieces
impeccable, had few opportunities of revising
his work after its first appearance in print, and
such opportunity may count for much, not only
because, as we have seen, it enables a poet to
profit by criticism, but for another reason which
I think will appeal to every penman.   In all
literary work it is a great aid to revision to be
able to see how the words look in type.   Literature is a means of communication from mind to
mind.   So long as the words remain in the author's
mind or in writing by his own hand, he cannot

bring to bear upon them quite the same detached consideration that becomes possible when they are transferred to cold print. The process of proof-correction fixes the attention and compels the author to put himself more vividly in the reader's place. The author becomes his own critic. Points of obscurity or ambiguity and possibilities of refinement which had hitherto escaped his notice occur to him, sometimes so largely that editors or publishers request writers to observe that pieces should not be rewritten on proof-sheets, while publishers protect themselves by a tax upon authors' corrections. Each new edition that goes to press gives a poet a new occasion for revision, and Keats had few such opportunities, but he had some, and in other cases manuscripts of his have been preserved from which it is possible to trace the stages in the poet's work. A fair-copy manuscript of *Hyperion*, now in the British Museum,[1] discloses many felicitous corrections introduced upon second, and sometimes upon third thoughts. One instance has been given on a previous page. There is another in the eighth and ninth lines of the poem. Keats is describing the silence round about the lair of Saturn. " No stir of air was there "—

> Not so much life as what an eagle's wing
> Would spread upon a field of green-ear'd corn.

[1] An account of this MS. was printed in the *Times* of October 10, 1904.

So it was first written. In the manuscript the lines were altered thus :

> Not so much life as on a summer's day
> Robs not at all the dandelion's fleece—

an improvement, as giving a better picture of stirless air ; but Keats was not yet quite satisfied, and the second line finally gave place to this :

> Robs not one light seed from the feathered grass.

Certainly an improvement again : " the feathered grass " is prettier than " the dandelion's fleece," and " not one light seed " is better, if only because more particular and more pictorial, than " not at all." The appeal to the mind's eye which is made more vivid by the substitution of a particular statement for a general has been noted several times already, and there is another instance a few lines further on in *Hyperion*. The Titaness, a goddess of the infant world, is being described :

> By her in stature the tall Amazon
> Had stood a pigmy's height : she would have ta'en
> Achilles by the hair and bent his neck ;
> Or with a finger eas'd Ixion's pain.

The picture of the Titaness taking Achilles by the hair was already perfect, but the reference to Ixion was felt to be too general, and Keats altered the last line, thus :

> Or with a finger stay'd Ixion's wheel.

Another piece which was greatly improved on

revision is the sonnet " To Sleep," one of eight
almost perfect sonnets, says Mr. Bridges :

O soft embalmer of the still midnight !
   Shutting, with careful fingers and benign,
Our gloom-pleas'd eyes, embower'd from the light,
   Enshaded in forgetfulness divine ;
 O soothest Sleep !   If so it please thee, close
   In midst of this thine hymn, my willing eyes,
Or wait the amen, ere thy poppy throws
   Around my bed its lulling charities ;
   Then save me, or the passed day will shine
Upon my pillow, breeding many woes ;
   Save me from curious conscience, that still lords [1]
Its strength for darkness, burrowing like a mole ;
   Turn the key deftly in the oiled wards,
And seal the hushed casket of my soul.

But now read this earlier version as found in the Dilke MSS. :

O soft embalmer of the still Midnight
Shutting with careful fingers and benign
Our gloom-pleas'd eyes embowered from the light ;
As wearisome as darkness is divine.
O soothest sleep, if so it please thee, close
My willing eyes in midst of this thine hymn,
Or wait the amen ere thy poppy throws
Its sweet death dews o'er every pulse and limb,
Then shut the hushed Casket of my soul,
And turn the key round in the oiled wards,
And let it rest until the morn has stole,
Bright tressed from the grey east's shuddering bourn.

Every alteration was an improvement.   The

---

[1] Mr. Forman' suggests (rightly surely) " hoards " for " lords," saying tha
Keats would very likely spell it " hords."

fourth line in the earlier version is commonplace ;
it was replaced by the beautiful

> Enshaded in forgetfulness divine.

The eighth line shows an almost equal improvement, and Mr. Buxton Forman has noted the
high poetic instinct which led Keats on second
thoughts to transpose the tenth and ninth lines
and place them at the end of the poem. But the
crowning example from Keats of the way in which
the greatest felicities sometimes come only on
second thoughts is to be found elsewhere. It is
in the lines of the " Ode to a Nightingale," which
have been often quoted, since Matthew Arnold
led the way in such sort, as standards of natural
magic in words and touchstones of perfection
in poetry. The poem was written one morning
under a plum-tree in a Hampstead garden, but
perfection did not come in the sudden glory of
a minute. The lines were first written thus :

> The same that oft-times hath
> Charm'd *the wide* casements, opening on the foam
> Of *keelless* seas, in faery lands forlorn.

A beautiful recollection, even so, of a favourite
picture, the Enchanted Castle of Claude ; but
any casements may be wide, and there is no poetic
suggestiveness in making them either wide or
narrow. And again " keelless " is an ugly
word which hisses, and it gives the imagination

less scope than the word which was substituted on revision :

> The same that oft-times hath
> Charm'd *magic* casements, opening on the foam
> Of *perilous* seas, in faery lands forlorn.[1]

Half the enchantment of the lines came with the poet's second thoughts. Not always, however, were the second thoughts of Keats the better. Lord Houghton was certainly right in giving us the manuscript version of "La Belle Dame sans Merci" in place of that which was printed in Leigh Hunt's *Indicator* :

> O what can ail thee, Knight at arms,
> Alone and palely loitering ?

So Keats first wrote. Who or what, one wonders, induced him to alter this opening to

> O what can ail thee, wretched wight,
> Alone and palely loitering ?

The earlier version sets one of the characters clearly before us in the opening lines, whereas the phrase " wretched wight " is conventional and not distinctive. " The Knight-at-arms," says Mr. Bridges, " gives the keynote of romance and aloofness from real life, and the suggestion of armour is of the greatest value to the general colouring." Moreover, as one of the editors of Keats has sagely remarked, we have already

---

[1] The original draft of the poem showing these revisions was published by Sir Sidney Colvin in the *Monthly Review* for March 1903.

been told that the wight was wretched by being asked what could ail him.   It is easier to understand, but not to approve, another alteration in the poem.   In describing the lure of the enchantress Keats had written :

> She took me to her elfin grot
>> And there she wept and sigh'd full sore,
> And there I shut her wild wild eyes
>> With kisses four.
> And there she lulled me asleep.

On revision for the press the lines were altered thus :

> She took me to her elfin grot,
>> And there she gaz'd and sighed deep,
> And there I shut her wild sad eyes—
>> So kiss'd to sleep.
> And there we slumber'd on the moss.

Presumably it was the " kisses four " and the fun which Keats himself had made of them that caused these alterations.   In sending the piece to his brother and sister, Keats had written : " Why kisses four, you will say, why four ? Because I wish to restrain the headlong impetuosity of my Muse : she would fain have said ' score ' without hurting the rhyme, but we must temper the imagination, as the Critics say, with judgment.   I was obliged to choose an even number that both eyes might have fair play, and to speak truly I think two apiece quite sufficient.   Suppose I had said seven, there would have been three and a half apiece, a very

awkward affair, and well got out of on my side."
The letter shows the poet in a pleasant light:
it is the sort of letter that Rossetti might have
written. But a sense of humour is one thing;
a fear of ridicule is another. The revised version
was tame compared with the first. Besides, when
it comes to counting kisses a poet should not
care a farthing for the possible cavil of crabbed
greybeards.

There is one place in Keats about which I am
never quite able to make up my mind:

A

Ah would 'twere so with many
A gentle girl and boy !
But were there ever any
Writhed not at passèd joy ?
To know the change and feel it,
When there is none to heal it
Nor numbed sense to steel it,
Was never said in rhyme.

B

But in the soul's December
The fancy backward strays,
And darkly doth remember
The hue of golden days.
In woe the thought appalling
Of bliss gone, past recalling,
Brings o'er the heart a falling
Not to be told in rhyme.

Which reading do you prefer for this third stanza
of the song " In a drear-nighted December " ?

" A " is the one that was printed, " B " was
found in a friend's album ;[1] and if the choice
had to be decided on the last four lines of each
version, there could be no question. The last
four of " B " are almost banal, and the phrase " a
falling " might have been used by Mrs. Gamp.
But the case is different with the first four lines.
Each of the other stanzas has " December "
in the first line and " remember " in the third.
Thus version B gains something by the contrasted
repetition of the words, and I have often wondered
whether, if Keats had lived to revise his poems,
he might not have combined the first four lines
of B with the last four of A.

Among the most interesting of *repentirs* are
those which one poet has made in consequence
of the criticism, or at the suggestion, of another.
There is a famous instance in Wordsworth's
" Thanksgiving Ode (1815)."   As first issued
(1816) the piece contained the following lines :

> But Thy most dreaded instrument,
> In working out a pure intent,
> Is Man arrayed for mutual slaughter,—
> Yea, Carnage is Thy daughter.

The temptation of rhyme had led the poet into a

[1] I copied the version from the *Athenæum* of September 15, 1883, to
which journal it was sent by Mr. Francis V. Woodhouse, who had found it
in a MS. book belonging to his brother, the friend of Keats. Sir Sidney
Colvin tells us, I see, that the version " cannot yet be regarded as entitled
to a place in the established canon of Keats's work " (*Times Literary Supplement*, May 2, 1918).

false step. Byron saw his opportunity and took it. The passage was pilloried in the seventh canto of *Don Juan* :

> Carnage (so Wordsworth tells you) is God's daughter ;
> If *he* speak truth, she is Christ's sister . . .

and Byron, in giving the reference, appended a pungent note : " This is perhaps as pretty a pedigree for murder as ever was found out by Garter King at Arms." The hit went home, and Wordsworth recast the passage thus :

> But Man is Thy most awful instrument,
> In working out a pure intent ;
> Thou cloth'st the wicked in their dazzling mail,
> And for Thy righteous purpose they prevail.

I have never made a close study of Wordsworth's *own* second thoughts ; but such as I have chanced to note are seldom improvements. If this be the case generally, it is what might be expected, for Wordsworth is of all great poets the most unequal, and his happiest things came by grace and not by reflection. A peculiarly unhappy thought occurred when he revised " the most majestic of his poems," [1] written originally under stimulus from the sixth *Aeneid*. " Laodamia " is Wordsworth's " one great utterance on heroic love," and the penultimate passage, as it first came to the poet, was worthy of the Virgilian echo which followed :

---

[1] F. W. H. Myers.

Ah, judge her gently who so deeply loved !
Her, who in reason's spite, yet without crime,
Was in a trance of passion thus removed ;
Delivered from the galling yoke of time
And those frail elements—to gather flowers
Of blissful quiet 'mid unfading bowers.
—Yet tears to human sufferings are due, etc.

So wrote the Muse, holding the poet's pen ; but the moralist afterwards took the passage in hand and sermonised it into this :

Thus, all in vain exhorted and reproved,
She perished ; and, as for a wilful crime,
By the just Gods whom no weak pity moved,
Was doomed to wear out her appointed time,
Apart from happy Ghosts, that gather flowers
Of blissful quiet 'mid unfading bowers.
—Yet tears to human sufferings are due, etc.

Lord Morley in his edition prints this later version; it is one of the many services rendered to Wordsworth by Matthew Arnold in his volume of *Selections* that he restores the earlier version. The well-known " Lines " on the expected death of Mr. Fox contained this passage :

A Power is passing from the earth
To breathless Nature's dark abyss ;
But when the Mighty pass away
What is it more than this
That Man, who is from God sent forth,
Doth yet again to God return ?

So the poet wrote at the time of inspiration, but

afterwards he reflected and altered the third line into this :

But when the great and good depart.

Here again Lord Morley gives the revised version, but Matthew Arnold restores the original, and his preference will, I think, be generally approved. The revised version tells us, it is true, that Wordsworth considered Mr. Fox to be a good as well as a great man, and the judgment is interesting, but it is added at the cost of poetic effect. The lines were written, as the poet's prefatory note tells us, during a walk at evening after a stormy day, and the poet had just heard the tremendous news that the death of Fox was momentarily expected. "Loud was the vale." "Thousands were waiting the fulfilment of their fear." It was the passing of the Mighty that was the note of the piece.

For one of his retouchings I once owed the poet some grudge. In the second volume of *Modern Painters* Ruskin describes how Wordsworth conceives a group of children as "rooted flowers" which

Beneath an old grey oak as violets lie.

I hunted and hunted and could not find the passage. I turned in my extremity to a friend, whose untimely loss was deplored by all students of literature—the late Professor Churton Collins. He was good enough to hunt and hunt also,

and at last pronounced with the emphasis
characteristic of him : " I tell you positively that
Ruskin is wrong ; the line is not in Wordsworth."
A few days later I asked a girl friend, who is
fond of Wordsworth, to see if she could find the
passage. By chance her edition was an early
one, and there in the original version of the
poet's " Descriptive Sketches among the Alps "
the passage disclosed itself. Wordsworth, not
knowing that his comparison of the children to
" rooted flowers " was to be the theme of an
eloquent eulogy in *Modern Painters*, had in the
most inconsiderate manner changed them, in all
subsequent editions, into the likeness of " lambs
or fawns," and placed them

> Under a hoary oak's thin canopy.

Such are the pitfalls which poets lay with their
retouchings, and such the long disappointments
and sudden joys of the commentator.

Sometimes a poet repents, but knows not how
to amend. There is a curious instance of this
incomplete repentance in the first line of Wordsworth's " We are seven." As originally printed
(*Lyrical Ballads*, 1798), the piece began thus :

> A simple child, dear brother Jim,
> That lightly draws its breath,
> And feels its life in every limb,
> What should it know of death ?

Very naturally, Wordsworth afterwards took out

" dear brother Jim." He thought the rhyme
to " limb " ludicrous, and the whole thing too
colloquial even for him. Besides, Coleridge
had suggested the line half in jest, and they had
let it pass—so Wordsworth says—only for the
fun of " hitching - in " a mutual friend whose
familiar name was Jim. But when the mild
little joke was played out, what was to take its
place ? The poet seems to have given it up,
and the first line appeared, rhymeless and incomplete, thus :

> ——A simple child,
> That lightly draws its breath, etc.

Coleridge, to whose frankness of self-criticism
I have already referred, was sometimes content
to confess a blemish or an altered opinion without
amending the lines. In an early poem he had
written :

> He knows, the Spirit that in secret sees,
> Of whose omniscient and all-spreading Love
> Aught to implore were impotence of mind.

Upon revision he let the lines stand, but appended this footnote : " I utterly recant the
sentiment, it being written in Scripture, ' Ask
and it shall be given you '; and my human
reason being, moreover, convinced of the propriety of offering petitions as well as thanksgiving
to the Deity." In one case, although altering
a line, he reprinted the original. The seventh

stanza of the "Ode to the Departing Year"
(1796) thus begins :

> Not yet enslaved, not wholly vile,
> O Albion !   O my mother Isle !

and the footnote to the first line is : " O doomed
to fall, enslaved and vile—1796." There is
something very winning in such frank memorial
of hasty judgment.

Second thoughts are best, says the proverb,
by way of a criticism of life. " Repentirs,"
says a critic of another art, " are always wrong."
Of poetry, neither statement can be accepted as
universally, or even generally, true. " The wind
bloweth where it listeth, and thou hearest the
sound thereof, but canst not tell whence it
cometh." The saying is true of every one that
is born of the Spirit of poetry. " What constitutes the true artist," says a master of style,
" is not the slowness or quickness of the process,
but the absolute success of the result " ; and,
" as with those labourers in the parable, the
prize is independent of the mere length of the
actual day's work." Beauty and truth may come
together and find the exactly right words in the
flash of a moment, or after many attempts. Yet
in the former case Tennyson's saying should be
remembered : " Perfection in art is perhaps
more sudden sometimes than we think, but then
the long preparation for it, that unseen germina-

tion, *that* is what we ignore and forget." Wordsworth wrote best when he revised least ; but who
can say how long he " went humming and booing
about " (as an old dalesman remembered him)
before he " murmured near the running brooks
a music sweeter than their own " ?   One thing
alone is certain in this matter—that poetry is an
art, and that " art is long." The new age is
sometimes impatient of perfection :

> Thundering and bursting
> In torrents, in waves—
> Carolling and shouting
> Over tombs, amid graves. . . .
>   *—Ah, so the silence was !*
>   *So was the hush.*

INDEX

Acton, Lord, *Lectures on the French Revolution*, on Ruskin, 34 ; *Letters to Mary Gladstone*, on Carlyle, 208, on the Fifty Best Books, 185, on Froude, 208

Addison, 198

Aeronautics, 152

Aeschylus, 182, 187

Akenside, 218

Alexander, Francesca, *The Story of Ida*, 31

Allen, George, 51

Allen, Grant, 73, 78, 81, 98

Allingham, William, 288

Alliteration, 43, 44, 50, 264, 281

Ancestry, in biography, 13

Anders-streben, 244

Ariosto, 182

Armstrong, Sir Walter, on Turner, 212

Arnold, Matthew, index to, wanted, 60 ; his favourite passages in literature, 186 ; obituary notice of, 125 ; poems, revision and rearrangement of, 297-301

particular works quoted or referred to :—Church of Brou, 294-6 ; *Culture and Anarchy*, 93 ; Empedocles, 292, 298 ; Epilogue to Laocoön, 244 ; *Essays in Criticism* (and other essays) on: Burke, 199, Dryden, 193, Heine, 103, natural magic, 306, New Journalism, 126, Ruskin, 34, 52, Shelley, 60, 204 ; Faded Leaves, 297 ; *Friendship's Garland*, 117, 122 ; Haworth Churchyard, 298 ; In Utrumque

Paratus, 25, 298 ; *Letters*, 18, 19 ; *Literature and Dogma*, 89 ; The Lord's Messengers, 101 ; The New Age, 317 ; Revolutions, 298 ; Selections from Wordsworth, 312, 313 ; The Scholar Gipsy, 299 ; To Marguerite, 297 ; Tristram and Iseult, 296 ; Switzerland, 297 ; Youth and Calm, 298

Art is long, 317

Asquith, H. H., on Prussian militarism, 165 ; on Ruskin, 34, 37

Attar, 275

Austen, Jane, 202

Avebury, Lord, 183

Babbage, Charles, 270

Back numbers, 80

Bacon, 34, 198

Balfour, A. J., on German militarism, 166

Bayle, 72

Beeching, Dean, 95, 99

Belgium, 165

Bell, Mackenzie, *Life of Christina Rossetti* quoted, 178

Benson, A. C., 95

Bentham, 169

Bentley, emendation of classical texts, 247 ; of Milton, 248

Best, Mr. Justice, 68

Bible as literature, 185

Binyon, Mrs., *Nineteenth Century Prose*, 48

Biographies, some of the best, 3, 5, 8, 10, 11, 13, 20, 21, 28, 29, 31 ; some of the worst, 31-2, 211

319

Biography, an art, 1-6 ; ancestry in, 13 ; arrangement, 19 ; author in relation to subject, 24 ; brevity, 6-9; candour, 20 ; composite biographies, 2 ; foils in, 29 ; hero-worship, 21, 29 ; history and, 9, 12, 23 ; indiscretion in, 18 ; individual character, 11 ; irony of (least known lives best worth knowing), 30 ; letters in, 15, 20, 24 ; politics and, 23 ; relevance in, 9-17 ; selection, 18 ; subject, 22-33

Birrell, A., 60, 113

Bismarck and Busch, 23

Blake, William, 81, 192, 242

Bobby, 148

Bodleian Library, 65

Bonfires for books, 65

Book Monthly, 74

Bookman's Inferno, 61 ; Paradise, viii, 81 ; Purgatory, 80

Books, and the war, v ; stitching of, 79 ; *versus* newspapers, 113

Bossuet, 186

Boswell's *Johnson*, 3, 5, 9, 11, 12, 25

Bowles, W. L., 179

Boyle, C., 247

Boyle, Dean, 298

Brest-Litovsk, negotiations at, 170

Bridges, Robert, on Keats, 190, 191, 192, 305, 307

Bright, John, Life of, 28 ; on good English, 139

British Empire, new name proposed for, 173

British Museum, Keats MS. in, 303 ; Reading Room, 198

Bromley, William, 69

Brontë, Charlotte, M. Arnold on, 298 ; in the *Cornhill*, 107 ; on Jane Austen, 202 ; *Villette*, 187

Brooke, Rupert, "The Old Vicarage, Grantchester," 302

Brougham, Lord, 148

Brown, Dr. John, 31

Browning, Mrs., and the *Cornhill*, 85 ; on the Magazines, 112

Browning, Oscar, 295 *n.*

Browning, Robert, 14, 199, 298 ; poems quoted or referred to :— *Ferishtah's Fancies* (Epilogue),

199 ; My Last Duchess, 8 ; A Light Woman, 27 ; *Parleyings*, 213 ; Rabbi Ben Ezra, 33 ; Old Pictures in Florence, 204 ; One Word More, 239, 240, 241, 270 ; *The Ring and the Book*, 3, 180, 198, 293 (Book vii. 935) ; Mr. Sludge the Medium, 1 ; A Toccata of Galuppi, 92, 233

Browning Society, 240

Burke, 175, 186, 199

Busch, Moritz, 24

Butler, Samuel, *Alps and Sanctuaries*, 180, index to, 72 ; *Evolution Old and New*, index to, 73, 74 ; *Note-Books*, on immortality, 58, on style, 39, 41

Byron, 198 ; and Turner, 218, 233 ; on the Huns, 159 *n.*; Childe Harold, 187, 218, 233 ; Don Juan, on Wordsworth, 311

Bywater, Ingram, 248

Cairns, Dr., Life of Dr. John Brown, 31

Callimachus, 223, 247

Calverley, translations from Theocritus and Virgil, 188

Campbell, Lord, 56

Campbell, Thomas, Hohenlinden, 159 *n.*

Caricature, 127

Carlisle, Lord, Journals, 181

Carlyle, Mrs., letter from Ruskin to, 36

Carlyle, Thomas, 198 ; index to his Works, 58, 70, 74 ; on books without an index, 54 ; on journalism, 117 ; *French Revolution*, 187 ; *Life of Schiller*, 32 ; *Life of Sterling*, 31 ; *Sartor Resartus*, 187

Carthage and Turner, 231, 245

Casaubon, Isaac, 247

Cavour, 147

Caxton, 198

Chatham, as a subject of biography, 15, 25, 26

Chaucer, 198

Cherfils, Christian, *Canon de Turner*, 59

Chesterton, G. K., on Browning, 14 ; on Dickens, 32
Cicero, 151, 179 *n.*
Clarendon, Lord, and disarmament, 17
Class Lists in literature, 176, 181, 190
Classical texts, 247
Claude Lorraine, 306
Claudian, 175
Clemenceau, M., 160
Club, The, 181, 182
Cobden, on Thucydides, 205
Coleridge, Derwent, 256, 258
Coleridge, Lord, 60, 268
Coleridge, S. T., revisions in his poetry, 251-9, 315 ; self-criticism, 252 ; Ancient Mariner, 251-9 ; Kubla Khan, 187 ; Ode to France, 194 ; Ode to the Departing Year, 194, 316 ; To a Friend (1794), 315
Coleridge, Sara, 252
Collins, J. Churton, 97, 123, 267, 313
Colvin, Sir Sidney, 94, 97, 109, 307 *n.*, 310 *n.*
Comte, on Tacitus, 207
Concise Oxford Dictionary, 168
Conrad, Joseph, *Lord Jim,* 180
Cook, Dutton, 94
Cornhill Magazine, genesis of, 81 ; George Smith and, 81, 82, 96 ; a set of, and its fate, 77-81 ; Alma Mater of the essay, 95 ; anecdotic interest, 107 ; biographical notes in, 103 ; buried copy in, 100 ; contributors to, 82, 83, 90, 97, 103 ; cover, 109 ; editors of : — the first, 82, second, 96, third, 98, later, 99, 100 ; first numbers, 83, 103 ; footnotes to history in, 105 ; illustrations, 108 ; note of, 92, 99, 111 ; novels in, 82, 86 ; prices, 102 ; title, 109
Cory, William, Amaturus, 129
Courage of literary opinions, 204
Cowell, Professor, 274
Crashaw, 178
Creep-hole, 163
Crimean War, 165, 168, 203

Croker, J. W., 57
Curzon, Lord, on Tennyson, 196
Cust, Henry, 138

Daily Mail, 153
Daily News, 114
Dante, 183, 187, 302
Darley, George, 282 *n.*
Delane, J. T., 123, 132
De Morgan, A., 151
Demosthenes, 207
De Quincey, 34 ; on Burke, 199
Dibdin, T., 223
Dickens, and the *Daily News,* 114, 118 ; on Thackeray, 90, 105 ; *David Copperfield,* 119 ; *Hard Times,* 118 ; Martin *Chuzzlewit,* 115, 116 ; *Pickwick,* 58, 115 ; *Pictures from Italy,* 114
Dickens Dictionary, 58
Dictionary of National Biography, 7, 32
Disraeli, Benjamin, as subject of biography, 27, 29 ; sayings of, 58 *n.,* 122, 209
Dixon, Canon, 203
Don Quixote, 58, 200, 201
Douce, F., 61
Doyle, Sir A. Conan, 157
Doyle, Sir F. H., The Private of the Buffs, 154
Doyle, Richard, 106
Dramatic criticism, 120, 121, 125
Dryden, Alexander's Feast, 193 ; Mrs. Anne Killigrew, 193
Dumont, M., 210

Edinburgh Review, 200
Editions de Luxe, 60
Edward VII., titles, 174
Eliot, George, 202 ; *Middlemarch,* 33 ; *Romola,* 103, 108
English language, as written by Controllers, 136 ; corrupted by journalism, 131 *seq.*
English men of letters, the twenty greatest, 198
Essays, 93, 94, 95

Fields, J. T., 91
Finberg, A. J., books on Turner, 211, 214, 234

Finish in art, 8, 54
First editions, 80, 107, 259
Fisher, H. L. A., v
FitzGerald, Edward, *Letters*, quoted or referred to, on :— Jane Austen, 202, Browning, 3, *Cornhill Magazine*, 83, George Eliot, 202, Scott, 201, 202, style, 40, Tennyson's revisions, 267, Thackeray, 203 ; Omar Khayyám, revisions in, 270-281
Flying, 106, 152
Forbes, Archibald, 126
Forman, H. Buxton, 305 *n.*, 306
Forster, John, and the *Daily News*, 114
Forsyth, W., *Captivity of Napoleon at St. Helena*, 56
Fortescue, Chichester, 16
Fortnightly Review, 186
Fox, Charles James, 13, 127, 204 *n.*, 312, 313
Franks, The, 159
Fraser's Magazine, 89
Freeman, E. A., and Stubbs, 119 ; on Arrian, 11 ; *Norman Conquest*, index to, 74
Froude, J. A., as editor of *Fraser's*, 89 ; Lord Acton on, 208 ; *Life of Carlyle*, 21 ; *Short Studies*, 60 ; on Tacitus (Lives of the Saints), 207
Fuller, Thomas, on indexes, 62
Furnivall, F. J., 38 *n.*

Garibaldi, books on, by G. M. Trevelyan, 28, 29, 105 ; blouses, 148 ; on militarism, 167
Garnett, Richard, on M. Arnold's Oxford poems, 301 ; on Carlyle's *Life of Sterling*, 31
Garrett, Edmund, 4, 5, 179 *n.*
Geographical licence in poetry, 293, 294, 295
George, D. Lloyd, 144 ; on :— Boloism, 160, comb and clean cut, 164, militarism, 166, profiteering, 170
German Emperor, on Huns, 159 ; on Contemptibles, 161
Gibbon, 198 ; his method of reading, 61 ; *Decline and Fall*, various estimates of, 205, 206, 208
Gibbs, Philip, *The Battles of the Somme*, 150, 151
Gillray, J., 127
Gladstone, W. E., as subject of biography, 10, 26, 29 ; Homeric studies, 88 ; on the best lines in poetry, 183, 184
Gladstone bag, 147 ; claret, 147
Globe newspaper, 123
Goethe, his place as poet, 183 ; scientific studies, 88 ; on his commentators, 240 ; on the arts, 243
Gollancz, Professor, 157
Gosse, Edmund, and the *Cornhill*, 97 ; *Life of Swinburne*, 198
Gould, Sir F. C., 127
Gould, Gerald, " Oxford," 276
Gray, Thomas, on Thucydides, 207
Great men, aloofness of, 25
Greek Anthology, epigrams quoted, 179, 247
Green, J. R., as journalist, 119, 122
Greenwood, Frederick, and the *Cornhill*, 96 ; as journalist, 123
Grundy, Mrs., and the magazines, 85, 86

Hallam, Henry, on Milton, 194
Hamerton, P. G., on Ruskin (*A Painter's Camp*), 87 ; *Life of Turner*, 212, 228, 238
Hamilton, Sir W., method of reading, 61
Hansard, index to, 57, 61
Hardy, Thomas, and the *Cornhill*, 86 ; on favourite passages in literature, 176, 186 ; on the corruption of English, 131, 137
Hare, Archdeacon, 32
Harrison, Frederic, on biography (*Among my Books*), 10 ; Gibbon, Herodotus, and Thucydides (*The Meaning of History*), 204, 206 ; Ruskin's—*Harbours of England* (*Tennyson, Ruskin, and Mill*). 53, style, 36, *Unto this Last* (*John Ruskin*), 46
Hay, Ian, 148
Heber, Bishop, hymns, 177

Heine, 88

Henley, W. E., *Hospital Outlines*, 89

Herbert, George, *The Temple* (Elixir), 55

Heredity in biography, 15

Herodotus, 21, 29, 204

Heron-Allen, E., *Some Side-Lights upon E. FitzGerald's Poem*, 275

Herrick, *Noble Numbers*, 179

Hill, Dr. Birkbeck, and the *Cornhill*, 97

Historians, which is the greatest? 204-9

Holland, Lord, 241

Homer, 184, 186, 204 *n.*, 223

Hooker, 34

Horace, 186, 260, 302

Horton, Dr. R. F., *Autobiography*, vii

Houghton, Lord, edition of Keats, 103

Hugo, *Les Misérables*, 201

Hunt, Leigh, and the Bank of England, 103 ; the *Indicator*, 307

Hymns, 177

Illustrations of the 'sixties, 108

Index, Indexing, an art, 56, 68 ; an indispensable adjunct, 55, especially to Collected Works, 58 ; principles of :—one book one index, 63, many titles, 64-6, how to be arranged, 66-72 ; as propaganda, 69 ; humour in, 72 ; impartiality in, 66, 69 ; pains and pleasures of, 75-6 ; punishments proposed for omission of, 56, 61, plea in defence, 61 ; saves foot-notes, 75 ; scale of, 74 ; use of, in tasting books, 75 ; who should make ? 72 ; makers to be named, 73

Interviewing, 4

Jargon, Jargoneers, 135, 137

Jebb, Sir R., on corrupt classical texts, 246 ; on Herodotus, 204 ; on Thucydides, 208, 209

Johnson, Dr., 199 ; as subject of biography, 5 (*see also* Boswell) ; on *Clarissa Harlowe*, 57 ; on Dryden, 193 ; on Milton and Gray, 204 ; on writing to be paid, 102

Joubert, Joseph, 268

Journalese, 106, 132, 135

Journalism, modern, satirised by Victorian writers, 114-20, but contributed to by them, 122 ; not a foe of good reading, 128-131 ; alleged corruption of English by, 131-5, responsibility and temptation of in this respect, 138, importance of the craftsman's conscience, 140; personalities in, 127 ; schools of, 139 ; sensational, 84 ; space given to literature, 124-6 ; superficial, and why, 120-2, 138 ; wide range of, 124

Jowett, B., 76, 207

Juvenal, 124

Keats, the five great Odes compared, 189-192 ; revisions in his poetry, 250, 256, 302-310 ; various references, 143, 198, 199, 261

particular poems quoted or referred to : — Autumn, 190, 191 ; Grecian Urn, 190, 191 ; Hyperion, 250, 303, 304 ; In a Drear-nighted December, 309 ; Indolence, 189 ; La Belle Dame, 307 ; Maia, 190 ; Melancholy, 190, 256 ; Nightingale, 190, 192, 306 ; Psyche, 190, 192 ; Sleep, 305

Kingsley, Rev. W., on Turner, 243

Kipling, *A Diversity of Creatures*, on Horace, 186

Kitchener, Lord, 146, 148

Lairesse, Gerard de, 213

Lang, Andrew, as journalist, 123 ; handwriting, 246

Larkin, Henry, 70

Latin poetry, the finest lines in, 187, 188; the worst line in, 189

Lee, Sir Sidney, *Principles of Biography* (Leslie Stephen Lecture), 4, 7, 13

Leighton, Lord, illustrations to *Romola*, 108

Lemprière's *Classical Dictionary*, 224
Leopold, Prince, 278
Lessing's *Laocoön*, 243
Letters as biographical material, 15, 20, 24
Lever, Charles, *Charles O'Malley*, 144
Lewes, G. H., and the *Cornhill*, 83 ; *Life of Goethe*, 20
Leyland, Mr., and Whistler, 244, 245
Literature, and journalism, 113 *seq.*; and the magazines, 98, 112
Local allusions in poetry, 301
Locke, 198
Lockhart, J. G., *Life of Scott*, 6 ; review of Tennyson, 260, 261
Lovelace, Richard, 9
Lowe, Robert, as journalist, 120 ; on the battle of Marathon, 205
Lowell, J. R., index to *Biglow Papers*, 72 ; " The Present Crisis " quoted, 142
Lucas, E. V., and the *Cornhill*, 95, 99
Lucca, 47
Lucretius, 182, 263
Luxmoore, H. E., on profiteering, 172
Lyons, Lord, Life of, 17
Lyrical Ballads, 251, 254, 314
Lytton, E. Bulwer, on Scott, 202

Macaulay, Lord, 198 ; death of, 107 ; fondness for literary class-lists, 181 ; *History of England*, 64 ; limitations of, 181, 204 ; quoted or referred to, on :— The Ancient Mariner, 256, Jane Austen, 202, Boswell, 3, Don Quixote, 200, Dryden, 193, indexing, 64, 69, 73, *Lays of Ancient Rome*, 181, order of poets, 182, Richardson, 57, Shakespeare's plays, 181, Thucydides, 206, *Vicar of Wakefield*, 200, Virgil, 187
Macaulay, Z., 209
MacColl, D. S., 214 *n.*
Mackail, J. W., *Life of William Morris* quoted, 52, 203
McKenna, S., *Sonia* quoted, vii
Macmillan, Alexander, 90

Macmillan's *Magazine*, 81, 90, 112
Madvig, J. N., 248
Magazines, literature and, 98 ; writing in, for fame and pay, 102
Magenta, 148
Maitland, F. W., *Life of Leslie Stephen*, 86, 94, 97, 100
Martial, epigram (i. 18), 147
Martineau, Harriet, 298
Maxwell, Sir Herbert, *Life of Lord Clarendon*, 17
May, Phil, 8
Medwin, T., *Conversations of Byron*, quoted (Shelley), 194
Mendelism, 65
Meredith, George, favourite passages in literature, 186, 187 ; " Love in the Valley," revisions in, 281-7 ; on Myers's *St. Paul*, 281 *n.* ; on Leslie Stephen, 94
Michelangelo, poems, 242
Mill, J. S., and Sterling, 32 ; on Ruskin, 37 ; style, 41
Millais, Sir J., illustrations to Trollope, 108
Milton, 198 ; Bentley and, 248 ; finest lines in, 184 ; Ode on the Nativity, 194 ; on good English, 137 ; place among poets, 182, 183 ; quoted by Turner, 215, 216 ; Tennyson on, 34, 184
Mommsen on Renan, 40
Monkhouse, Cosmo, on Turner, 224, 242, 245
Morison, J. C., on Gibbon, 208
Morley, Lord, and Burke, 199 ; as journalist, 123 ; *Life of Gladstone*, 27, index, 67, 74, quoted, 183 ; *Notes on Politics and History*, quoted, 20, 23 ; *Recollections*, 16 *n.*, 126, index, 75 ; on the four sacred bards (*Miscellanies*, Byron), 182 ; on journalism (*Compromise*), 117 ; on Mill's style (*Recollections*), 41 ; on the most melodious line (*Recollections*), 185 ; on Ruskin (*Studies in Literature*), 34 ; *Wordsworth*, 176, 312, 313
Morris, William, and Ruskin, 52 ;

and Miss Yonge, 203 ; on the artist's delight, 131, 141

Murray, Grenville, 106

Music, 244

Myers, F. W. H., favourite passages in literature, 187 ; on Tennyson, 197 ; on Wordsworth, 311 ; *St. Paul*, revisions in, 277-81

Napoleon I., 148

Napoleon III., 105

National Gallery, buried Turners, 211

New College Essay Society, vii

New English Dictionary (Oxford Dictionary), 120, 133 n., 146, 148, 161, 167, 170

New Journalism, 126

Newman, Cardinal, style, 38, 39 (Mozley's *Letters of J. H. N.* ii. 477)

Newnes, Sir G., 128

Newspapers, have they souls ? 91 ; traditional styles in, 95. *See also* Journalism

Newton, Lord, *Life of Lord Lyons*, 17

New Witness, quoted, 169

Nicoll, Sir W. Robertson, 298

North, Roger, *Lives of the Norths*, 11, 12 n.

Norton, C. E., on Carlyle and Froude, 21

Novels, serial publication of, 81 ; should they be indexed ? 58 ; which is the best ? 199-204

Ode, which is the best English ? 193-5

Officialese (*Times*, Aug. 9, 1917), 135

Oman, Professor, 147

Omar Khayyám Club, 138, 275

Opie, John, *R.A.*, 66

Osborn, E. B., *The Muse in Arms*, 142

Ossian, 218

Ovid and Turner, 223, 224

Paganini, 88

Palgrave, F. T., 271

Pall Mall Gazette, 122, 183, 185 ; of fiction, 116

Palmerston, Lord, 29

Pater, Walter, as journalist, 122 ; on Anders-streben in art, 244 ; on style, 40, 54, 316

Paul, H. W., *Men and Letters*, 268

Payn, James, and the *Cornhill*, 98, 99

Peeler, 148

Pindar, 194

Plagiarism, 293

Plato, 39, 301

Plutarch's Lives, 7, 9, 10, 12, 14

Poe, E. A., "To Helen" quoted, 205

Poetry, or music, the norm of the arts ? 244 ; the finest line in, 184 ; perfection in, 191, 316, 317

Poole's index to periodicals, 103

Pope, 198 ; his villa and Turner, 217

Presentation copies, 209

Proctor, R. A., 98, 106

Proof-reading, 302

Prout, Father (F. S. Mahony), 111

Punch, 161 ; on Turner, 235, 236

Purcell, E. S., *Life of Manning*, 21

Quarterly Review, 260, 282

Quercia, 47

Quiller-Couch, Sir A., on Keats's Odes, 190, 191, 192 ; on Jargon, 135

Quinet, E., and Matthew Arnold, 294, 296

Raglan, Lord, and Miss Yonge, 203

Raleigh, Prof. Sir W., on Boswell (*Six Essays on Johnson*), 3

Rawlinson, W. G., on Turner's poetry, 226

Reading, aids to, 61

Renan, style, 40

Revisions in poetry, 101, 249 *seq.* (*See further* Second Thoughts)

Rhodes, Cecil, 5

Riccio, Luigi del, 242

Richardson, Samuel, 57

Ritchie, Lady, *Blackstick Papers*, 93

Rogers, Thorold, 119

Rome and Turner, 226, 231

Roosevelt, Theodore, 155

Rosebery, Lord, *Chatham*, 13, 15,

25, 26 ; *Napoleon*, 56 ; on bonfires for books, 65

Rossetti, Christina, Advent, 178 ; Old and New Year Ditties, 178

Rossetti, D. G., Ave, 294 ; Blessed Damozel, revisions in, 287-92 ; Burden of Nineveh, 245 ; Last Confession, 293 ; Love's Nocturn, 292 ; on a passage in Ruskin, 53

Rossetti, W. M., on local mendacity in poetry, 293, 294

Rowlandson, T., 127

Roxburghe Club, 56

Ruskin, John, diaries and letters of, 36, 47 ; drawings of, 51 ; intellectual independence, 35, 36, 37 ; a letter to Mrs. Carlyle, 36 ; a master of English prose, 34 ; use of superlatives, 179

　Remarks of, quoted, on :—biography, 15, 30 ; Don Quixote, 200 ; Horace, 186; indexing, 75; journalism, 118 ; Leighton's *Romola* drawings, 108 ; Lockhart's Scott, 6 ; Myers's Poems, 278, 281 ; repentirs, 316 ; Rossetti's Blessed Damozel, 287 ; Scott's Novels, 201, 202 ; *The Story of Ida*, 31 ; Tennyson, 197, 269 ; Thucydides, 206 ; Turner, 218, 220, 222, 233, 240 ; *Vicar of Wakefield*, 200

　Particular works, quoted or referred to :—Collected Works, Library Edition, 36, 38, 42 *n.*, 47, 49 *n.*, 51, 53, 59, 74, 240 *n.*; *Crown of Wild Olive*, 45, 46 *n.*; *Fors Clavigera*, index, 72 ; *Harbours of England*, 53 ; Lecture on Style, 42-5 ; *Modern Painters*, 36, 43, 47, 49, 50, 52, 53, 124, 224, 313 ; *Munera Pulveris*, 89 ; *Poems*, 124 ; *Poetry of Architecture*, 35 ; *Præterita*, 35, 38, 51, 53 ; *Pre-Raphaelitism*, 222 ; *Unto this Last*, 43, 87, 173

　Style of : — formed early and natural to him, 35 ; pains taken, 38, in revising, 49 ; exact use of words, 38 ; early

manner and matter, 41-2, compared with later, 42-4, 47-9, 134 ; concentrated, 44-7 ; a word-painter, in what sense, 50-4

Ruskin, John James, 38 *n.*, 212

Russell, Sir W., 126

Saintsbury, Professor, 296, 301

Sala, G. A., 83, 117

Salisbury, Lord, as subject of biography, 27

Scott, Sir Walter, 198 ; quoted by Turner, 218 ; Waverley Novels, 13, key to, 58, which are the best ? 201

Second Thoughts of Poets, interest of, as studies in taste, 250, 259, 270 ; felicities often due to, 250 ; illustrations from :— Arnold, 101, 294-302, Coleridge, 251-9, 315-16, FitzGerald, 270-7, Keats, 250, 302-10, Meredith, 281-7, Myers, 277-81, Rossetti, 287-294, Shelley, 250, Tennyson, 101, 251, 259-70, Wordsworth, 310-15 ; not always best, 267, 269, 271, 307, 311, 316

Senior, Nassau William, 105

Shadwell, A., on profiteering, 172

Shakespeare, which are the best plays ? 182 ; *King Richard II.* quoted, 175 ; various references, 182, 183, 185, 198, 203, 248, 294

Shelley, on Coleridge, 194 ; text of, 248, 249 ; the Turner of poetry, 218 ; poems quoted or referred to :—*Alastor*, 219-20, 221, 222 ; *Julian and Maddolo*, 221, 222 ; *Lament*, 186 ; *Prometheus*, 218, 220, 221, 222 ; *Queen Mab*, 219 ; To Jane (Ariel to Miranda), 248 ; To Jane (The Recollection), 250 ; various references, 198, 199, 204

Shenstone, W. A., 98

Shrapnel, General, 149

Slip of the pen, the most unaccountable, 200 *n.*

Smith, George, and the *Cornhill*, 88, 81, 96, 99 ; anecdote of Leigh Hunt, 103
Smith, Reginald, 100
Smith, Sydney, 131
Smuts, General, v, 173
Sophocles, 182, 261
Southey's *Life of Nelson*, 8
Spectator on profiteering, 170
Spedding, James, 263
Spenser, 198
Spielmann, M. H., 41
Spiritualism, 84
Stanley, Dean, handwriting, 246
Statius, 189
Stead, W. T., 4, 126 *n.*
Stellenbosch, 149
Stephen, Sir Leslie, as editor of the *Cornhill*, 86, 89, 96, 97, 98, 100 ; his *Cornhill* essays, 93, 111 ; on journalism, 120, 122 ; on Lewes's *Life of Goethe*, 20 ; on Thackeray, 93
Sterling, John, 32
Stevenson, Robert Louis, and the *Cornhill*, 94, 95, 111 ; favourite passages in literature, 180 ; on Roger North, 12 *n.* ; style of, 39
Strachey, J. St. Loe, as editor of the *Cornhill*, 99
Stubbs, Bishop, 119
Style, 35, 39-42
Superlatives in literary estimates, injudicious, 176, but interesting, 177, and revealing, 179 ; some dealers in, 177, 199
Swift, 198
Swinburne, favourite passages in literature, 187 ; use of superlatives by, 177 ; quoted or referred to, on :—The Ancient Mariner, 256 ; Matthew Arnold, 298 ; FitzGerald's Omar, 271, 274, 275 ; Herrick, 178 ; Keats's Odes, 190, 192 ; Les Misérables, 201 ; Christina Rossetti, 177 ; Rossetti's Blessed Damozel, 287, 292 ; Tennyson, 196 ; Thackeray, 107
Sykes, Godfrey, 110
Symonds, J. A., and the *Cornhill*, 97 ; as journalist, 122 ; favourite passages in literature, 186 ; on the norm of the arts, 244

Tablet, 73
Tacitus, 205, 207-9
Taylor, Sir H., 194
Taylor, Jeremy, 34
Teddy, 154
Telegraphese, 106, 133 *n.*
Temple Bar magazine, 112
Tenniel, Sir John, 127
Tennyson, Alfred Lord, 199 ; his best poem, 195-8 ; range and variety of his work, 197 ; long period of productivity, 198 ; misprints in, 249 ; revisions in, 251, 259-70
Remarks by, quoted or referred to, on :—alliteration, 264 ; Jane Austen, 203 ; commentators, 240 ; first editions, 259 ; hissing in poetry, 267 ; hymns, 177 ; Keats, 192 ; Meredith, 282 ; poetical germination, 316 ; Scott, 202 ; the six greatest English prose writers, 34 ; Wordsworth, 184
Particular poems quoted or referred to : — Charge of the Heavy Brigade, 144 ; Charge of the Light Brigade, 269 ; Dream of Fair Women, 261, 269 ; In Memoriam, 195, 267 ; Lady of Shalott, 265 ; Locksley Hall, 260 ; Lotos Eaters, 263 ; Maud, O let not the solid ground, 129, O that 'twere possible, 196 ; Miller's Daughter, 267 ; Œnone, 187, 262, 268 ; On the Death of the Duke of Wellington, 194, 195 ; Palace of Art, 251 ; Poets and their Bibliographies, 260 ; Princess, 195, 196 ; Sea Dreams, 90, 268 ; Tithonus, 90, 101 ; To E. Fitz-Gerald, 270 ; To the Queen, 110 ; To Virgil, 189, 197 ; translations from Homer, 63, 102 ; Ulysses, 156 ; Vision of Sin, 270 *n.* ; You ask me, why, tho' ill at ease, 267

Tennyson, Hallam Lord, *Memoir* of his father, 3, 259, 270

Thackeray, as editor of the *Cornhill*, 82-9, 91, 95 ; the Thackeray touch, 91, 93 ; novels, 203 ; *Lovel the Widower*, 83, 107 ; *Pendennis*, 144 ; *Philip*, 117 ; *Roundabout Papers*, 83, 93, 103, 107 ; on Screens in Dining-rooms, 100 ; Thorns in the Cushion, 83, 89 ; on Charlotte Brontë, 107

Theocritus, 188

Thompson, Sir H., 84

Thomson's *Seasons*, 216

Thoreau, 180

Thornbury, Walter, *Life of Turner*, 211, 238

Thucydides, 12, 205-9

Times, The, 124, 135, 157, 161, 205 ; *Literary Supplement*, 124

Tindale, 198

Tit-Bits, 128

Tommy Atkins, 154

Tooke, Horne, 61

Traill, H. D., on Coleridge, 251

Treaty of Paris, 165

Trelawny, E., *Recollections of Shelley*, 248

Trench, Archbishop, *On the Study of Words*, 143, 169

Trevelyan, Sir George, *Early Life of Charles James Fox*, 13, 204 ; *Life of Macaulay*, 21, 159 *n.*, 183, 209

Trevelyan, G. M., books on Garibaldi, 28, 105 ; *Life of John Bright*, 28, 29

Trollope, Anthony, and the *Cornhill*, 82, 83, 85 ; on Millais's illustrations, 108

Turner, J. M. W., character of, 223, 238, 240 ; choice of mottoes for his pictures, 216, 218, 233 ; fond of poetry, 215 ; industry, 212, 213 ; interest in classical story, 224, 226, 231 ; landscape, views of, 228 ; lectures, 214 ; note and sketch books, 211-14 ; the Shelley of painting, 218-22

Pictures and drawings :—Apollo and the Python, 223 ; Caligula's Palace and Bridge, 232 ; Cephalus and Procris, 219 ; Childe Harold's Pilgrimage, 218 ; Corfe Castle, 225 ; Decline of the Carthaginian Empire, 232 ; Departure of the Fleet, 237 ; Dido building Carthage, 228 ; Evening Star, 234 ; Exile and Rock Limpet, 235 ; Fountain of Fallacy, 237 ; Garreteer's Petition, 234 *n.*; Greta and Tees, 42 ; Hannibal crossing the Alps, 231 ; Light and Colour, 237 ; Lulworth Cove, 225 ; Morning on Coniston Fells, 215 ; Opening of the Walhalla, 236 ; Poole, 225 ; Queen Mab's Grotto, 218 ; Shylock, 220 ; Slave Ship, 241 ; later Swiss drawings, 243 ; Téméraire, 220 ; Twilight at Harlech Castle, 215 ; Ulysses, 223 ; Venice, Going to the Ball, and Returning from the Ball, 233

Poetry of :— characteristics of, 224, 226, 229, 230, 241 ; examples of, in mottoes for his pictures, Fallacies of Hope, 223, 231, 232, 235, 236, 237, from his note-books, 217, 225, 226, 227, 229, 230, 234 ; reasons for his persistent attempts, 238 *et seq.*

Tyrrell, Professor, *Latin Poetry*, 188, 189

Van de Weyer, M., viii

Venice, and Turner, 231, 233

Virgil, 182, 187, 261, 311 ; the best lines in, 187, 188 ; the worst, 189

Voltaire, 187

Wace, Dean, 133

Walker, Frederick, illustrations in the *Cornhill*, 108

Walston, Sir C., on Ruskin, 50, 53, 59

War bulletins, 137

War correspondents, 126

War words and phrases, history summed in, 142-4; reflect changed or new military conditions, 144-6, 152, 163, and new economic and diplomatic conditions, 165 *seq.*; adapt names of famous men, 147-8, names of places, 148, names of inventors, 149; onomatopœic, 150, 152; humorous associations, 150; difficulty of fixing origin of, 155; adopted from abroad, 158-62

Particular words and phrases :— aerobatics, 152; aerodrome, 152; Anzac, 143; Archies, 151; aunties, 151; barbed-wire disease, 142; biplane, 152; Blighty, 157; Boloism, 160; Bolshevik, 162; Bosche, 158; camouflage, 159; clean cut, 164; C.O.'s, 163; coal-scuttles, 150; comb, combing out, 164; Conchies, 163; Cuthbert, 163; defeatist, 160; Dora, 150; duds, 145; dug-out, 144, 145; food hoarders, 162; funkholes, 163; gassed, 142; going west, 156; grandmothers, 151; Hamstertanties, 161; heavies, 144; Hun, 158; internationalism, 169; Jack Johnsons, 150; Kitcheners, 148; Leninism, 162; Lewis, 149; Maximalist, 162; militarism, 166; Mills, 149; monoplane, 152; Old Contemptibles, 161; over the top, 143; pacifism, pacifists, 168; pill-box, 151; pip-squeak, 150; plum puddings, 151; profiteering, 170; right of self-determination, 169; Sammies, 155; sausages, 151; shell-shock, 142; steam-roller, 143; Stokes, 149; strafe, strafing, 161; streamline, 153; tanks, 150; tear-shells, 142; Tony, 154; trialism, 162; volplane, 152; Waacs, 143; whizz-bang, 150; Wrens, 143; zoom, 153

Ward, Sir A. W., on the *Cornhill*, 97
Wardour Street English, 254
Watts-Dunton, T., 194, 198
Wedderburn, Alexander, 38
Wellington, Duke of, on authors, 209; use of his name, 148
Westminster Gazette, 164, 300
Wheatley, H. B., on indexes, 69
Whistler, 244
Whitley, W. T., 214 *n.*
Wilde, Oscar, as journalist, 123; on unreadable books, 216 *n.*
Williams, Basil, *Life of Chatham*, 26
Wise, B. R., 12 *n.*
Wood, Anthony à, *Athenae Oxonienses*, 8
Wordsworth, 198; his best ten years, 198; revisions in his poetry, 259, 310-15; particular poems, etc., quoted or referred to :—Advertisement to Thanksgiving Ode, Jan. 18, 1816, 167; Descriptive Sketches, 314; Laodamia, 311; Lines on Fox, 312; Lyrical Ballads, 254; Ode on Intimations of Immortality, 194; A Poet's Epitaph, 317; Prefaces, 89; Rob Roy's Grave, 171; Stepping Westward, 156; Thanksgiving Ode, 1815, 310; The world is too much with us, 184; Tintern Abbey, 184; To B. R. Haydon, 139; We are seven, 314

Yonge, Miss, *The Heir of Redclyffe*, 203

THE END